Jonathan Langstaff Forster

Biblical Psychology In Four Parts

Jonathan Langstaff Forster

Biblical Psychology In Four Parts

ISBN/EAN: 9783743382602

Manufactured in Europe, USA, Canada, Australia, Japa

Cover: Foto ©Lupo / pixelio.de

Manufactured and distributed by brebook publishing software (www.brebook.com)

Jonathan Langstaff Forster

Biblical Psychology In Four Parts

BIBLICAL PSYCHOLOGY.

IN FOUR PARTS.

BY THE LATE

JONATHAN LANGSTAFF FORSTER.

EDITED BY HIS SON,

HENRY L. FORSTER.

"The Lord God formed man of the dust of the ground, and caused him to breathe into his nostrils the breath of life; and man became a living soul."
(Gen. ii., 7.)

LONDON:

LONGMANS, GREEN, AND CO.

1873.

INTRODUCTION.

DURING the life of Jesus Christ on earth, he rebuked those then professing to be explainers of God's Word thus—"Ye have taken away the key of knowledge." With equal justice might a similar accusation be brought, in this age, against our theologians—"Ye have 'taken away the key of knowledge." The Arch-Deceiver has once more destroyed the simple truth by " Ye shall not surely die," by inculcating the immortality of the soul.

Every religion must be based upon its own psychology. The assertion that the deity is the soul of the world, when credited, tends to Pantheism. By this system, the human soul is declared a discerption from the divine soul, and to be merged, at man's decease, into the Universal Spirit. On the other hand, the religion which assumed the soul to be a demon, immortal and ever-existing, drifted its followers into calling man's body an encumbrance, and also into fatalism. This demon of Plato, an immortal soul implanted and apart in man, is unfortunately embraced generally in Christendom, and made a handle of consolation at the hour of death.

Alas! the principal doctrines of our inestimable Bible, so rich, so inexhaustible, so precious, have been for centuries smothered under the rubbish of a Heathen psychology; the Biblical psychology has, in the interval, remained latent and unknown.

This work is an attempt to shed light on the faith once delivered to the saints, amid the darkness involving it. The one wise God, who alone can impart knowledge, will condemn all in this book that is not of Him, and eternally keep His own truth.

HENRY L. FORSTER.

10, *Victoria Square,*

Newcastle-upon-Tyne,

24th September, 1872.

CONTENTS.

ERRATA.

Page 32, *for* "Zenophon's" *read* "Xenophon's."

Page 103, *for* "The objective perceptions" *read* "The subjective perceptions."

Page 181, *for* "τὸ ὂν" *read* "τὸ ἔν."

Page 221, *for* "Shunamite's" *read* "Shunammite's."

Page 227, *for* "St. John" *read* "John the Baptist."

At pages 50 and 51, the passage in Deut. xx., 16, has been misunderstood. The reader, in referring to his Bible, will find that the word *neshama*, in this verse, does not apply only to men, but to every animal. The Israelites had to deal with the nations "very far off" (verse 15) in a lenient manner; of these only the males had to be destroyed. But nothing that breatheth had, on the other hand, to be saved in the cities of the nations given to God's chosen people. Therefore, this (Deut. xx., 16) is a further testimony to the word *neshama* being applicable to both man and brute.

PART I.

THE LIVING SOUL.

Chapter I.

CHRISTIAN PLATONISM.

It is the common belief that the soul possesses a personality distinct from the body; also that the soul and spirit are identical. It is a philosophical doctrine that the body is an encumbrance to the soul, and that the latter would be better without it. According to many the soul languishes in the body as in a prison, and yearns after its native heavens; and upon the decease of the latter, it enters upon a career of immortality, and soars to worlds unknown; or, in the language of Schiller in his Tract upon the Connection of the Animal Nature of Man with his Spiritual, death unfolds itself from life as from its bud—matter resolves itself into its original elements —the soul issues forth to exercise its powers of thought in other spheres, and to contemplate the universe in other aspects.

Whilst the mental constitution and future destiny

A

of man involve many perplexing questions, the
minds of ancient philosophers were in proportion
curious and enquiring; nor is it surprising that the
opinions of such men have excited a corresponding
curiosity and interest in future generations. Revelation itself has been chiefly confined to an enun-
ciation of the Divine origin of our creation, and of
our personal immortal destinies, leaving still open
to investigation how they are to be reconciled with
its own language and the psychology of our nature.

"*Nec tamen quasi Pythius Apollo, certa ut sint et
fixa, quæ dixero, sed ut homunculus unus e multis,
probabilia conjectura sequens*" (Cic. Tusc., lib. i.,
cap. 9, sec. 17).

It is proposed in the present chapter shortly to
trace the origin of the present popular notions concerning the human soul, prior to entering upon
the further enquiry.

The model republic of Plato was partly deduced
from his views of the harmonious constitution of
the soul and body of man himself.

From his Timæus we may collect what were his
peculiar opinions as to the fitness of every part of
the human microcosm; how each member and
faculty was subservient to another; and how all
were subservient to the presiding mind: whilst it
is his definition of the latter which here more particularly invites attention.

In opposition to the doctrines of Parmenides,
Empedocles, and the Eleatics, who held the opinion

that the universe itself was eternal and was in short
the Deity himself, Plato with Anaxagoras taught
the sublime doctrine that a supreme and Almighty
Creator was the Author and Parent of all that exists,
and was himself, or conceived in himself, the ideal
archetype of all.

The doctrine of the eternity of matter, as held by
the old Philosophers, was founded upon the argument
as expressed by Lucretius, " *nullam rem e nihilo
gigni.*"

Plato, on the contrary, distinguished between that
which is eternal and always the same, and that
which is becoming or in a state of generation.

He, therefore, identified the visible universe with
the latter, as being perceptible by the senses, and
susceptible of continued modifications; wherefore,
" we say that some originating cause must be assigned to that which is in a state of generation"
(Stall. Tim. 114).

But as regards the rational soul, it being always
the same and indivisible, he held it alone, like its
archetype, to be eternal.   It must therefore, he
argued, have possessed a pre-existence, as well as
shall have a post-existence, independently of the
body.

The rational soul personified those ideas which
are now denominated subjective in contradistinction
to the objective ideas of the senses : such as the
ideas of God, of the sublime and beautiful, of
morality, and all such as do not enter from the outer

world by the senses. These Plato seemed to consider as identified with a previous existence, and to have originated in a higher and more perfect sphere.

He did not seem to perceive that our subjective ideas are themselves constituted of our objective ideas or sense perceptions; and, therefore, attributing to the former a higher origin than that of the latter, he embodied them in his ideal of the rational soul as characteristic of the immortal.

After creating the demons, or inferior deities, as Plato denominated the stars and planets, the Deity committed to each of them, in his peculiar sphere, the creation of all inferior races, whom he himself provided with souls according to their nature.

The inferior animals received mortal souls; but man, both a mortal or animal soul, representing his passions and organic propensities, and also a rational immortal soul.

That philosopher (in Timæus) also informs us, that the nobler and virtuous souls of men shall, upon the decease of the body, return to their original state of spiritual individuality in the sphere to which each pertains; or, according to their deserts, pass through successive transmigrations of creatures.

The human rational soul, which was characteristic of personal superiority and immortality, the Deity gave to each as a demon to occupy the most exalted position in his body. Αὐτὸ δαίμονα Θεὸς ἑκάστῳ ἔδωκε (Stall. Tim. 359).

He treats of this soul in such terms of independent personality, distinct and separable from the body, as purport to identify the individual to whom it pertained, after decease, as well as during life. In its several transmigrations the same identity continues; and, finally, the purified soul returns to the happy state of its first creation; otherwise it is devoted to a less felicitous portion in *Hades.*

Considering the exalted views entertained by Plato of the supreme Deity, and also of the rational soul of man, there is something inconsistent in his adoption of the Pythagorean metempsychosis; for, after making a broad distinction between the rational soul of man and the mortal soul of inferior creatures, he intimates the possibility of the former occupying the latter, which (in order to preserve identity) it must be supposed to do in its integrity.

That Pythagoras held the doctrine of a metempsychosis in the sense usually ascribed to him, appears to be corroborated by the explicit language of Plato in regard to the same doctrine (Stall. Tim. 182).

However irrational this doctrine may appear, such were not the characters or powers of the great men who professed it. Considering that all creatures are finally resolved into the elements from which they were originally constituted, these elements would again be set free to enter into the composition of new generations as well of animals as plants; and, if the souls of men were regarded as distinct personal demons, they were thus considered as susceptible of transference into other

bodies by this natural process of regeneration, or
παλιγγενεσία.

Plato regarded the human soul as a distinct personality, or demon, capable of preserving its archetypal identity when separated from its temporary
abode in the corruptible body.

Aristotle (De Anima, Trend.) appears to have
held a different opinion.   According to his view,
the body and soul in respect to personality are
inseparable; the organic faculty (δύναμις) is corporeal; the connection of the mind with the body
is its personal perfection; the combined faculty of
body and mind in action is ἐνέργεια.   The consubstantial faculty thus constituted is the perfect faculty.
The soul in relation to the body constitutes the
complete man ; the perfect being (ἐντελέχεια).

He regarded man as a compound being, and
considered that instead of dividing his nature the
phenomena alone should be distinctively regarded;
the physical, or those which were exhibited by his
bodily organism, and the dialectic or mental (De
Anima, cap. i., sec. 1, sent. 11).

"*Illud dialecticus, hoc physicus arripiet, philosophus
utrumque jungere sciet*" (Trend. Com. De Anima,
page 207).

Plato, considering the soul to be distinct from the
body, and as having a previous personal existence,
concluded that its highest cogitations were founded
upon memory, or innate ideas, the impress of its
archetype (In Menone and Tim.).

Aristotle, on the other hand, contended that it had no memory of anything beyond what had its affections in the body—that the spiritual energy or rational soul is indeed distinct, immortal, and eternal, whilst that which is the subject of the affections is mortal, and yet without this we are sensible of nothing (De Anima, cap. iii., sec. 5, sent. 2).

Hence it follows, as Trendelenburg remarks, that apart from our human nature we cannot recollect anything.

The Deity alone is the perfect and eternal mind, with whom all ideas are cognate. The human mind consists of that which thinks and that which is affected.

Aristotle thus seemed to regard the soul as a spiritual consubstantial agency; the body without it would be insensate, as the eye without it would be without perception, whilst the soul without the bodily organs would possess no personal individuality.

Philoponus appears to have understood him in this sense. Thus the various senses of the body were regarded as organic powers dependent upon mental energies.

Aristotle endeavours to demonstrate the mutual and necessary dependence of mind and body, and concludes that, if the soul could locally move of itself independently of the body, it might quit or return to the latter at pleasure. The very dead might

thus rise again, which he treats as an impossibility.
And he further supposes, that if the soul could thus
act independently, it might pass away from the
substance of the body altogether (De Anima,
cap. i., sec. 3, sent. 6).

The Peripatetics in general disbelieved in the
separate existence of the soul, and regarded the
Deity himself as the soul of the world, into whom
all departed spirits merged.

From what we have premised from the Timæus,
it is manifest that Plato held both a personal pre-
existence and post-existence of the individual soul,
although not in either case a human identity, but
an individual archetypal identity.

The body, according to the Platonic view, was
an encumbrance and source of pollution to the
soul; and, when it escapes its mortal prison, it
finds its future bliss not in any recognisable personal
identity with reference to its human personality,
but in the bosom of its tutelary sphere, or demon,
its first and best estate.

Cicero, in his Tusculan Disputations, fully and
eloquently debates the question of the immortality
of the soul; and, after discussing all that can be
said on both sides, he expresses himself as thereby the
more confirmed in its favour. In the absence of the
Revelation of the Resurrection from the dead, it was
much more consolatory to cherish such a hope, however shadowy, than to reject it. He sided with
Plato against those who held the opposite doctrine.

" *Errare mehercule malo cum Platone, quam cum istis vera sentire*" (Tus. lib. i., cap. 17).

Yet, he was equally perplexed with other philosophers as to what the future state of the soul, as the spiritual representative of the body, might be. " *Si cor, aut sanguis, aut cerebrum est animus, certe, quoniam est corpus, interibit cum reliquo corpore. Si anima est, fortasse dissipabitur; si ignis, exstinguetur; si est Aristoxeni harmonia, dissolvetur*" (Tus. lib. i., cap. 11).

Socrates, the early preceptor of Plato, seems to have held the personal immortality of the soul, as is apparent in the Phædo of Plato and the Tusculan Disputations of Cicero (Tus. lib. i., cap. 23); yet, he confessed himself to be by no means certain of this in his oration before his judges, when condemned to death, as mentioned both by Plato and Cicero ('Tus. lib. i., cap. 41).

The personal identity puzzled them all; and yet the personal identity was the faith of the popular superstition.

Thus Virgil, in his Æneid (lib. vi.), details the popular superstition as to the future destiny of the soul, when describing the scenes to which the Sibyl introduced Æneas in the infernal regions. He there recognized various well-known characters, and amongst the rest his own father Anchises. From this it is manifest, that a concrete personal identity was popularly regarded as being preserved by the departed, although not in their mortal bodies. He saw but their *manes : " tenues sine corpore vitas.*"

B

His account of the Cœlestis Origo of Life is rather Platonic than Pythagorean, referring it to a supreme Creator.

Principio cœlum, ac terras, camposque liquentes
Lucentemque globum Lunæ, Titaniaque astra
Spiritus intus alit, totamque infusa per artus
Mens agitat molem et magno se corpore miscet.
Inde hominum pecudumque genus, vitæque volantum,
Et quæ marmoreo fert monstra sub æquore pontus.
Igneus est ollis vigor, et cœlestis origo
Seminibus (lib. vi., 724-731).

Herodotus says, that the Greeks derived their knowledge of the immortality of the soul from the Egyptians. Plato, in his Timæus, gives an account of an interview between Solon and the Egyptian Priests, during which the latter supplied him with certain information concerning the ancient history of his own country. Plato himself also visited Egypt for the purpose of extending his philosophical enquiries; and, according to Pliny, the Greeks received a portion of their philosophy from the eastern Magi. The Israelites probably left behind them in Egypt no inconsiderable knowledge of their own traditions; and, the Greek philosophers and learned Jewish Rabbis of a future age were not unacquainted with each other.

When we consider that the Mosaic writings date from about fifteen centuries before the christian era, whilst the earliest of the Greek philosophers did not flourish until about nine centuries later, there was ample time for the dissemination of Hebraistic doctrines; these, if imperfectly understood, philosophic ingenuity might readily modify into the speculations which different philosophers developed according to their different views.

We thus meet with the divine attributes in the Orphic Hymns; and in the Greek mythology we read of the rebel wars of the giants against Jupiter, and of the Titans against Saturn. The heaven-seeking demons of Empedocles suggest a similar origin. The fable of Prometheus, the philosophy of Pantheism, and the doctrine of the universal spirit, or soul of the universe, in like manner arrest our attention; but we must look elsewhere for the origin of the mythology itself.

It is not improbable therefore, according to Grotius *de veritate* and Eusebius, that the opinions of the ancient heathen philosophers, and even the popular superstitions, may have themselves been the modifications of isolated truths widely disseminated by tradition amongst the Egyptians and Asiatics with whom the former held intercourse.

In a similar manner many Scriptural traditions have found their way into the books of the Buddhists and Brahmans. Sir James Emerson Tennent, in his Ceylon, vol. i., p. 518, adverts to the influences of Nestorian Christianity upon the genius and literature of Buddhism, and also to many striking coincidences which occur between the sacred books of both the Brahmans and Buddhists and the Jewish Scriptures, only to be accounted for by " the close proximity of a Jewish race in Affghanistan, the progenitors of the

Hebrew colony that still inhabits the Dekkan near
Cochin, known as the Black Jews of Malabar."

The doctrines of Plato were themselves essentially
eclectic, being a more enlightened reconstruction of
those held by some of his predecessors, attributing
the creation of all things to a supreme self-existent
Deity, the source of universal life and intelligence,
and from whose hands man received a soul, destined
to a future existence.

But then we have seen that his account of the
origin of the soul, and its future destiny, was very
different from the simple and more sublime narrative
of the Hebrew writings.

Notwithstanding this, there was sufficient in the
Platonic philosophy to attract the admiration of the
more learned of the early Christians; his doctrines
were accordingly held in great repute in the Alex-
andrian school, of which Origen was a distinguished
ornament; and, from the use which he made of that
philosopher's doctrines in endeavouring to reconcile
the learned Pagans to Christianity, Origen probably
conduced in no small degree to Platonise the general
views of Christians respecting the nature of the soul
and its future existence.

The hopeful and exalted views of Socrates upon
the same subjects, as delineated by Plato in his
Phædo and Phædrus, were well calculated to attract
the admiration of the early Christians, and are still
read with a greater interest than the more philosophic, but less enthusiastic conclusions of Aristotle.

The latter leave us in sepulchral gloom, whilst the former are full of immortality.

Justin Martyr and others of the early Christians, besides Origen, were versed in the Platonic philosophy; and, even before the time of our Saviour, the Jewish Rabbis were deeply tainted with Greek and Oriental speculations, as is apparent in the unscriptural views which abound in the Talmud and in the peculiar creeds of the sects of the Pharisees, Sadducees, and Essenes.

After the return of the Jews from the Babylonian captivity, the writings of their Rabbis became especially thus tinctured.

Aristobulus is said to have held pretty nearly the same views as Plato upon metaphysical subjects.

Philo held that there were two souls in man, in the sense of Plato, or the Magians; but he acknowledged that we do not know the nature of the rational soul, whether it be blood, or air, or fire, or whether it possess any material quality at all. The Hebraistic phraseology and doctrine of the sacred books had evidently, in his time, exchanged to a great extent their pregnant Hebraistic sense for Pagan ideas, derived from human speculation. The Oriental mysticism of the Magi, also, now began to manifest its influence in Jewish literature.

The peculiar dogmas of the Jewish sects upon the advent of Christ were modifications of Greek and Oriental philosophy. All their sects, except the Karaites, neglected their own scriptures for the writings of the Talmudists. The Pharisees, thus, adopted to a considerable extent the popular Greek idea of a *Hades;* the Sadducees denied the existence of spirits and the doctrine of a resurrection; the Essenes considered that the soul was immortal, and after death would pass to some place of reward or punishment without any resurrection of the body. The Karaites seemed to hold much the same doctrine as the Essenes (see Josephus, and Jennings' Jewish Antiq.).

Most of the early fathers of the church studied the Greek philosophy. The writings of Plato, Pythagoras, and Aristotle were in general highly esteemed by the fathers; they, however, viewed these writings otherwise than the Rabbis, inasmuch as the former sought in them a confirmation of Christianity, which the latter rejected.

The early fathers sought to propitiate the Grecian philosophers of the day, by showing an accordance between their philosophy and Christianity; but, in doing this, they laid themselves open to the charge of sometimes substituting the former for the latter; and of subjecting Christianity to the test of human reason, instead of rectifying the mere deductions of human ingenuity by the standard of revealed truth. So, the genuine doctrines of revelation were partially modified or superseded, by the speculations of philosophy.

Thus, whilst we denounce with Bacon " the unwholesome admixture" of religion and philosophy, we have very generally adopted some of the notions of the Greek superstitions, as an element in our mental philosophy, to the exclusion of the doctrines of inspiration itself.

Tertullian, Lactantius, and others of the patristic writers were aware of this tendency, and expressly opposed it.

Yet, whilst physiologists and metaphysicians have generally avoided any direct reference to Biblical authority, they have tacitly adopted what they understood to be a Biblical definition of the soul, whilst all the time it might be but a Platonic gloss.

Deeply versed in the Greek philosophers, Justin Martyr, Origen, St. Clement, St. Augustine and others employed that learning in illustrating the Christian doctrines concerning the Deity, the human soul, and our moral duties.

Origen appears to have grounded his opinion of the immortality of the soul upon his belief in its previous existence; but, he said, it was not determined by the Church whether the soul were eternal or not in a personal sense. He conceived that, after decease, it still retained some kind of body.

St. Augustine, in his Treatise " On the Quantity of the Soul," considered " that the soul derives its origin from God; it is simple and immaterial." He enumerated its various stages of development, from mere vegetable life to its perfection in the contemplation of truth itself, and its return to the great first cause (see Blakey's History of the Philosophy of Mind, and the authorities there referred to).

The school of the new Platonists, established at
Alexandria about the end of the second century,
had a material influence in the modification of
Christianity in accordance with Greek philosophy.
During many centuries afterwards Plato and Aristotle
maintained their ascendancy, not only in the schools
of science but of theology as well.

Upon reference to the Scriptural account of the
creation, we read that "the Spirit of God moved
upon the face of the waters;" and that God, after
creating man of the dust of the ground, "breathed
into his nostrils the breath of life, and man became
a living soul." It is impossible not to be struck
with the similarity of some of the notions of the
Stoical philosophers, which almost seem like a
modified tradition of this *Nishmath* or Divine
afflatus.

These imagined a certain ethereal fluid, that pervaded the universe, and was the cause of life and
animation in every living creature, being itself the
soul of the world and the very essence of the Deity
himself.

The soul of the Hebrew Scriptures thus became
identified with the spiritual creation of Plato; and,
the departing spirit has been invested with a beatific
individuality.

Dr. Reid and other modern metaphysicians appear,
consequently, to have regarded the soul as a personality distinct from the body.

The bodily organs are treated by such writers as
the mere instruments of the soul, or the windows

by which it communicates with the outer world; whilst the general opinion is, that the soul would be better without the body.

Pope's admired couplet is but a condensed translation of the Stoical sentiment, that the Deity is the cause of all life and intelligence, and is himself the soul of the world—

> " All are but parts of one stupendous whole,
> Whose body Nature is, and God the Soul."

Other modern writers repeat the same Pantheistic sentiment to admiring Christendom.

It is true that everything owes its origin to the Almighty Jehovah, who originated that *afflatus* which imparted life to all living. However, to regard all as but parts of Him, is to merge all created personalities in Him, and to abjure all individual freedom and responsibility.

Thus the Stoical, as well as Platonic, philosophers have perpetuated their disciples in Christendom itself; but the most common opinion, with regard to the human soul, has been rather Platonic than otherwise.

As Plato regarded the human soul to be an archetypal creation, implanted by the supreme Deity in the human body as a distinct demon or personality, destined to be again removed to another sphere, so the soul has in general been spoken of as a personality in man distinct from the body, and upon the decease of the latter retaining its distinct personality.

c

In general, the dissolution of the bodily tenement has been considered the deliverance of the soul from an encumbrance and state of bondage.

Plato's definition, contained in the following passage from his Axiochus, as quoted by Blackwall, literally expresses the modern idea of the soul. "For we are, indeed, a soul; an immortal being enclosed in a perishable citadel, the tabernacle which nature has provided as a protection from harm" (vol. ii., page 19).

At death, the soul is commonly said to escape from the fetters of mortality, and to carry with it all the mental faculties of the perfect man into another state of existence. The faithful are represented as passing to heaven to the participation of angelic happiness, whilst the unbelieving are consigned to personal retribution. More classical minds are content to consign the soul to a classical *Hades*, or intermediate state, until the resurrection of the body.

That the beautiful poetic metaphors and fancies of the ancient heathen should have found a response in the aspirations of modern poetry, and the popular sympathies of all times, is natural. It is pleasing to think that heaven is our "native place;" that death is the messenger of celestial life; that departed parents and children still hover round the family circle; and that the souls of the righteous already wear their crowns of immortality, and strike their golden harps before the throne of heaven. It is flattering to genius to think, that he may shake off death as dust from his wings, and soar at once through the empyrean.   And, had we no better hope than that which arises from our natural aspirations, we might prefer to err with the Pagan philosopher rather than embrace a merely speculative alternative.

CHAPTER II.

THE BIBLICAL SOUL AND BODY.

THE ancient traditions of the immortal destiny of the human race were preserved in mythology by its attributing to man after death a concrete personality, however shadowy—the shade being clothed with all the personal characteristics of concrete humanity. In this respect the poets followed the mythologic tradition, which was much more distinct than the philosophic theories.

The philosophers treated soul and spirit as convertible terms; mythology attached personal identity to the soul alone. Thus Homer,

Πολλὰς δ'ἰφθίμους ψυχὰς ῎Αϊδι προΐαψεν
'Ηρώων, αὐτοὺς δέ ἑλώρια τεῦχε κύνεσσιν
Οἰωνοῖσί τε πᾶσι (Il. lib. I., 3, 4, and 5).

Many brave heroes themselves he dismissed to Hades, and gave their bodies as a prey to dogs and every bird.

The word ψυχὰς represented the persons of the heroes, the shades, or *idola*, of Hades and Orcus. Whilst αὐτοὺς refers, in apposition, to their dead bodies left as a prey behind.

It was also ψυχὴ (Psyche) whom the Greeks

allegorised as a butterfly ascending from the lips of a deceased person.

Æneas, upon his descent to the infernal regions, beheld, amongst others, Deiphobus, the son of Priamus, exhibiting in his *manes* all the lacerations of his human body.

> Atque hic Priamiden laniatum corpore toto
> Deïphobum vidit, lacerum crudeliter ora;
> Ora, manusque ambas, populataque tempora raptis
> Auribus, et truncas inhonesto vulnere nares (Æn. lib. vi., 494).

The Stoics, imputing to the soul the characteristics of the spirit, were consequently led to adopt the theory of its absorption after the dissolution of the body into the universal spirit (τὸ ἕν). They thus, in ignorance of a resurrection doctrine, limited the individual personality of the soul to its human corporeity.

This doctrine was altogether inconsistent with the continuance of personal identity after death; therefore Plato supposed that the soul possessed a personality distinct from the body, from the encumbrance of which the soul was delivered by the dissolution of the latter.

Thus, whilst the ancient mythology treated the soul as the personal self, the philosophers in general considered it as synonymous with spirit, the principle of life, motion, and intelligence.

Hence modern (like the ancient) philosophy, discarding the absurdities of mythologic fiction, has in general identified soul with spirit, and, as Plato, attributed to the soul or spirit a personality distinct from that of the body.

Later philosophers speculated still further. Thus Plotinus, whilst he maintained the incorporeal substance of the soul, supposed, in conformity with classical tradition, that it was never altogether severed from what he called its idol or a sort of airy body; yet, in accordance with the spiritual philosophy, he fancied that it might quit, and leave in *Hades* alone, this airy body; whilst the pure spirit was, he thought, absorbed into the Deity. (Cudworth.)

Porphyry, on the other hand, adhered to the Pythagoric tradition, that the soul is always united to some body. Origen, Irenæus, and Tertullian were of the same opinion.

Others, again, with the Chaldaic philosophers, clothed the soul with imaginary vestments—some pneumatical, and others luciform; whilst Philoponus blended them into one; all which ideas they seemed to treat as in harmony with poetic tradition.

So consistent were the Platonic philosophers and many of the Christian Fathers in attributing post-corporeity to the soul, that their only disagreement was as to the nature of that body.

Hierocles went so far as to say, that the reasonable soul always possessed a cognate body proceeding from the Creator, but retained it in such way " that it is neither itself a body, and yet cannot be without a body."

Tertullian says of the soul, "if it be not a body, it is nothing." Arnobius argues, that the soul is wholly incapable of sensation or reflection without the body.

It seems to have been the general sentiment of the early Christian writers that the soul, after death, retained some sort of aërial personality, analogous to (and not less vague than) either the mythologic or Platonic ideas. All seem to be equally corroborative of the tradition of a future state.

The abnormal condition of death deranged the conclusions of the ancient philosophy, and perplexed the half Pagan and half Christian arguments of the theologians who succeeded.

The substance of the mythologic traditions seems to be, that man in some form of personal identity is reserved for a future destiny after the termination of his ephemeral human existence.

The philosophers for the most part have retained this tradition, but have invented theories of their own in its interpretation.

Although the heathen tradition of a future state harmonises, yet the meaning attached by them and their followers to the word 'soul' does not harmonise, with Biblical doctrine.

"Men," says Locke, "having been accustomed from their cradles to learn words, which are easily got and retained, before they knew or had framed the complex ideas to which they were annexed, or which were to be found in the things they were thought to stand for, they usually continue to do so all their lives; and without taking the pains necessary to settle in their minds determined ideas, they use their words for such unsteady and confused notions as they have, contenting themselves with the same words other people use; as if their very sound necessarily carried with it constantly the same meaning" (book iii., chap. 10, sec. 4).

Applying these remarks to the popular idea of the term *soul*, and then considering the same term as Biblically employed, it is necessary to advert as well to the original significance of the word itself as to the contexts in which it is used. For, as Blackwall well observes of the significance of the Hebrew language, "one word is often a good description, and gives you a satisfactory account of the chief and distinguishing property or quality of the thing or person named."

In the interpretation of Biblical literature, ecclesiastics have in general taken for granted, that the Greek psychology was equally as applicable to the Biblical as to the Pagan doctrines.

Whilst, therefore, we would refer with respect and deference to Horsley's Biblical Criticism, or Bloomfield's Digest, or Warburton's Divine Legation, and similar works of extensive research and erudition, we shall be disappointed if we expect to find in them anything like an independent psychological investigation of some of those subjects which are more or less interesting to all.

The language of the Hebrew Scriptures is so peculiar with regard to the characteristics of the soul and spirit, as naturally to suggest enquiry concerning its original significance. What is the import of the perpetual reiteration of 'the soul' in the Hebrew idiom? Why is *the soul*, like a pronoun or another person, so constantly the object of appeal? Why are those personal affections and characteristics, which are commonly considered to be animal and concrete, so constantly ascribed to *the soul?* Why are life and spontaneity and intelligence imputed to the spirit and not to *the soul?* Why are birds and beasts denominated 'souls,' whilst we have in general been told that they have no souls? Why do the Scriptures associate *the soul* with death and the grave, whilst we have been taught to believe that the soul of man is immortal? Where is the congruity of all?

That the language of inspiration possesses a psychological fitness to its doctrinal teaching, we may reasonably believe.

Stockius observes, that the word *nephesh* generally denotes 'the soul,' by which an animal lives, and, as by a primary instrumentality, acts as suits its particular genus. The word itself in its radical sense means 'to breathe;' and substantially it expresses 'the self,' or 'personality' of the breathing creature, hence the term animal (from *anima*), personal breathing soul, or self.

Parkhurst remarks, that "*Nephesh* has been

D

supposed to signify the spiritual part of man, or what we commonly call his soul. I must for my part confess that I can find no passage where it hath undoubtedly this meaning."

Gesenius states, that it specially signifies 'person,' as, " *the soul* that sinneth ;" " seventy *souls* ;" *gonaiv nephesh*, a slave-dealer (or *seelen-verkäufer*, a soul-dealer); *nephesh maith*, a dead soul or any dead person.

Richardson, in his Dictionary, refers to the Saxon etymology given by Ihre, in which the latter conceives there must be some connection between "sioel" (soul), and " sioelf " (self), perhaps from a Gothic root signifying the breathing person.

In accordance with these opinions we find in the Scriptures themselves, that *nephesh* specially denotes the 'personal individuality' as well of man as of brute.

Thus, in the account of the Creation, the term 'living soul' (*nephesh chaiyah*) is indiscriminately applied in the original to fish, fowls, beasts, living creatures of all species, and man.

There is no such distinction implied between the souls of men and brutes as is popularly understood. The radical import of a 'breathing personality' is equally applicable to all.

Nor is there any apparent reason why the same expression should not apply to the individuals of the vegetable creation, since they all breathe or absorb the constituents of the atmosphere. Parkhurst refers to an idiomatic phrase in Isaiah (x., 18) used in this sense.

The Greek word ψυχή is derived by Plato, in his *Cratylus*, from the act of respiration and refreshment by which the bodily life is maintained. Aristotle also adopts the same etymology (*De Anima*, chap. i., sec. 2, cl. 23).

The Platonic *rational soul* was the personal demon; his *animal soul* was the principle of life in the whole body. The Aristotelian *rational soul* was the characteristic of man, but probably could not survive the body in a personal sense; his *animal soul* was the vital principle. *The Hebrew soul* is the breathing animal itself; which, being used in a personal sense, became perverted by the heathen philosophers into a personal demon distinct from the body, or identified with a spiritual principle.

In order to maintain a distinction between the application of the term "soul" to brutes as well as to man, Plato and others supposed that there were two souls in man—the one the *animal soul;* and the other the *rational soul.* But our Scriptures make no such distinction. Indeed, as the subjective capacities of the mind are fundamentally dependent upon the objective, the separation of the one characteristic from the other would involve the dissolution of the very characteristics which such a distinction was intended to preserve.

The following personal affections are ascribed to *the soul*, as being organically experienced—Joy,

Grief, Sorrow, Valour, Gluttony (*Baal nephesh*), Hunger, Thirst, and Weeping. It is also said to die, and to be killed. (Ps. lxxxvi., 4; Is. xv., 4; Job xix., 2; Judg. v., 21; Prov. xxiii., 2; Prov. x., 3; Prov. xxv., 25; Ps. cxix., 28; Judg. xvi., 30; Num. xxxi., 19.)

Many of these senses, as of hunger, thirst, weeping, dying, and being killed, cannot be understood of *the soul* in the popular sense; whilst all of them are properly ascribed to it in the sense of corporeal personality, and not in that of an independent spiritual personality.

Similar affections are frequently, as Gesenius observes, applied to the heart, as the centre of their nervous influence, and as heartfelt personal emotions.

All the personal affections are also metonymically referred to the soul, or corporeal personality.

Thus, by a metonymy, *nephesh* denotes the natural affections and desires. "If it be your mind"—*Im yaish eth naphshechem* (Gen. xxiii., 8). "Who hath not lifted up his soul unto vanity" (Ps. xxiv., 4). "So panteth my soul after Thee" (Ps. xlii., 1).

The blood is also in some places symbolically identified with the soul or self. The blood retains and circulates the life. Thus "the soul of the flesh is in the blood" (Lev. xvii., 11), parallel with similar expressions in Gen. ix. Its symbolical significance is apparent from Lev. xvii., 14, where it is said that the blood of the sacrifice is "for the soul thereof;"

literally, "the soul of all flesh is its blood in its soul"—a part used symbolically for the entire personality. Thus the blood is equivalent to a holocaust. The murderer was required as a sacrificial atonement. All the bloody sacrifices were typical and have been absorbed in the sacrifice of Christ, whereby they were superseded and lost their ritual force.

The word *nephesh* (soul) has by a common metonymy, in several of the passages referred to, been translated 'life;' the word 'life' being used for the living 'self.'

The same metonymy occurs throughout the New Testament. To seek the young child's 'soul' is, therefore, translated 'life.' The person who lays down his 'soul' for another, lays down his 'life' for that other.

Nephesh (the soul) is also employed pronominally in the sense of the concrete self. "Let us not kill him"—*lo nachennoo naphesh* (Gen. xxxvii., 21). "The soul of the child came into him again," or "the child came to himself again" (1 Kings xvii., 22). "As her soul was in departing," or "as she was passing away" (Gen. xxxv., 18). "Let me die"—*tamoth naphshi* (Judg. xvi., 30). "Hell"—*Sheol*, the sepulchral state—"hath enlarged herself" *naphshah* (Is. v., 14). "Thou shalt make 'his soul' ('himself') an offering for sin" (Is. liii., 10). Joshua smote the cities of Canaan "and all 'the souls' (or 'them') that were therein" (Josh. x., 37). "His flesh upon him shall have pain, and his soul within him shall mourn" (Job xiv., 22), implying bodily suffering conjointly with personal grief—mourning within himself. "That 'the soul' (or 'a person') be without knowledge is not good" (Prov. xix., 2).

And so, in similar instances, the concrete personal import is manifest. There is no impersonation of the subjective, in contradistinction to the objective, soul.

The same pronominal sense is also applied to things as well as to living creatures, when there is a personified significance; as, with reference to idols (Is. xlvi., 2), or with regard to anything else, by a personal metaphor implying the object or subject itself.

For, although the word originally signified that which breathed, it ultimately symbolized the object or subject of discourse—its 'self' or 'personal identity,' or even its 'ideal.'

Thus, the North American Indians and other uncivilized tribes speak of 'the souls' of warlike and culinary implements accompanying their owners to their traditional land of spirits. Here 'the soul' is the *ideal* 'self.' They talk and think as if the hatchet or canoe itself will re-appear with the hero; yet they think not that the material thing will re-appear (any more than the Hebrews thought that the *nevailah* or dead body would), but that its *nephesh* or ideal will.

By an anthropopeia with reference to the divine

personality, it is also applied to God, "Him that loveth violence 'his soul' (or 'he') hateth" (Ps. xi., 5), "Jehovah hath sworn by himself" (Amos vi., 8).

Whilst the word *nephesh* is applied to the concrete personal self or its ideal, the term *nevailah* is used solely to express the mere carcass; *nephesh maith* (dead soul) implies a dead person; *nevailah* is the dead body.

Jehoiakim's dead body (*nivlatho*) was to be cast out without burial (Jer. xxxvi., 30); the carcass of the man of God slain by the lion was cast in the way.

The word *nevailah* itself implies that which is deciduous and falls to decay, and, therefore, has reference to 'the body' in contradistinction to 'the person.'

The distinction, then, between *nephesh* and *nevailah* is that which is to be observed between personal identity and the fleeting atomic body. The former is permanent, although also atomic; the latter is momentary and passing to decay. Yet both terms are alike applied to men and brutes.

Personal identity is maintained by atomic replacement, independently of atomic identity.

Thus the atomic soul representing personal identity is ever renewed, whilst the deciduous body is ever passing away. The octogenarian remains the same person as the child was.

The nearest analogy in our language to the Hebrew *nephesh* is when we use the word 'soul' in the sense

of 'a person;' as "a good soul," "my soul" (or self),
"every soul perished in the wreck," and in the
various pronominal constructions of the word "self."

In the Greek classics, ψυχὴ is commonly used in
the same literal personal sense as *nephesh*, as before
exemplified; but it also bears a corresponding metonymical sense. The phraseology is Hebraistic; and
the Lexicon of the learned Parkhurst furnishes the
following illustrations,—from Zenophon's Cyropaed.,
lib. iv., τὰς ψυχὰς περιποιησάσθε, "Ye have saved
your *lives*" (the metonymical *soul* or *self*); from
Aristophanes, Nub. line 711, τὴν ψυχὴν ἐκπίνουσι,
"They drink my *soul*" (or the typical *blood*);
Virgil applies *anima* in the same metonymical sense,
purpuream vomit ille animam (Æn. lib. ix., 349).
The principle or agency of life was supposed to
be in some sense specially dependent upon or identified with the blood.

The senses in which the word 'soul' is employed by
the philosophers are dogmatic exceptions.

In the New Testament the word 'soul' is always
used in the Hebraistic personal sense. Our Saviour
says, "What is a man profited if he shall gain the
whole world and lose his own *soul?* or what shall a
man give in exchange for his *soul?*" (Matt. xvi., 26);
but in a parallel passage in Luke ix., 25, it is written,
"What is a man advantaged, if he gain the whole
world and lose *himself?*" which in the Syriac version
is rendered, "lose his soul," the exact Hebraism for
himself, with regard to his future destiny.

The passage in Psalm xvi., 10, "Thou wilt not leave my *soul* in hell" (*Hades*, or the sepulchral state), is expressly applied to a personal resurrection in Acts ii., 27, 31.

Thus, also, we understand in a concrete personal sense such expressions as the following, "Let every *soul* (person) be subject unto the higher powers" (Rom. xiii., 1); "Three thousand *souls*" were added to the church, "And fear came upon every *soul*" (Acts ii.); "Eight *souls* were saved by water" (1 Peter iii., 20); "My *soul* is (or, 'I am') exceeding sorrowful, even unto death" (Matt. xxvi., 38).

"I will say to my soul, Soul, thou hast much goods laid up for many years; take thine ease, eat, drink, and be merry. But God said unto him, Thou fool, this night shall thy soul be required of thee" (Luke xii., 19, 20). Now *the soul in the abstract spiritual sense* does not eat and drink; it is *the concrete self* which eats, drinks, and dies.

The salvation of *the soul* is always spoken of as a personal condition in relation to the future destiny of *the individual.* Thus the 'health of the *soul*' is a phrase emphatically employed in apposition to that of the corruptible *body* (3 John, 2).

To "save a *soul* from death" (James v., 20) is to save *a person*, and is parallel to the expression, "Thou shalt both save thyself, and them that hear thee" (1 Tim. iv., 16).

In all such instances, with which the Scriptures abound, the Hebraistic phraseology is pronominally

E

significant of personal identity in the concrete
(either natural or spiritual) body.

It may be mentioned, so as to avoid circumlocu-
tion, that the foregoing form of expression has become
vernacular. We speak of being stirred to the 'very
depths of our *souls*,' thereby meaning that we are
moved in 'all our thoughts and feelings.' When
the early Christians are said to have been as "one
soul," we conceive a unison of sentiment and interest
as if they had been 'one person.'

In chapter xviii., 12, 13, of the Apocalypse there
occurs the expression—"the merchandise of bodies,
even the persons of men" (τὸν γόμον σωμάτων, καὶ
ψυχὰς ἀνθρώπων); this is parallel to the expression
nephesh adam ("persons of men") in Ezek. xxvii.,
13.

In a metonymical sense the terms 'soul' and
'spirit' have sometimes a distinctive doctrinal import, as respectively typical of the natural and
spiritual states of the human conscience, into which
the Word of God penetrates as a discerner of the
thoughts and intents of the heart, "piercing even
to the dividing asunder of 'soul' and 'spirit,' and
of the joints and marrow" (Heb. iv., 12).

The personal body in the present state is the
natural body, and is in general so translated; hence
the natural man does not receive the things of the
Spirit of God, because they are foolishness to it and are
only spiritually discerned by the spiritual teaching
of the Word of God (1 Cor. ii., 14); the wisdom

of the natural person is "sensual" (James iii., 15) ;
on the contrary, whatsoever ye do ye should do it as,
from a personally regenerated nature, to the Lord
(Col. iii., 23) ; for the natural soul or person is
without divine instruction and without the Spirit of
God.

Whilst *the soul*, with respect to a living person,
implies corporeal personality, it is also used in
reference to personal identity in a future state. But,
although the same expression of 'the soul' is applied
to brutes as is applied to man, the limitation of the
resurrection doctrine to the latter intimates the distinction existing between the idiosyncrasies and
future destinies of the man and those of the brute.

The expression σῶμα ψυχικὸν (personal body) is
distinctively used to denote that body of personal
identity which shall be raised a spiritual body
(σῶμα πνευματικόν), in contradistinction to the corruptible body (*nevailah*) which shall not be raised
at all. Yet it is with entire propriety said of the
σῶμα ψυχικὸν or personal body, " It is sown in corruption, it is raised in incorruption ;" because the
corruptible or natural body, when sown, possesses
a personal identity the same and as complete as
the spiritual body shall. Isaiah (xxvi., 19) intimates
his hope of a resurrection under the very term
nivlathi, which refers to the corruptible body, parallel
to St. Paul's language, "this corruptible must put
on incorruption ;" some expositors, however, apply
this portion of Isaiah's book prophetically to Christ.

The patriarch Job also intimates his belief in a personal resurrection, when he says, "In (from) my flesh (*mibsari*) shall I see God"—from his resurrection body ; "It is sown in corruption, it is raised in incorruption."

The body was in the Hebrew denominated *"gaiv"* with respect to its substance, and in this sense (which is applicable to the spiritual as well as to the natural body) the apostle Paul speaks of waiting "for the adoption, to wit, the redemption of our body" (Rom. viii., 23)—the σῶμα ψυχικὸν (1 Cor. xv., 44) or personal body, the *gaiv* and not *nevailah*. Thus the translators of the Hebrew New Testament have appropriately adopted the former term, *gaiv*, for 'body' in this passage. *Gaiv* is synonymous with σῶμα, generally used in speaking of the substantial body (*vide* 1 Cor. xv).

The natural body shall be exchanged for a spiritual body, and the corruptible for an incorruptible.

These conditions literally and fully satisfy the ancient and common arguments as to the immortal destiny of man.

The common arguments as to the immortality of the soul do not, in fact, establish its immortality, but its fitness for immortality, and its intuitive consciousness of such fitness.

Professor McCosh, in his work on the Intuitions of the Mind, remarks, "But as to whether the dissolution of the bodily frame is a sufficient cause of the decease of the soul, as to whether it may abide when the bodily

frame is disorganised, this is a question to be settled
not altogether by intuition, but by a number of other
considerations, and more particularly by the conviction that God will call us into judgment at last, and
is most definitely settled after all by the inspired
declarations of the Word of God. But it is pleasant
to observe that there is an original conviction
altogether in unison with this derivative belief, a
conviction leading us to look on self as permanent
unless there be a cause adequate to its dissolution"
(page 151).

As our intellectual intuitions point to a fitness for
an immortal career, so do our moral intuitions of
right and wrong lead us from the inadequacy of
human retributions to anticipate, in accordance as
well with mythology and reason as with Scripture
itself, a day when the ways of the Just One
shall be justified in the presence of all mankind.

Kant and Chalmers are both mentioned by McCosh
as concurring in the force of the moral argument in
favour of the immortality of the soul. The present
enquiry would rather incline us to substitute the
words 'immortal destiny' for 'the immortality' of
the soul.

The ordinary aim of philosophers has been to
establish the doctrine of personal immortality by a
development of our nature from the mortal to the
immortal, as if our immortal destiny were to be
attained by a process of natural development; as if
the decay and removal of the mortal body were the

process by which the immortal should be set at liberty from a state of imprisonment to emerge, like the butterfly from the chrysalis, into a spiritual and angelic transformation.

Whatever might have been the metempsychal conditions of the paradisiacal state, we have now to deal with a condition of our nature altogether changed; our hopes of a future life and altered nature are based upon Biblical promises, which have been fulfilled in one man (an assurance of their fidelity to all humanity), seeing that Jesus Christ brought life and immortality to light by his personal resurrection from man's existing natural state.

A nice and consistent distinction is thus preserved throughout the whole of the Sacred Writings between the terms used to designate the mere body or carcass, the spirit, and the living or dead soul or self—the individual concrete personality.

In accordance with this, St. Paul, in concluding his first epistle to the Thessalonian Church, addressing them corporately, prays, according to the accurate translation of an excellent divine and sound philosopher referred to by Blackwall, "The very God of peace sanctify you entirely in every part; and may the whole of you, the spirit, the soul, and the body, be preserved blameless to the coming of our Lord Jesus Christ."

He applies to the Church in a corporate sense the constituents of individual personality (yet in a manner only applicable to a continuous body), as an aggregate body whose individual members by their unanimity appeared to think and act as one soul, and of which the Holy Ghost was the animating spirit. It was only in this sense that the apostle's prayer was pertinent.

Another text, which is often misinterpreted, is further illustrative of this appropriate verbal distinction. Our Saviour said, " Fear not them which kill the body, but are not able to kill the soul; but rather fear Him which is able to destroy both soul and body in hell" *Gehenna* (Matt. x., 28).

The two sentences are antithetical, and cannot be better explained than by a parallel passage in Luke (xii., 4, 5), "Be not afraid of them that kill the body, and after that have no more that they can do; but fear Him, which after he hath killed hath power to cast into hell" *Gehenna*.

Men may kill the body, but cannot cast into hell. God can do both. Therefore, rather fear Him who, after the extinction of the mortal body, has power over the future destiny of the individual.

By not adverting to the Biblical distinction between body, soul, and spirit, a popular confusion has arisen, which has practically fused soul and spirit into one idea, analogous to the Platonic demon.

The distinctive meaning of spirit remains to be considered.

The Greek philosophers preserved in their language the original terms; but, ignorant of the Scriptural doctrines of the Fall and Resurrection, they lost the distinctive meanings of the terms themselves.

Tradition had preserved the doctrine of a future state in the popular superstitions; but philosophy, rejecting the absurdities of poetic fiction, either ignored a future state altogether, or sought to account for a perpetuation of personal existence after death upon what appeared to be more rational principles. Reasoning well upon the powers of the human intellect, philosophers inferred its fitness for immortality; and, ignorant of a promised resurrection, they speculated upon a personal existence, after the decease of the body, in another personality independent of the body. They thus clothed the departing spirit with the name and attributes of the Hebraistic soul.

It is curious to observe how consistently the Greeks, both in their philosophy and mythology, have attributed personality to the soul and not to the spirit, even whilst they treat of the soul under spiritual terms; however, in this spiritual treatment of the soul they were really right according to our own Scriptures, inasmuch as it is the soul (the Self or individual) that shall be raised a spiritual body. It is to 'the soul' the personal identity attaches, and not to 'the spirit.'

In the Bible the word "soul," we have seen, is invariably and physiologically significant of corporeal personal identity, either in the natural body or the spiritual body. It is never used in the Platonic sense, personifying the subjective ideas in contra-distinction to the objective. The doctrine of its immortal destiny necessarily involves that of a personal resurrection, which circumstance is more or less clearly intimated throughout our Hagiographa, and, in connection with the doctrine of the future destiny of the soul, fulfils all the conditions of philosophic argument.

The philosophic soul is a mere ideal abstraction. The mythologic soul is the shadow of the reality faintly recognised in the dim twilight of tradition. The soul of Scripture is the concrete personal identity itself. It is the personal body ($\sigma\tilde{\omega}\mu\alpha\ \psi\upsilon\chi\iota\kappa\grave{o}\nu$). It eats, drinks, thinks, and acts; it has its joys and its sorrows, health and sickness; and finally it dies, and all its thoughts perish.

The 'soul' is this substantial 'Self,' which throughout life is ever coming, never gone; whilst the corruptible is ever passing away. It is this corporeal personal identity which is apostrophised in the Hebraistic phraseology and in our own vernacular. It is this 'Self' which, raised a spiritual body ($\sigma\tilde{\omega}\mu\alpha\ \pi\nu\epsilon\upsilon\mu\alpha\tau\iota\kappa\acute{o}\nu$), shall emerge from the gloom of the sepulchral Hades and stand before the Throne of Eternal Justice; which shall wear the Crown and bear the Palm; and which realises even now by an act of faith—more than poetic fancy or philosophic theory—the sublime foreshadowings of Revelation.

NOTE.

As the previous chapter was passing through the press, the Editor noticed in the *Contemporary Review* for December, 1871, a most excellent article by the learned Max Müller, "On the Philosophy of Mythology," out of which the following is an extract:—

"I shall try by at least one example to show how mythology pervades, not only the sphere of religion or religious tradition, but infects more or less the whole realm of thought.

"When man wished for the first time to grasp and express a distinction between the body, and something else within him distinct from the body, an easy name that suggestd itself was *breath*. The breath seemed something immaterial and almost invisible, and it was clearly connected with the life that pervaded the body, for as soon as the breath ceased, the life of the body became extinct. Hence the Greek name ψυχή,* which originally meant breath, was chosen to express at first the principle of life, as distinguished from the decaying body, afterwards the

---

* "The word ψυχή is clearly connected in Greek with ψύχω, which meant originally blowing, and was used either in the sense of cooling by blowing, or breathing by blowing. In the former acceptation it produced ψῦχος, coldness; ψυχρός, cold; ψυχάω, I cool; in the latter ψυχή, breath, then life, then soul. So far the purely Greek growth of words derived from ψύχω is clear. But ψύχω itself is difficult. It seems to point to a root *spu*, meaning to blow out, to spit; Lat., *spuo*; Goth., *speivan*; Greek, πτύω, supposed to stand for σπύω. Hesychius mentions ψύττει = πτύει, ψυττόν = πτύελον. (Pott, Etym. Forsch., No. 355.) Curtius connects this root with Greek φυ, in φῦσα, blowing, bellows, and with Latin *spirare (i.e.*, spoisare). Stahl, who rejected the division of life and mind adopted by Bacon, and returned to the Aristotelian doctrine, falls back on to Plato's etymology of ψυχή as φυσέχη, from φύσιν ἔχειν or ὀχεῖν, Crat. 400 B. In a passage of his 'Theoria Medica Vera' (Halae, 1708), pointed out to me by Dr. Rolleston, Stahl says :—'Invenio in lexico graeco antiquiore post alios, et Budaeum imprimis, iterum iterumque reviso, nomenclaturam nimis quam fugitive allegatam : φυσέχη, poetice, pro ψυχή. Incidit animo suspicari, an non verum primum nomen animæ antiquissimis Græcis fuerit hoc φυσέχη, quasi ἔχων τὸ φύειν, e cuius vocis pronunciatione deflectente, uti vere familiariter solet vocalium, imprimis sub accentibus, fugitiva enunciatione, sensim natum sit φυσ-χή φσυχή, denique ad faciliorem pronunciationem in locum φσυχή, ψυχή. Quam suspicionem fovere mihi videtur illud, quod vocabuli ψυχῆς, pro anima, nulla idonea analogia in lingua græca occurrat; nam quæ a ψύχω ducitur, cum verus huius et directus significatus notorie sit refrigero, indirectus autem magis, spiro, nihil certe hæc ad animam puto" (p. 44).

incorporeal, the immaterial, the undecaying, the immortal part of man—his soul, his mind, his Self. All this was very natural. When a person dies, we too say that he has given up the ghost, and ghost, too, meant originally spirit, and spirit meant breath.

"The Greeks expressed the same idea by saying that the ψυχή had left the body,* had fled through the mouth, or even through a bleeding wound,† and had gone into Hades, which meant literally no more than the place of the Invisible ('Αἰδης). That the breath had become invisible, was matter of fact; that it had gone to the house of Hades, was mythology springing spontaneously from the fertile soil of language.

"The primitive mythology was by no means necessarily religious. In the very case which we have chosen, philosophical mythology sprang up by the side of religious mythology. The religious mythology consisted in speaking of the spirits of the departed as ghosts, as mere breath and air, as fluttering about the gates of Hades, or ferried across the Styx in the boat of Charon.‡

"The philosophical mythology, however, that sprang from this name was much more important. We saw that *Psyche*, meaning originally the breathing of the body, was gradually used in the sense of vital breath, and as something independent of the body; and that at last, when it had assumed the meaning of the immortal part of man, it retained that character of something independent of the body, thus giving rise to the conception of a soul, not only as a being without a body, but in its very nature opposed to body. As soon as that proposition had been established in language and thought, philosophy began its work in order to explain how two such heterogeneous powers could act on each other—how the soul could influence the body, and how the body could determine the soul. Spiritualistic and materialistic systems of philosophy arose, and all this in order to remove a self-created difficulty, in order to join together again what language had severed, the

* Ἀνδρὸς δὲ ψυχὴ πάλιν ἐλθεῖν οὔτε λεϊστὴ
Οὐδ' ἑλετή, ἐπεὶ ἄρ κεν ἀμείψεται ἕρκος ὀδόντων.
II. ix. 408.

† ἐιὰ δ' ἔντερα χαλκὸς ἄφυσσεν
Δηώσας · ψυχὴ δὲ κατ' οὐταμένην ὠτειλὴν
Ἔσσυτ' ἐπειγομένη.
II. xiv. 517.

‡ 'Ter frustra compressa manu effugit imago,
Par levibus ventis volucrique simillima somno.'
Virg. Aen. ii. 792.

living body and the living soul. The question whether there is a soul
or spirit, whether there is in man something different from the mere
body, is not at all affected by this mythological phraseology. We
certainly can distinguish between body and soul, but as long as we
keep within the limits of human knowledge, we have no right to speak
of the living soul as of a breath, or to speak of spirits and ghosts as
fluttering about like birds or fairies. The poet of the nineteenth
century says :—

> 'The spirit does but mean the breath,
> I know no more.'

And the same thought was expressed by Cicero two thousand years
ago : 'Whether the soul is air or fire, I do not know.' As men, we
only know of embodied spirits, however ethereal their bodies may be
conceived to be, but of spirits, separate from body, without form or
frame, we know as little as we know of thought without language, or
of the Dawn as a goddess, or of the Night as the mother of the Day.

"Though breath, or spirit, or ghost are the most common names
that were assigned through the metaphorical nature of language to
the vital, and afterwards to the intellectual, principle in man, they
were by no means the only possible names. We speak, for instance,
of the *shades* of the departed, which meant originally their shadows.
Those who first introduced this expression—and we find it in the
most distant parts of the world—evidently took the shadow as the
nearest approach to what they wished to express; something that
should be incorporeal, yet closely connected with the body. The
Greek εἴδωλον, too, is not much more than the shadow, while the
Latin *manes* meant probably in the beginning no more than the
Little Ones, the Small Folk.* But the curious part, as showing
again the influence of language on thought, an influence more powerful
even than the evidence of the senses, is this, that people who speak
of the life or soul as the shadow of the body, have brought themselves
to believe that a dead body casts no shadow, because the shadow has
departed from it; that it is, in fact, a kind of Peter Schlemihl.†"

---

* *Im-manis*, originally not small, came to mean enormous or mon-
strous.—See Preller, "Römische Mythologie," p. 72 *seq.*

† "Unkulunkulu; or the Tradition of Creation as existing among
the Amazulu and other Tribes of South Africa." By the Rev. J.
Callaway, M.D. Natal, 1868. Part I., p. 91.

CHAPTER III.

THE BIBLICAL SPIRIT OR GHOST.

WHEN we read the allegoric fable of Prometheus, who is said to have stolen fire from heaven, and therewith imparted animation to the moulded clay of the human form, or when we advert to Virgil's *Cœlestis Origo* of Life, we cannot but ascribe such parallelisms, distorted as they are, to the older source of divine revelation.

The Pythagoreans and Stoics held that the Deity was the soul of the universe, and that Jove personified the omnipresent principle of life. Anaximenes regarded air and spirit as identical.

Aristotle adverts to the Orphic Hymns, which represent the soul (in the sense of spirit) being inhaled with the air from the soul of the universe; φησὶ γὰρ τὴν ψυχὴν ἐκ τοῦ ὅλου εἰσιέναι ἀναπνεόντων, φερομένην ὑπὸ τῶν ἀνέμων (De Anima, cap. i., sec. 5, clause 15).

Trendelenburg, in his commentary upon the passage referred to, quotes a few phrases to which Aristotle adverts: Ἄνεμοι οὐ τὰ φυτὰ μόνον ἀλλὰ πάντα ζωογονοῦσι (Geoponicus). Πνοιαὶ ψυχοτρόφοι (Orph. Hymns, xxxviii., 22); and adds, *Id nobis*

*quœrendum restat, Orphica utrum Animam a primo
spiritus ductu et primo hoc quasi ventorum commercio
an a continua respiratione traxerint,* p. 289.

Thales, the wisest of the Seven Sages, said that
all things were full of the Gods.

The Hebrew Scriptures, paramount in time and
authority to all recorded philosophy, inform us of
the omnipresent Spirit and the Divine *afflatus,* and
that it is God " in whose hand is the soul of every
living thing, and the spirit *(ruach)* of all mankind"
(Job xii., 10).

The Spirit of God was brooding *(merachepeth)*
on the face of the primeval waters (Gen. i., 2., and
Deut. xxxii., 11).

The generic meaning of the word *ruach* signifies
the air as well as spirit, and the breath of our
nostrils (Lam. iv., 20; Num. xi., 31).

This term *ruach* (spirit) is generally expressive of
an invisible agency, which, like the air, is only
detected and characterised by its phenomena. Thus,
it is sometimes the 'spirit' of life, or the agency productive of life; sometimes it is the 'spirit' of wisdom
and knowledge, or the mysterious agencies producing
those cognitions which characterise an intelligent
being; or it is sometimes synonymous with doctrine
as the result of the preceding; at another time it is
the 'Spirit' of God, enunciatory then of His personal
agency whether mediate or immediate, whilst the
Holy 'Spirit' is always only declarative of His
immediate personal agency.

The phrase, " the Spirit of the Lord," is sometimes adopted in an idiomatic sense with reference
to a whirlwind (2 Kings ii., 16), also to a blighting
air (Is. xl., 7), apparently thereby intimating, in the
expressive phraseology of the holy tongue, that the
natural agencies are ministerial to the divine agency.

The laws and properties of matter would, doubtlessly, from the first conduce to consummate the
work of harmonious arrangement in what was
originally without form and void.   And, perhaps,
the phrase, " the Spirit of God," may imply, in the
idiomatic sense referred to, a mighty wind and other
secondary agencies moving upon and swaying the
primeval deep.

Sanchoniathon is supposed to have derived some
of his historic records from the Mosaic cosmogony.
Hesiod borrowed from the former, and Ovid from
him.   Thus, many things in the classic pages of
antiquity read almost like a paraphrase of the Mosaic
writings :—

> Ante Mare, et Tellus, et quod tegit omnia Cœlum,
> Unus erat toto naturæ Vultus in Orbe
> Quem dixere Chaos; rudis indigestaque moles (Ovid).

Amongst others, the poets Hesiod, Ovid, and
Virgil preserved the popular tradition of the Divine
origin of all things, the Divine *afflatus*, and a future
state or restitution.

The chaotic sphere, as at first introduced to us,
was unfit for the abode of organic occupants.

At the Almighty fiat light pervaded the atmos-

pheric gloom, the vapours dispersed, and the habitable earth appeared, preparatory to the introduction
of organised beings at successive creative *Eons.*

When, at length, the Almighty Creator fashioned
man from the dust of the ground, "he breathed into
his nostrils the breath of life *(nishmath chayim),*
and man became a living soul;" or more literally,
"he 'caused him to breathe' into his nostrils the
breath of life."

But, as other forms of organised life are in the
original Hebrew also denominated 'living souls,' we
must necessarily infer that they became so by the
same special agency; because like effects must be the
result of a like cause.

Yet we are not to infer, that the element in which
an animal lives, or which it inhales, is itself the
agency of life; for, unlike the physical agencies
which are developed solely in created matter, life
may be abstractedly identified in all its special
characteristics with the eternal Deity before created
things had existence. Angelic natures are also
represented as pre-existing; and their revealed
characteristics manifest, in a high degree, whatever
moral and intelligent characteristics we attach to
the vital agency.

Advanced science, moreover, leads us to the belief
that the sun, and the other considered spheres, are
constituted similarly to our own planet, and that the
same physical agencies and laws regulate the whole.

As we find a characteristic import attaches in the

Hebrew phraseology to the word *nephesh* (soul), so equally distinctive characteristics attach to the word *ruach* (spirit), whether natural or Divine.

The phrases "breath of life" and "spirit of life" are correlative. "The breath of the spirit of life," *nishmath ruach chayim* (Gen. vii., 22). Breath is dependent upon life, and life upon breath, in their physiological relation. The phrases "spirit of life" and "breath of life" seem not merely to imply the material agency, but something more.

When dead persons are reanimated, it is said " the spirit of life from God entered unto them" (Rev. xi., 11).

In Ezekiel's vision of the dry bones, when the flesh came upon them, still they lived not, " because there was no spirit (*ruach*) in them." But as soon as the 'spirit' was breathed into them from the four winds " they lived, and stood upon their feet, an exceeding great army" (Ezek. xxxvii., 8-10).

In the prophet's vision of the Cherubim the spirit animated the emblematic wheels which moved with them, "for the spirit of life was in them" (Ezek. i., 20).

The spirit of life is treated distinctively with the winds *(ruchoth)* which it accompanied, and as an agency separate from what it animates. A vital agency received with the breath of life, it enters the inanimate form, and man becomes a living soul; he becomes the conscious being, the voluntary agent. Thus, whether the Adam be regarded as a primordial creation, or as the mature development of an inferior type, the distinctive agency is equally applicable.

The verbal distinction between ' body,' 'soul,' and ' spirit' implies also a substantive and characteristic difference.

Body and soul possess each an objective character, correspondent with their verbal definition. The former refers to the deciduous character of the *nevailah*, and the other to the breathing character of the *nephesh*. But the spirit *(ruach)* possesses no such objective characteristics; there is no symbol by which it, as an immaterial agency, can be materially represented. It can only be designated by analogy with reference to its immaterial characteristics. An invisible agency productive of vitality, spontaneity, and sensibility, is something *sui generis.* So far as it is invisible and only discernible by its phenomena, it is analogous to the pneumatic agencies. "The wind bloweth where it listeth, and thou hearest the sound thereof, but canst not tell whence it cometh, and whither it goeth" (John iii., 8). Hence the term *ruach*, which primarily refers to the wind, is by analogy expressive of the invisible spiritual agency both of God and man. It is distinguishable and Biblically distinct from both body and soul.

If the word *neshama* (breath) in some passages of the canonical books refer to man alone, it is not by way of contradistinction to the brute creation; it is because man is the sole subject of allusion in those passages. As, with regard to the total extinction of the Canaanitish cities mentioned in Deuteronomy, the men alone were to be destroyed, and alone could be intended by the command " thou shalt save alive nothing that breatheth" (Deut. xx., 16). In its general import *neshama* is equally applicable to the breath of both brute and man.

The names of some animals, mentioned in Leviticus, are identified with the same root as this word *neshama*, and are supposed by eminent authorities to have been so designated with reference to some peculiarity of breathing. Thus, in Leviticus (xi., 3), *tinshemeth* (the breather), rendered " mole" in our authorised version, is a species of lizard according to Bochart and others; this reptile was believed to live upon air, and has a habit of inflating itself when disturbed.

" All flesh died that moved upon the earth, both of fowl, and of cattle, and of beast, and of every creeping thing that creepeth upon the earth, and every man : all in whose nostrils was the 'breath of the spirit of life' *(nishmath ruach chayim)*, of all that was in the dry land, died" (Gen. vii., 21, 22). Here the brute and the man seem clearly to be both comprehended under the same categorical expression of, " all in whose nostrils was the 'breath of the spirit of life'" *(nishmath ruach chayim)*.

The same *afflatus* that made man "a living soul" is equally applicable to the inspiration of all other " living souls," as modified by the idiosyncrasy of each.

The agency of life and intelligence in the brute is as mysterious and marvellous as that which is developed

in man. Their objective senses are essentially alike;
and, it is impossible to separate the subjective capacities—the special characteristic of man—from the
objective senses, these latter being fundamental to
the subjective.

Physiologists are generally satisfied, on scientific
grounds, to define 'life' as the active state of an
organic being; but to leave the question here is to
subject it either to the deduction that life is a property of organic matter, or that the spirit is the
philosophic Divinity himself. The Biblical doctrine
is more distinct, treating life as a distinctive agency
cognizable by positive characteristics.

That molecular matter, under suitable conditions,
manifests the phenomena characteristic of the physical agencies, and that organised matter, under
suitable conditions, exhibits the vital and even the
sensible and intellectual phenomena, is undoubtedly
and physiologically true. To say that these are
owing to the will of God is no less true; and, moreover, it is a truism and nothing more.

But upon this ground we thereby ascribe all these
phenomena either to material conditions or to the
direct interposition of the personal Deity.

By the former alternative we reduce the whole
to conditions of matter—not even excepting the
sensible and intellectual phenomena, which are synchronous and commensurate with the vital,—and
adopt the very dogma of Priestley, that they all
are properties of organic matter in some form.

By the other alternative we become Pantheists;

inasmuch as we impute not only life but its synchronous characteristics, as developed by sensitive and
ideal spontaneity and consciousness, to the direct
personal spontaneity and consciousness of the Deity.
Individual spontaneity and responsibility are thus
merged into so many developments of the Deity.

In treating of life physiologically it is, doubtlessly,
proper to confine its definitions to the physiological
phenomena. Physiologists, therefore, define the
conditions under which the phenomena of life are
manifested, and enter into the correlation of the
vital and physical agencies or forces. The Divine
power is manifested in all, and originates them all.

But, independent of the physiological phenomena, there are manifestly other characteristics of
life which are distinctively psychological and possess
no material analogies. We can no more cease our
enquiries with the physiology of life, than physiologists can be satisfied with the mere annunciation
of a vital principle.

Fundamental to the physical phenomena manifested in living organisms, there is an agency,
probably a secondary agency, that originates them.
It is something more than a merely material condition. The normal organism did not live until it
was caused "to breathe the breath of life." An
agency was thus introduced or developed with more
than merely material characteristics; there were
organic spontaneity and sensation, or consciousness.
These characteristics are apparently identified with

the Biblical spirit of life as a distinct psychological agency.

We are not told that this spirit is the Deity himself, but a spirit imparted by the Divine agency synchronously with the breath of life. A spirit, it may be, kindred to his own, for "we are his offspring;" spirit of spirit; an imparted, not a created agency.

At our death, "Then shall the dust return to the earth as it was : and the spirit shall return unto God who gave it" (Eccl. xii., 7). The dying believer is said to resign his spirit into the hands of God (Acts vii., 59, &c.).

It is thus, again, treated as a distinctive and separable agency, upon the presence of which life depends, and not as a mere condition. It is an agency susceptible of being given and taken away.

And yet, with Christian propriety, a man commends his soul (or Self) with respect to his eternal destiny to God, and his body to the dust.

The phraseology of the gospels, in relation to the death of Christ, is probably altogether of parallel import with the Old Testament doctrine. When, as expressed by St. Luke, Christ resigned his spirit or breath into his Father's hands, he afforded an example which Stephen in his martyrdom shortly afterwards followed, and which is worthy of every believer. But, with simple reference to the event itself, Christ, says St. Matthew, "yielded up ($\dot{a}\phi\tilde{\eta}\kappa\epsilon$) the ghost;" St. Mark says, $\dot{\epsilon}\xi\dot{\epsilon}\pi\nu\epsilon\nu\sigma\epsilon$, He expired;

and St. John says, Christ "gave up the ghost" παρέδωκε τὸ πνεῦμα.

The Psalmist, in commending himself to God's care, said, "Into thine hand I commit my spirit" or breath *ruchi* (Ps. xxxi., 5).

Job exclaimed, "Man giveth up the 'ghost,' and where is he?" *veyigva adam veaiyo* (Job xiv., 10).

Skinner and Junius consider that 'ghost' and πνεῦμα and *spiritus* originally meant breath or air, and that upon the conversion of the heathen to Christianity the term 'gast' and its congeners were applied *ad animas et angelos* in the popular sense.

The resuscitation of the dead is always mentioned as a miraculous event, or as the result of the Divine interposition through an agency divinely communicated to the individual.

The Shunammite's son was miraculously restored to life by the prophet Elisha. Lazarus revived at the command of our Saviour, "Lazarus, come forth;" Jesus took the ruler's daughter by the hand, "and the maid arose;" after His resurrection, "many bodies of the saints which slept arose, and appeared unto many."

Thus, life is represented as the result of a special agency divinely communicated to, or produced in, the organic body, and not as a property of matter, nor as the result of the ordinary physical or atomic agencies. Breath and life by the Divine interposition synchronously return; the Lord "formeth the spirit of man within him" (Zech. xii., 1); "He giveth to all life and breath" (Acts xvii., 25); "the inspiration of the Almighty (*nishmath Shaddai*) giveth them understanding" (Job xxxii., 8).

The Divine origin of organic life, as a distinctive agency, is testified to by the heathen in the sense of an Omnipresent Principle—hence, the *Chemosh*, or all-pervading vital agency of the Moabites, personified as Saturn by the Latins, the *Pater omnipotens æther* of Virgil, and the philosophic soul of the world.

As all living beings breathe, or appropriate the atmosphere in some manner, and as life and breath are commensurate with each other, the vital agency is with sufficient propriety denominated the spirit or breath of life, irrespective of any supposable atmospheric identity.

From the various contexts of the words *neshama* and *ruach* ('breath' and 'spirit'), it might be surmised, that the former implies the inspiration or breath, and that the latter is a consubstantial agency. So they frequently become convertible terms and parallelisms.

The manner of their use seems to illustrate some such radical distinction.

The Greek word Ζωὴ signifies the life itself, from ἄω to breathe; equivalent to *nishmath ruach chayim*, the breath of the spirit of life.

Elihu, in addressing Job, said, "The Spirit of God hath made me, and the breath of the Almighty hath given me life" (Job xxxiii., 4). Spirit and breath are obviously parallelisms.

In Isaiah (lvii., 16) a similar parallelism occurs, "The spirit should fail before me, and the breaths which I have produced."

The same word 'spirit' (*ruach*) is applied equally to men and brutes.

The human spirit, not by way of distinction but emphatically, is called the spirit of God (*ruach Eloa*); because, as Gesenius observes, it was breathed into man by God, and again returns to Him. But, it must be remembered, that such phrases have only special reference to man, whilst he is the special subject of the narrative; the same spirit, as implying the agency of vitality and intelligence, is in all living organisms equally and essentially Divine— "They have all one spirit" *ruach* (Eccl. iii., 19).

"Who knoweth the spirit (or breath, *ruach*) of man that goeth upward, and the spirit (or breath, *ruach*) of the beast that goeth downward to the earth?" (Eccl. iii., 21).

Pronaque quum spectant Animalia cœtera terram,
Os homini sublime dedit; cœlumque videre
Jussit, et erectos ad sidera tollere vultus. (Ovid, Lib. I.)

The natural attitude of man is erect, and his breath ascends; that of beasts, as a general characteristic, is prone, and their breath descends. But their attitude does not affect their psychology. "One thing befalleth them: as the one dieth, so dieth the other; yea, they have all one spirit" *ruach* (Eccl. iii., 19).

The Greeks recognised the same characteristic, when they denominated man ἀνθρωπος—a being who looks upward; or, as Herder describes him, *ein über sich, ein weit um sich schauendes Geschöpf.*

Neither man nor beast is ever called a spirit. They are always represented to be under its influence as an agency, and dependent upon it for life and intelligence.

Possibly, the Platonic doctrine of a *rational soul,* and the exploded doctrine of innate ideas had something to do with originating the popular distinction between the spirits of men and brutes.

That distinction, it would seem, must be sought in some other characteristic than that of the agency which imparts life and intelligence. Their different physiological idiosyncrasies suggest a sufficient disparity, without any compromise of their distinctive destinies, or of the Divine wisdom and power.

The characteristics of vitality are identified in all living organisms. There is no creature possessed of vitality, that does not in its own way, according to its idiosyncrasy, manifest automatic spontaneity and sensibility or response. Even plants, as well as animals, indicate something analogous to sensuous perception, directing them in the selection of their appropriate nutriment; it is more than atomic attraction or chemical affinity. There is a functional activity in the selection and organic assimilation of nutriment, which is only identified with the living organism. Some of the sensitive plants furnish

curious instances of a sensibility analogous to a
conscious instinct.

Spontaneity and sensibility are correlative and
synchronous, and are commensurate with vitality in
the whole and every part of the creature. They are
thus identified with the same indivisible agency,
the spirit of life.

We are therefore led to search for the characteristics
of vitality in the conduct of the living creature itself.
All its organic functions are automatic; all its actions
are spontaneous. Every sense is conscious of that
which addresses it. The entire being is instinct with
spontaneity and consciousness. The characteristics
of the spirit of life, in the whole and every part of
the entity, are spontaneity and consciousness.

It was probably from this characteristic spontaneity, that the ancients associated the idea of motion
with life, so often adverted to by Aristotle. It is,
perhaps, what Thales meant, when he said that mind
contained self-will or motion.

Spontaneity is developed in all the automatic
functions of the organic economy; whilst, in the
ideal functions, it becomes identified with the special
will and desires of the mental economy.

That which moves and acts from an inherent
cause, independent of all other and external causes,
manifests spontaneity. A spontaneous agency is
an originating power, akin to the spirit of Him who
originated all things. *Omniaque sentiens et movens,
ipsaque praedita motu sempiterno* (Cic. Tus. i., 27).

Again, Cicero very forcibly remarks, "*quidquid est illud, quod sentit, quod sapit, quod vivit, quod viget, caeleste et divinum, ob eamque rem aeternum sit necesse est*" (Tus. i., 27, s. 66).

This may well apply to the spirit, as an agency imparting vitality, conciousness, and spontaneity, but not to the concrete organic personality apart from that agency.

The doctrine of vibrations, as elaborately theorised by Hartley, may account for the transmission of sensuous impressions, but can never supply the *primum mobile*, automatic spontaneity, which involved that philosopher himself in perplexity.

Consciousness in like manner is developed in every special organic function, in every sensation, and in all the cognitions of the several senses. It is an ancient maxim, that we know nothing but what has first been in the senses. All wisdom and knowledge are the complement of such cognitions and of their subjective combinations and modifications. All are resolvable into sense consciousness, which is fundamental to them. Thus consciousness itself is an attribute of the spirit of life. "There is a spirit in mankind, and the inspiration of the Almighty giveth them understanding" (Job xxxii., 8).

All animals manifest objective perception, but man alone developes subjective conception. In him alone the spiritual agency becomes the spirit of wisdom and knowledge, properly so called, whether in a doctrinal or natural sense.

The passions and emotions are equally the result of conscious sense impressions, as the cognitions which give rise to them. Every passion, or condition of sense excitement, is the result of some sense perception. Every emotion is the accompaniment of some ideal subjective impression or conception. They resolve themselves into the same spiritual characteristics. All are personal organic affections, and subject to all the modifications of idiosyncrasy.

The objective impressions, received by the senses, are material impressions (τὰ παθητικὰ); but, in the living organism, those impressions are attended with synchronous consciousness or sensitiveness, as well as with automatic spontaneity.

This marvellous agency, manifested in the living organism, does not operate beyond, or independent of, the organic faculties. According to the idiosyncrasy of the organism, consciousness appropriates the sensuous impressions, and spontaneity directs and controls.

Howsoever we may designate the impressions or influences of external objects, we are not conscious of them out of ourselves. If the nerve of any sense be severed, the external communication is intercepted, and no conscious impression is received. The conscious impression, howsoever designated by us, is therefore an internal and not an external consciousness: yet, it is an internal consciousness of something concrete and external.

It is the living self, in the concrete, which is thus

conscious and spontaneous. Life, spontaneity, and consciousness are commensurate with each other, and are identified with the same agency.

As applied to the senses, we may term these characteristics ideal spontaneity and consciousness; but every organ of the living person manifests, physiologically, its own spontaneity and consciousness or sensibility.

If we adopt the term 'idea,' not in the Platonic sense, but rather in the general sense in which Locke used it, ideal consciousness implies, not only the objective ideas received by the senses, but those mentally acquired or formed by reflection upon the former by the intuitive power which we possess of combining, comparing, or analysing the objective or sense impressions.

All forms of knowledge and wisdom, in their natural sense, are fundamentally constructed of our internal conscious sense impressions and their subjective modifications. None of these states of consciousness arises from any probable or known property or form of matter; but all are so essentially different from the phenomena of inanimate matter, and are so identified with the living organism, as also to identify themselves with the agency of life itself.

Under these considerations, the Biblical phraseology appears peculiarly illustrative of the mental phenomena.

The spirit is spoken of as indicative of the will, as

well as of wisdom and understanding; for instance, "The spirit indeed is willing" (Matt. xxvi., 41), and "He that hath no rule over his own spirit" (Prov. xxv., 28). Spontaneity, in its subjective and objective forms, is indicated; although, in the Bible, all these terms are generally applied in a doctrinal sense.

Sometimes the same word 'spirit' is used metonymically, the effect being expressed for the efficient cause; as, when Pharaoh's spirit is said to be troubled, or Paul's spirit to be stirred within him; although, in reality, it is in such cases the organic personality which is moved. The agitation in the one case, and the emotion in the other are personal affections.

Spirit is, by a metonymy, sometimes synonymous with life, sometimes with disposition or doctrine, and at other times with the various perceptions and passions of personal character; but it is always as the causal agency upon which they depend. The cause and effect are correlative.

The phraseology is idiomatic, and based upon a latent psychology.

The living personality (or soul) is thus contemplated as a compound being, constituted of the concrete organism and a consubstantial spiritual agency as the co-efficient of the former.

We must, therefore, look for our mental intuitions, not in an abstract inner man corresponding to the popular soul and independent of the organic being,

but as they are developed by the compound living
organism itself, their results being modified by the
idiosyncrasy of each individual.

The characteristics of the spirit *(ruach)*, as
applied to the Holy Spirit, are essentially similar;
and they are indicative of an external independent
agency, in contradistinction to the spirit of the
creature. By the Holy Spirit (an agency distinct
from man's spirit), the will of the Creator influences
the will of the creature; by the Holy Spirit, God
enlarges the cognitions of man beyond the perceptions of common life; by the Holy Spirit, He helps
human infirmities; and by it, holy men of God spake
as they were moved. A prophet is styled a 'man
of the Spirit' *ish ruach* (Hos. ix., 7). The Holy
Spirit is in this way identified with the divine personality. It is the Deity in action.

Spirit is represented as acting upon spirit, the
spirit of God specially influencing the natural
spirit, as an agency auxiliary to it. The spirit of
ordinary life is controlled by an extraneous and
Divine influence for special purposes. The interposition of the Deity himself in mundane affairs is
implied by the agency of the Holy Spirit. The spirit
of man becomes ministerial to the Spirit of God.

The Holy Spirit is an agency so distinctive, that
it was capable of being taken from one and given
to another; as, when it was taken from Saul and
given unto David—thereby implying something
more than a mere personal mood, or frame of mind.

Indeed, prayer has been addressed to the Deity in all historic periods, from a conviction that He interposes, occasionally, by special influences upon, the minds of his creatures, and in the operations of nature. Civilized and barbarous alike look above in the hour of extremity. He who said, "Let there be light, and there was light," "Peace, be still! and there was a great calm," may not always act scientifically, yet must always be admitted to operate, in his special interpositions, consistently with Omniscience and His own prerogatives.

All the different forms of idiomatic phraseology, in which the term 'spirit' is employed as indicative of the will or of wisdom and knowledge, in their several applications to personal endowments or special gifts, are characteristic of the same spirit, either human or divine as the case may be. In a natural sense, they are identified with the same spirit of life ; in a divine and doctrinal sense, they are the special gifts of one divine agency, "There are diversities of gifts, but the same Spirit." (1 Cor. xii., 4).

The physiological characteristics of life are, equally with the psychological and Biblical, demonstrative of a distinctive agency. Thus, Hunter experimentally proved that the coagulation of the blood, when drawn from the body, was the organic result of the vital agency, and not mere coagulation or a physical phenomenon.

He also, by his experiments with the common

1

hen's egg, demonstrated that its preservation from freezing under the atmospheric influences of extreme cold, and the maintenance in it of a uniform warmth, notwithstanding surrounding changes of temperature, were peculiarly characteristic of the vital agency; in like manner putrescence was hindered, whilst that which was de-vitalised speedily decomposed.

The phenomena, however, of each organ are functionally peculiar; that is, each organ spontaneously developes the vital phenomena peculiar to its particular functions.

The word soul was generally applied, by the ancient philosophers, in the sense in which spirit is Biblically used. Aristotle attributes the phenomena of life to the agency of the soul (*De Anima*, cap. ii., sec. 1, sent. 4 and 8; and cap. ii., sec. 4, sent. 3). Thus, it is the principle (ἀρχή) of motion, also of sight to the eye, and of perception in all the senses. Moreover, Plato, although he treats of the soul in terms of personality as an incorporated demon, also imputes to it, as the animal soul, the vital phenomena (Phædo).

Hence, apart from the Divine personal agency, vitality, spontaneity, and sensibility are the Biblical, as well as the psychological, characteristics of the vital agency: or, seeing that vitality is commensurate with the two latter characteristics, we may say, that automatic spontaneity and sensibility are the characteristics of the vital or spiritual agency as developed in organised matter. So that, wherever there is life, there is also physiologically and psychologically automatic spontaneity and sensibility in some form ; each of these two is synchronous and commensurate with the other, and characteristic of the same agency.

There is ideal spontaneity or volition, when some thought or action is voluntarily produced; there is functional spontaneity, or what is commonly called involuntary thought or action, where the latter arises from some stimulus other than ideal spontaneity.

There is ideal sensibility, which is generally understood in the sense of consciousness; there is functional consciousness, in the sense of local sensibility or sensation, of which we may not be ideally conscious, as in many of the internal organic movements or the motor nerves of a paralysed limb.

Yet all consciousness resolves itself into organic sensibility, as diversified in the several senses and centres of nervous sensibility, the brain alone being apparently the centre of ideal sensibility.

Every organ possesses its own function ; and, therefore, according to its function, so are spontaneity and sensibility developed in itself and all its nervous radii.

These positions are abundantly corroborated by the experiments of physiologists, and are, for the most part, very clearly enunciated by Lewis in his Physiology of Common Life, and entirely accord with the characteristics biblically ascribed to the spirit as a distinctive agency.

We are not to think of 'the spirit' as of anything concrete; for it bears no material analogy. It is identified with the phenomena of life.

It is also identified with that second or ulterior consciousness in man, which has been conjectured to be associated with the grey matter surrounding a portion of his brain, and which characterises the intellect. This mysterious consciousness embraces in itself the consciousness of all the senses. Like an inner man it receives the report of each of the senses as to what each perceives of the outer world; and yet, it knows nothing of the outer world, except what it thus receives. But, what it thus receives, it spontaneously or at will combines or analyses, so as, by the processes of reason and dialectics, to build up and modify the entire fabric of knowledge and philosophy.

What that agency is, and how it operates, are amongst the secret things which belong only to the Omniscient.

Others as well as the Stoics, moderns as well as the ancients, have treated the spirit as the Divinity himself—the Soul of the World. But this is not the Biblical doctrine. It is stated to be Divinely originated, and its characteristics are analogous to those of the Divine Spirit.

There is no alleged discerption from the universal spirit, as held by some of the ancient philosophers. Even in a physical relationship, the offspring cannot be pronounced a discerption from its parent. Where

there is no diminution of identity, there is no discerption. Much less can there be a discerption from
the Divine Spirit, which is always the same, and
everywhere present. It is analogous to the miracle
of the widow's cruise of oil, always pouring out,
yet always full.

Neither is the spirit represented as a communication of personality in the pantheistic sense, otherwise
it would be tantamount to a participation in the
fulness of the Deity, and inconsistent with all individual independence and responsibility on the part
of the creature, contrary to the whole tenor of
revelation and experience.

The spirit of life and intelligence, not only animates the visible creation, but also the angels in
heaven, and those which are held in "chains and
darkness." It is, therefore, altogether inconceivable
that the Divine Spirit, in a personal sense, can be
identified with the spirit by which any of his creatures,
however exalted or however fallen, lives and moves.

It is a spirit imparted by the Creator, yet without
any discerption from, or identity with, his own distinctive Holy Spirit, by which his personal attributes
and influences are manifested and communicated.

The suspension or preternatural application of the
secondary or natural laws, in the phenomena recorded
as miraculous, vindicate the existence and authority
of a paramount intelligence and power—a great
First Cause, who is not the soul of the universe, but
its Parent and Ruler.

"The wind bloweth where it listeth, and thou hearest the sound thereof, but canst not tell whence it cometh and whither it goeth." So is it with the mysterious agencies within us and around us, whether divine, physical, or vital; their natural and revealed phenomena are alone demonstrable.

Chapter IV.

THE ATOMIC AND ORGANIC AGENCIES.

"The worlds were framed by the Word of God, so that things which are seen were not made of things which do appear" (Heb. xi., 3).

The visible universe was created from something else than itself, from something else than anything pre-existing, even from nothing.

It was not fashioned, as supposed by some of the ancient philosophers, like the work of an artificer, by a merely plastic modification or arrangement of pre-existing materials. As stated by Plato in his Timæus, the world was in a state of generation or becoming, and must have had a beginning; or, as more plainly stated in the Hebrew Records, "In the beginning God created *(bara)* the heavens and the earth." God *created* these; He *did not make* them from something already existing; the Hebrew words for 'create' and 'make' are quite distinct.

Yet, when we have said this, we are as far from answering the question, what is matter? as that of, what is spirit? neither can we explain or conceive, any more than Democritus could, how it was possible to create or shape out of nothing. It is sufficient for us to know that a Self-existent and Almighty Being said, "let there be," and it came to pass.

In what form matter was originally created, is beyond the reach of human research. But, that the visible universe has assumed its present appearance under the plastic influences of agencies which still operate, is both agreeable to the Mosaic cosmogony and in accordance with all its phenomena.

We discriminate between the vital and physical agencies, according to the phenomena which they develope; notwithstanding, they may be but modified results and exponents of the same unseen secondary essential agency, as they certainly are of the primary Divine agency which worketh all in all. The mysterious spontaneity, with which they all under suitable circumstances invariably obey certain demonstrable laws, seems to indicate, in all, an affinity to that which is itself originating and not orignated, to that causality which, behind the veil, moves the mechanism of the visible universe.

Without the operation of the physical agencies upon the various atoms of matter, according to their nature, the material universe might have ever remained a chaotic mass, unsuited to the purposes of an organic creation; yet, we have no reason to believe, that matter ever existed under such conditions. Every atom of matter, according to experimental philosophy, constitutes a centre of force. The tendency of the atomic, or (as they are generally denominated) physical, agencies has ever been to

promote such a material arrangement of the terrestrial elements, as would best adapt them to the
purposes referred to. There are thus the indications
of a primordial ultimate design on the part of the
Creator, that an organic creation should succeed the
inorganic; but, there is no proof, that the one should
be the development of the other.

If we can discover that the same agencies are
operating in other planets, we may infer that they
also are intended to become or are already the
abodes of an organic creation.   If, on the other
hand, there be a planet like the moon, probably
coeval with our own planet, in which we only
perceive evidences of material agencies, we may
have reason to conclude, that organic beings are
not a natural development of mere matter and
material agencies, but the result of a separate and
distinctive creation—that the lunar surface, perhaps,
presents to us the phase of a material world, such
as might be before its being clothed with an organic
creation.

According to the laws of chemical affinity, electricity, and gravitation, the varied stratification of
rocks, modified by the elements with which they
were surrounded, became consolidated and arranged;
and when, amidst the igneous and electrical convul-
sions of nature, heterogeneous compounds occurred,
the same agencies or forces again operated by disintegration to restore harmony out of seeming
confusion. So certain are these laws, that, under

given conditions, the same affinities invariably recur. Pure carbon, spontaneously, assumes the crystalline form of the diamond; and, other molecular matter spontaneously shapes itself into other crystals or strata. But the agencies or forces effecting these changes are atomic; we only detect them by their action upon atoms or molecular matter.

Thus, whilst automatic spontaneity is characteristic of living organisms, an analogous spontaneity is characteristic of the physical agencies affecting inorganic matter.

No individual atom changes or grows of itself: but, by a spontaneous agency or a self-contained force, several kindred atoms agglomerate or crystallise, or a body composed of several heterogeneous atoms is disintegrated. On the other hand, the most minute organic cell is automatic and generative. Never does matter assume, by means of the laws of atomic matter, the form of the organic being; this, from its heterogeneous constitution, is altogether opposed to, and inconsistent with the spontaneous tendency of the physical agencies. So much so is this the case that the organic body, under their uncontrolled influence, becomes rapidly disintegrated and disorganised.

It was reserved for a subsequent and distinct act of creative power, when the habitable globe was prepared for the advance, to call into existence the organic orders of creation in their various *Eons* of succession.

Whether they succeeded each other in the order of a nascent, as inferred by Darwin and others, or of a creative development, as Biblically recorded, does not, perhaps, necessarily disparage the character of Omnipotence and Omniscience in the Creator of all. If we believe in the prior existence of angelic beings, we cannot deny them a superior and independent origin.

By an anthropopeia, the Creator is said to have "breathed into man's nostrils the breath of life" (Gen. ii., 7); but, in a strictly causative (or *hiphil*) sense, we may say, "God *caused* him to breathe;" or, as in the vision of dry bones, "I will *cause* breath to enter into you" (Ezek. xxxvii., 5), whereupon man became a living soul or breathing personality. "He giveth to all life and breath" (Acts xvii., 25).

Thus the agency, which renders the organic being automatic, is itself represented as primordially derived from a source external to that being; but, by the act of breathing or absorption, it becomes functionally esoteric, and organically automatic. Supposing vitality were a property of matter, or an inherent agency independent of external causation, the creature would have been a living personality before he commenced to breathe, and the breath would have been a functional accessory; because, in that case, life must have been a property inherent, and not an agency *ab extra*.

As air is physically as well as vitally essential to the plant, so air is physically as well as vitally essential to the animal functions.

"The oxygen we extract from the atmosphere during inspiration is as much food as the flesh and farinacea which we introduce into the stomach, and the purposes it has to fulfil are equally important. If possible, they are more so; for the introduction of air into the animal economy begins with the first breath of life, and continues unceasingly until death closes the scene. Moreover, the oxygen introduced into the system, not only combines with the elements of food to construct, to build up the tissues of the economy, it also combines with them in other proportions during their disintegration and elimination; when, having served their turn, they die and are thrown out. Hence, the absolute necessity for an abundant supply of pure atmospheric air. For want of it, nutrition must flag; for, on the one hand, the construction of new tissues is defective; and, on the other, the elimination of those that are worn out is imperfect" (Dr. H. Bennet on Nutrition).

Wherefore, respiration being indispensable to the functions of the natural body, the latter is denominated a breathing personality *(nephesh)*.

But, in this sense only can we say, that the atmospheric elements are necessary to the maintenance of the natural body. For, if we substitute another body, such as the immortal, in the place of the mortal body, we cannot in like manner conclude that the atmospheric elements are equally, if at all, essential: in this case, vitality must be dependent upon an agency which is not identical with the material atmosphere.

The physical agencies, so far as not dependent upon the atmospheric elements, are capable of being developed *in vacuo*. As there are other beings besides those who occupy the habitable earth, and who may exist in other atmospheres or without any material atmosphere at all, we cannot conclude that air (any more than that water) constitutes the vital agency; these elements are essential to the functional existence of animal and vegetable life in their terrestrial state, but may not be so to those bodies which are spiritual and celestial.

Many species of animalcules afford instances of life sustained under greater extremes of temperature and varieties of atmosphere, than is known with respect to superior orders of beings. M. Pastein (in the *Comptes rendus* of Feb., 1861) describes certain animalcules, like small cylindrical rods, moving in undulations, which he discovered in the butyric fermentation : and he adds, "not only do these infusoria live without air, but air kills them. Carbonic acid does not affect them." Yet does not the fermentation, amidst which they live, imply the presence of air ?

Every organism has its peculiar element, which is essential to its normal conditions. The vital characteristics are the same in each, however diversified their functional development. As there are beings which live in air, others which live in water, and others which live in either, so there may be others which require neither, and some creatures which can exist in an atmosphere that would be destructive to most organisms. In like manner, there may be higher types of creation in other systems, to whom the spirit of life alone is the breath of immortality —an essential agency to which we cannot apply any physical test.

None of the planets in our firmament is supposed to possess an atmosphere similar to that of our earth. The chemical conditions and density of each are peculiar. So that, should organic life exist in other planets besides ours, it must be under conditions and modifications suitable to each, and different from our own; nevertheless, the agency of life may be the same in all.

In the present state, life is commensurate with breath ; therefore the spirit of life, as expressive of the vital agency, is correlative with the breath of life.

The plant and animal must be in a condition, and under circumstances, favourable to functional action, in order to develop vitality. The seeds of plants are preserved dormant, for a considerable period, by exclusion from the influence of the external elements; afterwards, when these seeds are exposed under suitable circumstances, vegetation commences. The animal frame cannot be so preserved, because its normal condition cannot be maintained, unless in the analogous form of the ova of animalcules.

M. Seguin, of Paris, is said to have enclosed

several toads in plaster, and after twelve years to
have found four of them alive. We can account
for the endurance of hibernating animals by the
torpor of their ordinary functions, and consequently
the less amount of aliment and air which they require. It may be thus with the fishes and reptiles
preserved in the moist clay of dried up ponds in
tropical climates until the next rain, the moisture
being the atmosphere of their torpid condition.
But the total exclusion of any animal or animal-
cule from air and moisture for several years, with
impunity, bears no analogy to the hibernating state,
and only an imperfect analogy to the condition of
the seed. Functional activity having commenced,
it would scarcely seem possible to exclude creatures
sufficiently from the action of the physical agencies
which are already developed within them. Their
normal condition would thereby be disturbed, without being renewed as it is in the merely torpid
state; whilst in the seed or ova it has never been
affected at all.

The reappearance of the rotiferi and other animalcules, after being allowed to remain in the dry sedi-
ment of a vessel for any lengthened period, may
perhaps be rather attributed to the germination of
their ova than the revival of deceased carcasses.

It is difficult to conceive how the normal conditions of an animal imbedded in rock, as sometimes
reported of toads, can be preserved from the fate of
the fossil.

Mr. James Samuelson, in a paper read before the British Association in 1863, mentioned, that "he had taken rags imported from various countries, and shaken the dust from them into distilled water, which he then exposed to the atmosphere." The general results of a microscopical examination of these fluids showed, that in the dust of Egypt, Japan, Melbourne, and Trieste life was the most abundant, and the development of the different forms was very rapid. Amongst these were some new species of rhizopoda and infusoria, and an interesting ciliated worm shaped form, which he believed to be from the larvæ of some other infusoria.

He said that, if he were correct in supposing the germs of the living forms, which he had described, to be present in the dust conveyed by the atmosphere, it was worthy of notice that these germs retained vitality for a long period, of which he could not pretend to define the limit. In his experiments they outlived the heat of a tropical sun, and the dryness of a warm room during a whole winter. But, in cases in which Dr. Ponchet was concerned, they must have retained their life two thousand years; for he obtained his germs from the interior of the Pyramids of Egypt, and they survived in an oil bath of four hundred degrees of heat.

It is not to be inferred from this, that the individual animals actually lived throughout these periods, but that their germs or ova retained their normal conditions like the seeds of plants; so that, when exposed under suitable circumstances to the atmosphere, they became vitalised as organic creatures, probably soon to die and be succeeded by new generations.

Sometimes infants apparently still-born, and persons apparently drowned, if medically treated before their normal conditions have undergone a change, are recorded as having had respiration imparted or restored. Dr. Marshall Hall refers to cases of resuscitation after the elapse of fifteen minutes or more. But, probably in such cases, some latent organic vitality, some muscular action of the heart susceptible of renewed activity, may still have been retained; for, as the vital conditions extend from the simplest form of cell life in the animal structure to the entire fabric, some portion may for a time retain functional vitality, when it has ceased to be manifested in its organic integrity. In order that vitality may be developed and perpetuated, the organic conditions must be normal, and the external circumstances must be suitable. When the normal conditions of the plant or animal are disturbed, or destroyed by disease or accident, the organic fabric becomes inevitably consigned to the ruthless agencies of death.

The organic phenomena are dependent upon the presence of the vital agency. The automatic functions of every organ are dependent upon it. The processes of the assimilation of food, and the propagation of species result from it. The offices of

all the senses are identified with it. Without this
vital agency, the organic body becomes incorporated
with the rest of the material creation, and is then
evidently subject to the atomic laws alone, and no
longer to those which govern the living organism.

If we confine our attention to the intellectual
characteristics of humanity, we are apt to conclude
that they indicate those of a spirit superior to that
communicated to the rest of the animal creation.
They all alike indicate in various degrees objective
sensibility; but man alone manifests subjective capacities. Yet sensuous spontaneity, indicative of a
will, is in all creatures dependent upon cerebral
action. In the lower animals, as well as in man,
there exists an objective will; but in man alone is
subjective volition developed, making him how like
a God, in his rational processes! This, however, is
dependent upon the subjective functions of the same
organ, and is not attributable to a different spirit;
for, "they have all one spirit." The mental characteristics of all vary with their cerebral idiosyncrasies
as animated by the spiritual agency, upon which
vitality itself depends. Each organ developes its
own functions, and the same spirit animates the
whole and every part of the fabric with spontaneity
and sensibility of its own.

In the organic being alone do the characteristics
of spontaneity assume the functions of the voluntary
agent; nevertheless, this special development of
spontaneity is confined to the ideal senses. A ship

does not sail against the wind; nor does a stone roll up hill : these spontaneously conform to the unalterable laws of mechanics and gravitation. But the smallest living organism is enabled at its will to resist, and even to reverse, the physical tendencies of atomic gravity and motion; not that it does so by the force of mere volition, but through the medium of organic powers which the will of the creature spontaneously exercises.

The sun cannot but shine; the chemical affinities cannot but act; the heart cannot but beat; howbeit, the ideal functions of the voluntary agent assert a control over the conduct and motions of the individual, in the guidance of all his senses to do or not to do. In atomic and functional spontaneity, as contradistinguished from ideal, there is no will except to obey certain fixed laws of development.

The different relations, in which the organic and atomic agencies or forces manifest themselves in the organic being, are discussed by Dr. Carpenter in an interesting paper upon "The correlation of the vital and physical forces" contained in the Philosophical Transactions for 1850.

The vital or organic agency is characterised by phenomena, which the physical or atomic agencies alone cannot produce. Remove the vital agency by death, and the physical agencies do not furnish any compensation; on the contrary, they speedily operate by the ordinary physical laws to disintegrate the organic structure.

" If the condition of the tissues in a plant is such
as to cause it to be changed by the play of the ordinary chemical affinities, it can only retain its normal
character so long as it is performing vital actions;
and when these cease, it either undergoes decay
(which is the case with the softer tissues), or it
becomes transformed into a substance which resists
decay."

Dr. Carpenter moreover shows, that in the living
organism the physical agencies are modified in their
action by the vital agency. The facts, which he
adduces, "indicate that every integral part of the
living fabric possesses within itself a capacity of being
so acted on by external agencies, that the very forces,
which would tend to decompose and destroy it if it
were dead, only excite it to vital activity if it be alive."

" In many of the highest plants, and also in
animals, we witness movements of fluid through a
capillary network, which must be wholly, or in part,
due to the vital relations of the fluid and the tissues
through which it is carried, no physical agency being
capable of entirely accounting for these movements,
and some of them taking place under circumstances
which, as in the case of the rotation within the cells
of the chara, etc., seem to exclude the idea of such
an agency. The forces concerned in the growth,
development, and movements of animals appear to
be essentially the same as those whose existence has
been traced in plants."

He considers, that the different vital phenomena

are but different manifestations or modes of the same force; yet, that the vital agency and physical agencies are not identical: he treats these statements as demonstrated by the results of experiments.

The physical agencies, acting upon the nerves of sense, develope their peculiar functions in much the same way as material objects produce in each sense its peculiar impression. Thus nerve force, "operating upon a certain special form of apparatus," developes electricity; and electricity, transmitted along the sensuous nerves, developes nervous force and the phenomena of each particular sense. Mechanical force, applied to each of the nerves of sense, does the same; and heat and light produce analogous results.

Whatever force the physical agencies exert upon a living organism, the vital force by a reverse action reciprocates.

Heat is not identical with the vital force; although, for its development, a certain temperature is necessary in all organised beings, whether vegetable or animal. The animal system so far generates its own heat, that (suitably to its powers of locomotion) it accommodates itself to a greater variety of climates than the vegetable.

From this power of generating animal heat, life is commonly designated the vital spark or celestial fire; howbeit the heat is not the vital agency, only its consequence proceeding from the chemical union of oxygen with carbon and hydrogen. Hence, and from the importance of light and warmth for the development of vitality, fire became symbolical of the agency.

Dr. Carpenter "no more regards heat as the vital principle, or as itself identical with the vital force, than it is identical with electricity, or with chemical affinity." The pre-existence of a living organism is necessary to the development of all the physiological phenomena. We never find the phenomena of organic matter developed by inorganic matter. To say that heat, electricity, and the chemical affinities, are not identical with the vital agency, is tantamount to saying that the phenomena of the atomic agency are not identical with those of the organic agency.

"Starting with the abstract notion of force, as emanating at once from the Divine will, we might say that this force, operating through inorganic matter, manifests itself in electricity, magnetism, light, heat, chemical affinity, and mechanical motion; but that, when directed through organised structures, it affects the operations of growth, development, chemico-vital transformation, and the like; and is further metamorphosed, through the instrumentality of the structures thus generated, into nervous agency and muscular power." In other words, the Divine will is represented by a spontaneous agency, distinct from matter, developing itself variously according to certain laws in or upon organic as well as inorganic matter.

Dr. Carpenter further shows a correlation between all the manifestions of the vital agency, as variously developed in the different functions of the living organism, and a resultant correlation between it and the physical agencies as they act and react upon each other in producing the several functional phenomena. There is in this way a functional distinctiveness indicated in the characteristics of the vital agency developed in the organic being, and in the physical agencies atomically developed in the same being. Yet all operate, correlatively and necessarily, in producing the phenomena manifested in the organic entity.

Deprived of the functional agency, the atomic agencies operate to disintegrate the organic being. On the other hand, the functional agency suspends or modifies the ordinary operations of the atomic agencies, and tends to replace what they remove. Thus the atomic body is ever fleeting, whilst the body of personal identity (the Soul or Self) is ever maintained.

As we find a correlation between all the vital phenomena variously developed in the organic functions, so we perceive a similar correlation between its psychological phenomena. Thus the spontaneity of the senses is identical with the spontaneity of all the bodily functions. As the eye cannot but see, so the other senses and organic functions cannot but perform their parts in the vital economy; each operates spontaneously in its own way. We cannot expect one organ to perform the part of another. We cannot expect the stomach to perform the functions of the brain. Therefore, as the ideal functions are developed in the brain and not in any other organ, we may expect to find spontaneity and consciousness manifested in some other way in the brain than in any other organ. This accords with that modification of spontaneity ideally manifested in volition, whereby the several sensuous motions and ideal processes are regulated.

In like manner ideal consciousness is only developed in the brain, whilst local sensitiveness is manifested in every physical organ. Although we may not be ideally conscious of what is passing in the heart, the stomach, or other corporeal organ, yet from the spontaneous local adaptation to local accidents, as manifested by the *vis medicatrix* and in similar ways, a local sense analogous to local consciousness is developed sufficiently to identify the same vital agency with the same characteristics in each and every organic function. Whence, the vital agency of physiology is identified with the spiritual agency of psychology. Spontaneity and consciousness, under their several correlative functional developments, are as much the characteristics of the one as of the other.

The physical and vital or spiritual agencies are intimately associated in the organic creature. They do not neutralise each other, but in some respects reciprocally modify each other's development. The tendency of the physical agencies, in the absence of the vital, is to disintegrate the organic structure. In the living organism, the spiritual or vital agency maintains the integrity of the system by replacing, through the functional processes of nutrition, what the physical or atomic agencies have exhausted or removed.

Thus there is a perpetual alternation, and, as it were, balancing of forces between the physical and vital or atomic and organic agencies in every organic being; the one displacing atom by atom, and the other replacing cell by cell. The body is always fleeting; the soul, the personal identity ever coming.

In the primeval state when all things were pronounced to be very good, we may suppose that this tendency, in at least the human system, might be progressive or metempsychal from the natural to the spiritual body; because, with respect to man, death is spoken of as abnormal. However, that perfection no longer exists; the physical agencies ultimately triumph, in reclaiming for the dust of the earth the wonderful being who once trod it under his stately step.

The spiritual or organic agency may be metaphorically termed the angel of life. The physical or atomic agencies are, in the present state, the messengers of death.

The physical agencies triumph over the individual. The organic agency triumphs in the perpetuation of the race.

But, in "the time of the restitution of all things," when this mortal shall have put on immortality, we shall witness more than the primordial perfection of the individual in the glory and power of the body that shall be—the body that shall no more hunger or thirst, shall no longer be subject to waste or decay. The balance of forces is restored. The ambrosia of immortals is the fruit of the symbolic Tree of Life.

We shall probably then, and not until then, comprehend the mysteries of a spiritual body—the incorruptible and immortal—the bush that ever burns and never is consumed.

PART II.

—:o:—

PERSONALITY.

—:o:—

PART II.

PERSONALITY.

CHAPTER I.

SELF.

FROM the time of Plato, the soul has generally been treated as the spiritual impersonation of the rational being enshrined in the corruptible body. Plato's idea has, however, been modified according to the various definitions adopted by Christian philosophers.

Locke defines *Self*, as "that conscious thinking thing (whatever substance made up of, whether spiritual or material, simple or compounded, it matters not) which is sensible, or conscious of pleasure and pain, capable of happiness or misery, and so is concerned for its self, as far as that consciousness extends" (book ii, chap. 27, sec. 17).

"Nothing but consciousness can unite remote existences into the same person, the identity of substance will not do it. For whatever substance there is, however framed, without consciousness, there is no person: and a carcase may be a person, as well as any sort of substance be so, without consciousness" (book ii., chap. 27, sec. 23).

The substance of Locke's argument pursued in the following sections of the same chapter seems to be, that the "thinking thing" within us constitutes the conscious *Self*, whilst the material form may change or become unconscious or die; and therefore, the same material person, apart from the "thinking thing" or spirit, may no longer be identified with the conscious *Self*.

"The same numerical substance is not considered as making the same *Self;* but the same continued consciousness, in which several substances may have been united and again separated from it, which, whilst they continued in a vital union with that wherein this consciousness then resided, made a part of that same *Self*" (sec. 25).

"This personality extends itself, beyond present existence to what is past, only by consciousness" (book ii., chap. 27, sec. 26). According to this definition, personal identity is excluded during any portion of our existence to which consciousness does not extend.

If self-consciousness is to be regarded the constituent test of personal identity, it does not appear what is to become of the *Self* during intervals of want of consciousness. Therefore, instead of self-consciousness being the constituent, it would rather seem to be our sole individual evidence of personal identity. A thing may exist without our knowledge of it, through deficiency of proof. Personal identity must necessarily be continuous, although during some portion of our lives we may become unconscious of it. The force of Locke's argument upon self-consciousness is rather, that it is our only personal assurance of our own identity, than that our personal identity depends upon it.

In another place, he speaks of the "ignorance we are in of the nature of that thinking thing that is in us, and which we look on as ourselves." Then he says, "But taking, as we ordinarily now do (in the dark concerning these matters), the soul of a man for an immaterial substance, independent from matter, and indifferent alike to it all, there can, from the nature of things, be no absurdity at all to suppose that the same soul may, at different times, be united to different bodies, and with them make up for that time one man" (book ii., chap. 27, sec. 27).

In his Controversy with the Bishop of Worcester, he further defines his idea of the nature of soul and spirit. "To what I have said in my book, to show that all the great ends of religion and morality are secured barely by the immortality of the soul, without a necessary supposition that the soul is immaterial, I crave leave to add, that immortality may and shall be annexed to that which in its own nature is neither immaterial nor immortal, as the apostle expressly declares in these words, 'For this corruptible must put on incorruption, and this mortal must put on immortality'" (book iv., chap. 3, sec. 6, note).

Moreover he considered, that the act of thinking was inconsistent with the idea of self-subsistence, and therefore must have a support, or subject of inhesion, or a substance ; and so he says, " we have a proof of a thinking substance in us, which in my sense is a spirit."

He afterwards adds, " Perhaps my using the word spirit for a thinking substance, without excluding materiality out of it, will be thought too great a liberty, because I leave immateriality out of the idea I make it a sign of. But in the present case I think I have great authorities to justify me. The soul is agreed, on all hands, to be that in us which thinks."

He then illustrates his meaning by reference to Cicero's Tusculan Questions, and the 6th Book of Virgil's Æneid, where the latter speaking of the soul says *Dum spiritus hos regit artus*, and the former says *Vita continetur corpore et spiritu.* Whence and from other passages he considers it plain, that " they called an active, thinking, subtle substance, out of which they excluded only *(corpus)* gross and palpable matter, *spiritus."* *Tanta ejus tenuitas ut fugiat aciem* (Cic. Tus. Ques., lib. i., chap. 22).

From all which it is clear, that Locke, with the ancient as well as modern philosophers, understood soul and spirit as identical. Whether the soul were regarded to be united to some form of matter or not, still the immortality of the soul was identified with that of the spirit in the sense of a personal immortality independent of the body.

It is true, as Locke elsewhere shows, that we have not, and cannot have with our finite understandings and experience, any primary scientific knowledge of either material or spiritual bodies. Although he is cautious in expressing any very definite idea concerning the soul, yet upon the whole he conceives the soul to be immortal and to represent, by its union with some unknown substance, our personal spirituality, which in a personal sense may survive the body.

Descartes expressed his conviction of our personality by the celebrated aphorism, *cogito ergo sum*. What he intended by this is not very obvious. That which thinks must be an existing entity. He probably intended, as Professor McCosh remarks, to express no more than Dugald Stewart did by ' an intuitive consciousness of the personal self;' or than Sir Wm. Hamilton does when he says, we are conscious of the *Ego* as " a self-subsistent entity" (Lect. 19).

The thinking *Ego* of these and other metaphysicians is evidently the " thinking thing" of Locke, an abstract thinking personality.

Reid remarks, in his Essay on the Organs of Sense, " We have reason to believe that when we put off these bodies, and all the organs belonging to them, our perceptive powers shall rather be improved than

N

destroyed or impaired. We have reason to believe, that the Supreme Being perceives everything in a much more perfect manner than we do, without bodily organs. We have reason to believe, that there are other created beings endowed with powers of perception more perfect, and more extensive than ours, without such organs as we find necessary. We ought not, therefore, to conclude that such bodily organs are in their own nature necessary to perception; but rather that by the will of God our power of perceiving external objects is limited and circumscribed by our organs of sense; so that we perceive objects in a certain manner, and in certain circumstances, and no other. If a man was shut up in a dark room so that he could see nothing but through one small hole in the shutter of a window, would he conclude that the hole was the cause of his seeing, and that it is impossible to see in any other way?"

Nos enim ne nunc quidem oculis cernimus ea quae videmus; neque est enim ullus sensus in corpore: ut facile intelligi possit, animum et videre et audire, non eas partes, quae quasi fenestrae sunt animi (Cic. Tus. lib. i., chap. 20, sent. 46).

Such was essentially the Platonic theory, and that the purgation of the soul was only to be thoroughly attained by its separation from the body; and in accordance with this assumption, it was considered that the organic senses were merely an encumbrance to the soul (Phædo, secs. 32, 33).

Reid illustrates his opinion in the same way as

Cicero did. It is therefore probable, that their views of the soul's distinct personality independent of the organic body were pretty much alike; but such is also the common idea of modern philosophers and theologians, whether right or wrong.

That this was likewise Kant's idea is to be negatively inferred when he says, that our inward sense gives us no perception of the soul itself as an object. *Der innere Sinn giebt zwar keine Anschauung von der Seele selbst, als einem Object (Kritik der reinen Vernunft, p.* 34). The soul is not an object of sense.

If we follow out the views above conveyed concerning the soul, we necessarily arrive at the same conclusion obtained by Reid and Plato, that the soul would be better without the body; in short, that the soul, being united to some substance which preserves its own identity, may survive and altogether dispense with the body. Our perceptive and rational powers together with the recollections of the past and self-consciousness being in a manner transferred to this inner self, which is at once the " thinking thing" within us and our self-personation, the Platonic idea is fully realized in the modern mind. The question is, thereupon, once more revived, why were we sent into these bodies at all? Nevertheless, whilst perception may not be dependent upon the bodily organs, individual personality may.

There is also a stoical or pantheistic view of the soul, that finds its modern disciples chiefly in Germany. This may partly result from the abstract idealistic doctrines of Hegel and Fichte; who, by disconnecting our ideas from the concrete, tend to identify the conscious Deity with the ideal developments of conscious humanity, thus negativing that individual personality which the Platonists maintain.

As before observed, Plato drew a distinction between the rational soul of man and the animal soul of the brute creation. He does not appear to have duly appreciated, that the perceptions of the senses are fundamental to the origin of all our ideas. He, therefore, identified the characteristics of our subjective ideas with the rational soul of man, and those of our objective ideas with the animal soul.

There is a distinction made between soul and spirit by H. Zschokke in his *Selbstschau* (part ii.), which very nearly corresponds with that made between the animal and rational souls by Plato. This popular work can scarcely be regarded so much a philosophical enquiry as a theoretical rhapsody ; yet it probably represents an acceptable opinion, and is replete with beautiful and lofty thoughts.

" As the plant in its possession of life ranks above what is lifeless, so the brute is superior to the vegetable world ; for it manifests in its movements something more than the plant ; it expresses a feeling of pleasure and pain ; it perceives the things round about it ; it has a soul.

"So man possesses a soul like the brute ; for he is conscious and feels like it" (*Auch der Mensch ist beseelt wie das Thier ; denn er gewahrt und empfindet wie dieses*).

" He is endued with life as the plant ; his body

is a union of substances and forces, as every other
body; but there is in him a yet higher power,
through which he is conscious of himself, surveys,
grasps, understands all things, and by means of
which he recognises a law of morals and holiness
inapplicable to brutes and plants. In man dwells
a consciousness of liberty by which he opposes the
impulses of life itself, even the appetites of the soul.
It is more than soul, it is the spirit"—*Da ist
mehr als nur Seele; da ist der Geist"* (*Selbstschau*,
part ii., page 10).

"Sense or feeling, in the common acceptation of
the term, is the utterance of the soul, and is found
in man, and more or less in the souls of beasts"
(page 14).

"The spirit does not thus feel; it is simply knowing, thinking" *das Wissende, Denkende* (page 15).

"Only a small portion of living material forms
are soul-gifted; only brutes and men upon earth
perceive and feel. All other creatures stand and
move as if dead, without being conscious of themselves or other things around them"—*alle andern
Schöpfungen stehn und wandeln, gleichsam wie Todtes;
ohne sich selber, oder das Uebrige um sich her zu
gewahren* (page 160).

It is true that all living things do not possess
ideal perception, yet the very plants manifest
functional sensibility or consciousness.

In the order of creation, "man appeared at last
a higher being; his *Ego* is the God-thinking spirit"
(page 206).

It is evident that Zschokke applies spirit in the sense of the rational soul of Plato. He treats life as an agency common to all organic beings; the soul as another agency or sensible substance common to men and brutes; and the spirit not only as the rational part of man, but as constituting his personality, and in this sense surviving his body. But further on he says that the soul, as if more than an agency, constitutes as it were the body of the spirit.

Again, his distinction between soul and spirit resolves itself into the common distinction between objective and subjective ideas, and nothing else. It is merely expressing in another form the popular distinction between men and brutes; for instance when it is said, that men have souls but brutes have none, that men possess subjective capacities of mind but brutes are merely objective.

Yet after all, we cannot precisely discriminate between men and brutes by the absence of all subjective ideality in the latter, but only by the absence of a subjective capacity; for, although they do not seem to possess a discretionary control over their ideal modifications amounting to a subjective capacity, many of their instincts are as rational in their results as if they were dictated by a knowledge of geometry and mechanics, such as those of the bee, the beaver, birds in the construction of their nests, the spider in its contrivances to ensnare its prey, and many others. So that ideally we must admit, that brutes manifest to some extent the same spirit as man, if such ideas be characteristic of a spirit different from that which animates the senses common to all, as assumed by Zschokke. They do things by an instinctive sense, which man can only solve by reason ; yet, this instinctive sense is as much identified with their perishable organisms, as their organic senses are. The great Mechanician of the universe has stereotyped in them single or simple problems, whilst man's subjective capacities are free to solve all problems ; his ideas, like moveable types, arrange themselves according to his will.

Since the time of the publication of Locke's Essay on the Human Understanding, it has in general been conceded that our objective or sense ideas are the primary source of all our knowledge. They are fundamental to all our rational or subjective knowledge. We possess no subjective ideas, however complex or exalted, which cannot be resolved into objective experience.

The objective perceptions of man may be compared to a second consciousness or ultimate perception of the sense ideas. Whether this further perception can be identified with a further or superior central organization, it is perhaps difficult to demonstrate ; but that there is a difference in the cerebral organization of man and all other creatures is itself demonstrable.

It has been conjectured, with some appearance of probability, that the grey matter is the seat of intellect. Johnston, in his Chemistry of Common Life, remarks, " The grey matter, though so small in quantity, is supposed to be the seat of intellect and the source of all nervous power. Softenings, tumours, and abscesses may exist in the white part of the brain—a portion of it may even be extracted —without seriously or universally affecting the mental powers; but compress the grey part ever so little, or otherwise alter or disturb it, and you, at the same time, seriously interfere with the processes of thought and disturb the intellectual sanity of the individual" (vol. ii., p. 405, edition, 1855). There is a small and modified grey matter about some portions of the brains of some animals that may, in like manner, have relation to their instincts; but in man it is universal, and seems directly to affect his intellectual powers.

Now, subjective ideas, by their fundamental dependence upon the sense ideas, appear a second or ultra consciousness. They seem to identify a second consciousness and spontaneity, which are related to and deal with the sense ideas as these are related to and deal with the objects themselves, and which are not developed by other creatures than man beyond the limits of their unalterable instincts.

The objects of sight and hearing, and of the other senses, do not remain in man as such; but, by a second or further spontaneity and consciousness, he becomes conscious that they are those particular objects, and modifies them again by further processes of collocation and comparison, in like manner as the senses are affected by the original objects.

Animals objectively perceive the same colours and sounds which man does; they, however, only see them as objects, whilst man further perceives them as characteristics of the objects already impressed upon his senses—he recognises in them ideal qualities. As the higher instincts of animals are identified with their physical organisms, there seems to be reason to conclude that the subjective capacities of man are also identified with his physical organism.

Whilst, therefore, the soul of man is *partly* characterised by its objective tuitions and experience, the souls of brutes are, on the other hand, *solely* characterised by analogous tuitions and experience.

The objective senses of brutes are as marvellous as, and some of them more acute than, the senses of man. The consciousness and spontaneity of the one are as spiritual and immaterial as those of the other; and the instincts of some creatures are even more accurate and wonderful than the results of reason itself.

If the objective perceptions of man are identified with his soul, so the objective perceptions of brutes are identified with their souls. If the objective perceptions of the one are identified with a spiritual and immortal agency, so must the objectivity of the other be identified with nothing less.

If the objective perceptions of man would be improved without the body, we might equally infer that the objective perceptions of brutes would be likewise improved by liberation from their bodies:

and further, if the personal immortality of man is to be inferred from the immaterial conditions of that agency which imparts perception and spontaneity to him, so may a similar inference be deduced with regard to that which imparts perception and spontaneity to brutes. Yet the similarity of the agency, which vitalises and intellectualises each, fails to establish of itself the personal immortality of either.

The rational or Platonic soul of man cannot, according to our experience, be disjoined from the objective faculties; because man's rational or subjective ideas are in fact composed of and based upon his objective perceptions.

The diversity, therefore, between the souls of men and brutes seems to result from their different intuitive idiosyncrasies, man alone possessing the faculty of subjective ideal combination and analysis. As all creatures are affected by whatever affects their respective organic idiosyncrasies, both men and brutes may be alike dependent upon the latter for their respective individualities.

Such a dependence is especially striking with regard to memory. For, although we might conceive it possible, that all our sense perceptions are modified by the affections of the senses through which they present themselves to the inner self (whatever that may mean); yet we might expect, that the inner self, representing the immortal substance of the soul as assumed by Locke, should ever afterwards retain a recollection of such perceptions, unaffected by the subsequent affections of the mere organic sensorium. This, however, is not so; the original perceptions or ideas are still liable to be as much affected by the subsequent affections of the organic sensorium as upon their first perception. A fever, or a blow, may obliterate temporarily, or altogether, a series of recollections. Similar phenomena are appealed to by the materialists, in support of Priestley's theory that life and intelligence are peculiar properties of organic matter.

That which is a property of matter in any form is inherent to it. If vitality and intelligence be properties of organic matter, they should continue to be inherent to it so long as any portion of the normal organism remains; but we do not find this to be the case. They should also have synchronised with the creation of the organism itself. Vitality and intelligence are, therefore, characteristics of an agency separable from organic matter. Nevertheless these, as the characteristics of a distinctive spiritual agency, are identified with the idiosyncrasy of the organic personality of all the orders of organic entities. The individual *Self* of each entity is identified only with its idiosyncrasy in the concrete.

Before the child becomes acquainted with the terms of language, it is intuitively conscious of what affects its *Self* as an organic being. When the adult thinks of *Self*, it is in the concrete; he does not think of himself as an abstraction. Whatever affects his organic being affects himself. When he thinks, he thinks of some actual sense or subject of cogitation that occupies his attention. He does not think of anything else than of what he experiences. We individualise ourselves from others in the concrete.

"We know *Self* as having being, existence. The knowledge we have in self-consciousness is of a thing, a reality" (McCosh on the Intuitions of the Mind, p. 149 and notes).

The exponent of *Self* is a subjective act of the mind, exerted by self identification in the midst of others.

We are intuitively conscious of seeing, hearing, touch, taste, and smell; so also is the brute creation. Each is objectively and intuitively conscious of what affects itself. But, it is the human subjective power of individualising oneself, by an intuitive comparison and contrast with others, as a concrete independent being, that makes the difference. We are thus subjectively conscious of the separate and individual *Self*. The brute has no such abstract consciousness.

We are thus conscious of our individual objectivity and subjectivity in contradistinction to those of others. We are also conscious of our individual powers and actions, and of being individually acted upon as individual objects in the midst of surrounding powers and agencies.

The brute possesses an objective intuition or

sense of what affects itself, yet no subjective abstract conception of it.

Again, exerting our abstract analytical intuitions, we experimentally perceive, that this individuality is composed of senses and organs, the complement of which makes up the whole man—that this frame is composed of matter possessing all the properties of matter, but influenced by an agency possessing characteristics of its own, imparting vitality, spontaneity, and consciousness—and that the whole together constitute the perfect *Self*, analogous to the ἐντελεχεια of Aristotle, the *animus ad corpus relatus*.

If we reverse the enquiry, and, instead of basing it upon the phenomena of the organic senses, we were to ground it (as preferred by some) upon the ideal phenomena alone, we should in the end arrive at the same conclusions.

The objective ideas or perceptions in both man and the inferior creation manifest a similar origin, as shown by Locke; the subjective modifications of these ideas are peculiar to man.

Now, these objective ideas precisely correspond with our sense ideas, which are the basis of all our subjective ideas. Hence, if man could under any circumstances dispense with his organic senses, without such a substitute as that of the spiritual body, we are again driven to the inevitable conclusion that brutes might also aspire to the same ideal personality.

Therefore, it would appear upon the whole, that the Biblical living soul, as constituted of the concrete body and the consubstantial spirit, is more in accordance with the phenomena of common life than the soul of either the Platonic or modern philosophy.

The demon of Plato and the shade of mythology were quite consistent with the religious creeds of the Greeks and the generality of pagan nations of all periods. They are the symbols or exponents of a tradition of the immortal destiny of man, whether passing through the purgations of a metempsychosis, or more directly transferred to Elysium, Orcus, or some other state of personal immortality.

The Universal Spirit of the Stoics and of all Pantheists is equally consistent with their disbelief in the personal perpetuity of either men or brutes. The Veda says :—"That Spirit, from which these created beings proceed; through which having proceeded from it, they live; toward which they tend, and in which they are ultimately absorbed; that Spirit study to know; that Spirit is the Great One" (Sir Wm. Jones on Asiatic Philosophy).

Before any particular views regarding 'the soul' can be advantageously examined, the meaning intended to be conveyed by the users of that word must be mastered. The Greek mythologists understood one thing by the term 'soul'; the philosophers understood another thing; and the Hebrews, from the entire Biblical context, seem to have understood something to which the former meanings only bore an ideal analogy. The Biblical doctrine of a personal resurrection from the dead is only consistent with the conditions of the *Hebrew* soul and spirit.

Every religion is based upon a psychology of its own.

CHAPTER II

SPIRITUAL PERSONALITY.

THERE was in the Gospel period (and there still exists) a vulgar belief in apparitions, such as ghosts or spirits, described by Philoponus. There also prevailed amongst the heathen certain philosophic tenets, respecting demons or inferior gods presiding over different departments of the universe and the destinies of men.

When Peter, after his deliverance from prison by angelic interposition, knocked at the door of the house where his friends were assembled, they refused at first to credit Rhoda's report of his identity, but said, "it is his angel"—either his tutelary demon or *famulus*, or that aerial similitude which the vulgar fancied sometimes appeared premonitory to the decease of the person represented (Acts xii.). But neither our Saviour nor his apostles ever said anything to sanction such notions.

When Christ's disciples beheld him walking on the sea, they said, "it is a spirit" (or apparition, φάντασμα), and "cried out for fear" (Matt. xiv., 26). The Pharisees implied a belief in such a spirit when they said of Paul, "if a spirit or an angel hath spoken to him;" for they confessed both of these agencies, whilst the Sadducees believed in neither of them (Acts xxiii., 8, 9).

The common notion of a spirit, even in the present day, is of something subtle and aerial, unsubstantial and immaterial. Spirit, as an agency, may be subtle and immaterial; but, as identified with personality, it appertains Biblically to either the natural or spiritual body.

We cannot see or hold communion with what is not amenable to the senses. We cannot form the remotest idea of what "eye hath not seen, nor ear heard" (1 Cor. ii., 9). Nay, the common ideas themselves of a spirit, however subtle and aerial, are essentially material; because our very conceptions of it are those of something that possesses form and active and passive power, which imply something material however indefinite, something based upon the objective and subjective perceptions of our senses.

The heathen notions of a spiritual world probably originate in the traditions of a future state; they depict an ideal founded upon their gross experiences of the real. If some of the South Sea Islanders or North American Indians expect personally to survive in another state of existence, they represent it surrounded with adjuncts ideally similar to those which have constituted the subjects of their experience in the present life. Themselves, with their instruments of war and the ornaments and furniture of their dwellings, are reproduced or remodelled like the flittings of a dream; these they may term and deem to be the souls or spirits of men, of kettles, clubs, and hatchets, whilst really they are only their fanciful ideals.

Locke remarks, "It is worth our consideration whether active power be not the proper attribute of spirits, and passive power of matter. Hence may be conjectured, that created spirits are not totally separate from matter, because they are both active and passive" (book ii., cap. 23, sec. 28). Indeed the expression 'spiritual body' itself implies a substantial form; this we cannot realise, except that it be some modification of matter other than the natural one, a substantial form adapted to a spiritual state—a state in which the spiritual agency shall be more fully and pre-eminently developed, as we suppose it is in the angelic nature.

We nowhere find the human spirit spoken of as a personality otherwise than in the human body, or when the natural body shall be raised a spiritual body. "The spirits of just men made perfect" (Heb. xii., 23) are in the heavenly Jerusalem in their resurrection bodies, as also represented in a prosopopœia in the vision of St. John in Patmos, as well as throughout the Revelation Choruses. There is no recorded instance of the disembodied spirits of the departed holding intercourse with the living. In the miraculous resuscitation of Lazarus and others, the individuals lived again; but, the

Scriptures being silent concerning any replies made by them to curious questioners, we are left to conclude that nothing important to our faith or consolation was elicited—or, perhaps, that they were like persons awoke from a dreamless sleep.

Enoch and Elijah were translated so that they should not see death. But, as the corruptible body cannot inherit the incorruptible kingdom, their bodies were doubtlessly changed, " in the twinkling of an eye," into the spiritual bodies of their glorified state. Moses, who appeared with Elias on the Mount of Transfiguration, had probably been translated immediately after his decease, in accordance with what is said of him by the apostle Jude and a Rabbinical tradition. They appeared corporeally with our Lord, under some recognisable characteristics; but not as disembodied spirits.

All the revealed angels appeared in a corporeal form, visible to the eye, audible to the ear; and, whilst in general accommodated in appearance to terrestrial communion, they were yet received as ministering spirits from the King of heaven, accredited by the credentials of supernatural powers and attributes. The angel who conversed with Manoah and ascended in the flame of the altar, or the angels who appeared at the tomb of our Lord and before the lightning of whose countenances the Roman soldiers became like dead men—besides all the other instances recorded throughout the sacred narratives —were beings manifesting concrete unmistakable bodies; they all had a body possessing properties and powers which distinguished it from the natural body, but probably identified it with the spiritual.

We never read of an incorporeal angel. An angel was sometimes invisible until the eye of man were opened; for example, the angel who stood in the way before Balaam. Satan is represented a concrete being, in the temptation scenes of Paradise and Palestine; yet, his influences are generally recognised without himself being personally perceived. Under such influences were some of the demoniacs tormented, as recorded in the gospels.

The only apparent exception to corporeal spiritual personality is in the first Epistle of St. Peter (iii., 19) where Christ is said to have preached by his Spirit, in the days of Noah, unto "the spirits in prison" ($\tau o \hat{\iota} \varsigma$ $\dot{\epsilon} \nu$ $\phi \upsilon \lambda \alpha \kappa \hat{\eta}$ $\pi \nu \epsilon \acute{\upsilon} \mu \alpha \sigma \iota$). The phraseology is, in this verse, anomalous; and, in construing it as well as such words as $\psi \upsilon \chi \eta$ and $\dot{\alpha} \delta \eta \varsigma$, we should be governed more by the Hebraistic sense and doctrine of the Scriptural context, than by the ordinary classical meaning of the words.

When it is said, in St. Paul's Epistle to the Galatians (iii., 8), that the gospel was preached before ($\pi \rho o \epsilon \upsilon \eta \gamma \gamma \epsilon \lambda \acute{\iota} \sigma \alpha \tau o$) unto Abraham, it is understood in a typical or spiritual sense with reference to his faith in the Divine promise, evinced by offering up his son Isaac. So, likewise, Christ or the gospel was typically or spiritually preached to the old world by Noah's act of faith in building the ark.

But, with respect to St. Peter's phrase "the spirits in prison," the best exposition is perhaps to be found in the Hebraistic ideas, latent in the Greek words; and thus the Syriac version, being cognate with the Hebrew, is the most likely to enunciate the true reading. Here we find, "And he preached to the souls which are held in *Sheol;* those which of old were not obedient in the days of Noah" (*Vacrez lenaphshotho ailen dachidon wai bashyul, &c.*): whence it would seem that the Greek word "spirits" was used as a substitute for "souls," and "prison" for "*Sheol*" or *Hades.* The translation would then read "to those persons who are now in the sepulchral state or dead," as defined in the sixth verse of the following chapter. In this rendering, the consistency of the passage is apparent. Instead of preaching to disembodied spirits, the persons themselves were typically addressed by Noah's act of faith in building the ark; and, these being dead when the apostle wrote, he mentions that they are "now in *Hades*" or the sepulchral state (1 Peter iii., 19).

That 'the sepulchral state' is the generic translation of *Sheol* and *Hades*, is confirmed by the best lexicographers, although the poetic Greeks and Platonising Christians attach to them also a mythological meaning.

Our Saviour's argument, addressed to the Sadducees "touching the resurrection of the dead," that God said "I am the God of Abraham, and the God of Isaac, and the God of Jacob," established in a

forcible manner that doctrine, but not, as often
understood, the present personal existence of those
patriarchs in a disembodied state (Matt. xxii., 31, 32).
Indeed the latter position would have proved too
much. It 'would have indicated the possibility of
a personal existence without a resurrection. But
when he added, on the assumption of the personal
extinction of the deceased as understood both by
Pharisees and Sadducees, "God is not the God of
the dead, but of the living," he proved the necessity
of a resurrection in order to the fulfilment of God's
promises to the patriarchs individually in the kingdom of the resurrection; for only then could He
become, in the sense intended, the God of the living
patriarchs. Moreover, in St. Luke's gospel (cap.
xx., 37), Christ is made most clearly to state the
matter in this way:—"Now that the dead are raised,
even Moses showed at the bush, when he calleth the
Lord the God of Abraham, and the God of Isaac,
and the God of Jacob." Observe, the only reason
given is "that the dead are raised"—not that the
patriarchs were then existing. Similarly St. Mark
narrates this argument:—"As touching the dead,
that they rise: have ye not read in the book of
Moses, how in the bush God spake unto him, saying,
I am the God of Abraham, and the God of Isaac,
and the God of Jacob?" (cap. xii., 26). Here
Christ distinctly infers that God is the God of the
patriarchs, because they *will* rise—not because they
were then living.

It is sometimes argued, that, if God as a Spirit

sees and knows all things, therefore the spirit of man, when divested of the organic nature, may also see and know all things even better than in the body. Yet the Spirit of the Deity is Biblically identified with Divine personality, of which we cannot form the slightest conception, there being no analogy between the personality of the Deity and that of any of His creatures. In God's mind the universe ideally subsisted before ever it was called into existence. The human mind is the reverse; with it no ideas are innate.

We know not that the spirits of men or angels have any individual being, apart from their natural or spiritual bodies; and, there is certainly no argument in favour of such a possibility, which is not equally applicable to the separate spiritual existence of all organic entities.

Nor can verse 8 of the fifth chapter of the second Epistle to the Corinthians, rendered in the sense of being absent from the body is to be present with the Lord, nor another analogous passage in the first chapter of the Epistle to the Philippians (verse 23), bear a literal interpretation. As popularly understood, they are only explicable upon the Platonic theory. We must, therefore, look to another canon of interpretation, which can only consistently be that the doctrinal death, as a final condition, is abolished, and, by an act of faith, the kingdom of the redeemed, in the resurrection state, coalesces with the condition of the dying believer. But, it is very doubtful, whether the passage in Philippians is correctly translated. The words, τὴν ἐπιθυμίαν ἔχων εἰς τὸ ἀναλῦσαι, καὶ σὺν Χριστῷ εἶναι, rendered in our authorised version, "Having a desire to depart, and to be with Christ," would perhaps be better translated by—"Having a desire for the returning, and to be with Christ" (as given by Mr. Davidson in the Rainbow Magazine for December, 1871). In Luke xii., 36, the word ἀναλύσει is not translated 'depart,' but 'return.' The early Christians were always wishing for and looking forward to the second coming of Christ; to this, therefore, might St. Paul be alluding. The words ἀνὰ and λύω, from which ἀναλῦσαι is derived, mean to 'loose back again'— that is, to return.

The eloquent arguments adduced by Cicero and other writers, ancient and modern, in support of the immortality of the soul as a spiritual personality distinct from the body, are corroborative only of the distinction between matter and spirit, and of the adaptation of man to a superior state; but they are totally defective for the establishment of the perpetuation of an incorporeal personal identity (Cic. Tusc., lib. i., cap. xxvii., and the Phaedo of Plato).

The apparent necessity of providing a body for what was termed the disembodied spirit of the deceased, in order to perpetuate his individuality, probably induced the Pharisees themselves to adopt much of the Greek philosophy. So that many of them substituted the doctrine of the Pythagorean metempsychosis for the latent resurrection doctrine of their own Sacred Writings (Jos. Antiq. Jud., lib. xviii., cap. i., sec. 3, &c.; Bk. of Wis., cap. viii., v. 20; and Matt., cap. xvi., 14). The adoption of the Platonic philosophy by Philoponus, and the patristic and eclectic writers, led them, in like manner, to substitute the ideal for the real, and to conclude that the soul (in the sense of spirit) retained, after death, some kind of airy, luciform body, perpetuating its personal identity.

Yet, without the Christian doctrine of a resurrection from the dead, we should be left in no better position than the ancient heathen. For, whilst the doctrine of redemption is the foundation of our hopes as sinners, the doctrine of the resurrection is the only actual and substantial foundation of our hope of a personal individual immortality.

After man was formed from the dust of the ground, he received, with his first *afflatus*, that agency which quickened him into the living soul—namely, the Spirit of Life—without which his sense impressions would have remained as ideally unconscious as the photographic material is of the picture, or the vibratory material of the sound produced upon it. All our ideas, so far as we can trace them, seem to be organic impressions made by material objects, accompanied with consciousness, yet not in the sense understood by Helvetius or the materialists, but as imparted by a co-efficient spiritual agency. We cannot conceive the same phenomena to occur, in a

personal sense, in pure spirit; nor how the latter
can assume a personal character, except as God has
made us. He has given us members and organs
which constitute individual personality, with its
synchronous life and intelligence.

When we think of the separation of Self from
the corruptible body in the mythological sense, we
still think of it in the concrete, and cannot otherwise realise it in our minds. We think of it as an
objective individuality, active as well as passive,
capable of sensation, of motion, and of rest. It is
the same whether we do so with reference to a
resurrection or not, because we cannot otherwise
realise the individual. The Self, if it continue to
subsist, must do so either ideally or really in some
sort of corporeal identity.

Persona originally signified (as Archbishop
Whately observes in his Treatise on Logic) a mask
worn by actors on the stage, representing the
character in which they acted. It came ultimately
to imply the person or individual himself. The
character cannot be separated from the individual,
but is identified with him. We therefore understand, that the term personality represents the
individual being, known by his individual mask or
person, of an objective as well as subjective character.
It is the Hebrew *nephesh*, the living soul represented
by the living man.

The impressions and emotions of our nature are
conscious physical affections; and, without them,

there would be no personal impressions or emotions whereof to be conscious.

Accompanied with the spiritual co-efficient, we find all the senses receive their impressions and perform their functions subject to physical influences and laws; and, in the combination and processes of ideas under the agency of volition, we find them characterised by physical analogies.

We have no need to transfer the physical impressions to an ideal substance, because the phenomena are all complete by the spiritual agency being consubstantial and synchronous.

When we use the term "physical impressions," we are not to confound it with the idea of a pictorial imprint; for that could at most be only applicable to our visual impressions. We must rather suppose, that the sense impressions consist of vibratory impulses; these, when once received, originate in the sensorium a susceptibility of their being again revived by the spontaneous processes of the mind.

This organic susceptibility is frequently affected by accident or disease. Sir Wm. Hamilton refers in his lectures to several remarkable instances. One of these instances is that of a gentleman, who, after an attack of fever, totally forgot the Latin language; another is of a servant girl, who in her delirium could repeat correctly several passages from Hebrew, Latin, and other authors, of which she had not shown any previous knowledge—it was ascertained that she had acquired it many years previously from a theologian with whom she had resided. Indeed, it would appear, from many well authenticated illustrations, that the mind is permanently impressed with every idea it has ever received; which idea may again be revived under favourable circumstances, indicating the dependent conditions of the intellect.

All our subjective ideas are combinations and modifications of the simple ideas received by the senses. The processes of this modification follow the laws of synchronous ideas. The statement of mesmerists, that one person can by an act of volition on his part communicate his thoughts to another person, is inconsistent with this position; because they thereby make an act of volition the vehicle of ideas which are fundamentally sense ideas. Therefore, such ideas must either originate from the ordinary mental processes, or be imparted symbolically, and not by a bare act of volition in the mind of another person.

It is, however, said that some persons have, by actual or approximate contact with others, produced catalepsy of the limbs and mental prostration; and, whilst the patient is in this state, an extraordinary control over his actions has been (or feigned to be) exhibited by the mesmerist. Ostensibly the patient is made to sing, dance, sit down, or rise up and walk at the discretion of the operator upon his giving a sign or word of command. But, instead of these phenomena being attributable to the communication of thought or ideas by an act of volition, they are probably the result of a personal sympathy or animal magnetism, productive of a state of somnambulism. At all events there is no evidence of a transference of ideas, otherwise than as a somnambulist might himself obey the impulse of what he might incoherently see or hear in the abnormal condition of his partially wakeful senses. The primary phenomena are physical and not psychological.

If the soul, in the vulgar sense, were a spiritual personality, of which the body were the mere instrument for receiving and imparting external communications, we might infer that its thoughts during sleep would be perfect in themselves, and the phenomena of dreams would appear unaccountable. But, if on the other hand all our ideas be conscious sense affections or impressions or modifications of them, we can readily understand, that consciousness will only attach to those ideas which are identified with the portions of our organism disturbed or partially awake.

If a portion of the brain in connection with any of our senses be removed, or if any sense be destroyed or paralysed, we so far lose a portion of ourselves that we are conscious there is nothing to supply the deficiency.

It is very obvious from the cries and motions of dogs and cats during sleep, that they are occasionally affected by dreams; which we might fancy sometimes to be of a predaceous character. Their external demonstrations are, however, at all times in keeping with the objective natures and individual idiosyncrasies of the animals.

The anomalous images and thoughts occurring in dreams are altogether based upon sense ideas, which at some time or other we have received; but these, arising in a partial and incongruous order, analogous to what happens in a fever and insanity, produce abnormal modifications and results. We live the past over again, and meet our departed friends. We see such phantoms and preternatural imagery as we have been accustomed to hear or read of. Perhaps, we may even fancy, in our minds, persons and places altogether novel; yet these, being human and terrestrial, are never actually alien to what has been familiar to us.

The subjects of our thoughts are in like manner those of experience. Now and then the ideas occurring during sleep are so perfect, in the absence of distracting external suggestions, that a process of reasoning is more completely achieved than during our waking hours. It is possible that the origin of the dream cannot be sometimes traced; thereupon the dream itself, by its subsequent fulfilment, might appear to have been a supernatural suggestion. Such a solution may probably be applicable to some of the prophetic dreams and visions recorded in Scripture.

In all the ordinary mental phenomena, the psychological conditions appear to follow the physiological.

If we can separate the conscious affections of the
senses and bodily organs from the senses and organs
themselves, then, as Aristotle argues, the soul (in
the sense of spirit) is divisible into corresponding
senses and organs. But we never find them separated;
and, if we cannot separate them, then the soul (in
the sense of spirit) is not divisible, but the same
in every part (De Anima, cap. i., sec. 1). Οὐδὲν
ἧττον ἐν ἑκατέρῳ τῶν μορίων—χαὶ τῇ ὅλῃ (De
Anima, cap. i., sec. 5, cl. 26).

Moreover, the same spiritual characteristics of consciousness and spontaneity appear in all the sensuous
and organic affections. The physical and spiritual
characteristics, although diverse, are universally and
constantly synchronous. Thus the mental and functional affections are neither altogether physical nor
altogether spiritual, but partake of each quality.
Whence we are led to infer, that the body and spirit
are co-efficient and consubstantial.

Immediate consciousness synchronises with the
exercise of each sense; wherefore to contend with
Berkeley and Fichte that we are not immediately
conscious of external objects (the *non Ego*), but
only mediately by the impressions they make upon
the intermediate organ, is to treat the personal
mind, or *Ego*, as a sort of inner man taking account
of the shadows on his chamber wall. Whereas consciousness, being (as before shown) the co-efficient
of each sense, is synchronous with perception.

The material sensorium, being in physical *rapport*

with the material world, communicates through the
external senses directly with it, either by contact,
or the vibratory impact of light or air; and the
consubstantial spirit is synchronously conscious.
So that the ideal perception is as immediate as the
organic impression. The *Ego* of Fichte is looking
into a mirror, where he beholds only the reflex of
surrounding objects; instead of this, the mirror is
itself instinct with consciousness, and is itself the
Ego.

But Fichte goes a step further; and, because we
are only conscious of our ideas, he seems to question
whether we possess sufficient evidence for enabling
us to know the origin of our ideas—whether our
ideas may not originate in the mind itself, without
reference to an outer world at all!

Every form of idealism resolves itself into the
generally admitted fact, that we know nothing
except of what we are ideally conscious. But,
whence do we derive those impressions of which we
are conscious, unless through the several senses?
Where these are defective, we are conscious of
nought that is dependent upon them. Our evidence
of the external world is a sensible evidence; but it is
not entirely of one kind; all we know and believe is
dependent upon various kinds of evidence, historical,
mathematical, hearsay, or personal. Our personal
knowledge is furnished by the senses, each according
to its special function. We are not to look for
tangible, or for ocular, or audible evidence only.

All that we can hope to ascertain by the most subtle enquiry is concerning what is communicated, and by what practical laws our ideal consciousness and ideal processes are regulated.

If we can separate any portion of the organic affections from the organs themselves, we may for the same reason separate the whole; because, as before said, the spirit is the same in every part. According to a common way of speaking, the animal affections are assumed to be separable from the rational; or, in other words, the rational soul of the Platonists is separable from the animal soul of their system, and the subjective part of man from the objective. In this manner a theory was constructed, by which it was thought that the higher or rational characteristics of man might survive those grosser parts which are animal and mortal. Howbeit this distinction is not discoverable in the pages of Revelation, nor is it consistent with the phenomena of those higher mental characteristics denominated the subjective.

The subjective powers of the human mind seem to be so entirely based upon the objective, that the one cannot be separated from the other. If, therefore, the former are separable from an organic substance, whether natural or spiritual, the other must be so as well. If they are separable in man, the argument would include that they are separable in the inferior orders of creation also.

But the Grecian sage, not adverting to this mutual

dependence, inferred that man possessed a rational
soul which, as a personal demon, distinguished him
from all other creatures. Yet this rational soul is
identical with the subjective part of our nature,
and is not a distinct and separable entity or demon;
since it is nothing in itself but a power or characteristic function, whereby our sense ideas are capable
of modification.

It is by force of the spiritual agency that the
several senses in men and animals perform their
functions. But, seeing has reference to the eye,
and hearing to the ear, and so forth; when, therefore,
these organs are decomposed, the terms seeing and
hearing lose their *rapport* and become unintelligible.
The agency may survive, but is no longer a personal
agency; otherwise, the individual characteristics of
brutes, as well as of men, might be said to survive.

The same popular views, previously expressed, are
also very commonly varied by considering the soul
to represent the animal life alone, or the animal
characteristics generally; and the spirit to represent
the rational soul of Plato, or the higher characteristics of the human nature. Nevertheless, this
involves precisely the same contradictions and
difficulties as the former doctrine; because, not
only is it opposed to the language and sentiments
of Revelation, but also, because the spirit in this
sense symbolises solely the subjective faculties, and
does not constitute the whole man any more than
the Platonic soul or demon does.

If spirit be understood to designate a spiritual body of some description, conformably with the spiritual and angelic body of Scripture, in which the future man shall unite in the converse and choruses of the heavenly state, then by such a belief as the preceding we would appear to anticipate the doctrine of a personal resurrection, and those Biblical passages representing it as a future reality become literally unintelligible.

Supposing the spirit were divisible, and possessed in itself personal attributes independently of a body whether natural or spiritual, then would the body as to such independent personality be superfluous, and a resurrection be likewise superfluous. The archetypal image of the human creation would be superseded by a Platonic myth.

During life, the body and spirit appear always to exist and act synchronously; the organic distinctiveness is corporeal, divisible, and manifold; the spiritual agency is indivisible, and possesses the same consciousness and spontaneity in each and every part. It is equally so in the vital functions of every bodily organ, and in the ideal functions of the several senses where they terminate in the brain.

All human knowledge is received by the senses, and by reflection upon what is so received; we cannot otherwise acquire any knowledge whatever. None of our ideas appear to be innate. The Biblical recognition of the concrete self is quite in accordance with this hypothesis. The organic senses can only be affected by objective impressions; whilst the spiritual co-efficient imparts spontaneity and a consciousness or cognition of the sense impressions, and of nothing else.

Since the time of Locke there have been few who entertained the notion of innate ideas; yet it is not quite clear whether the views of the spiritual part of our nature held by Zschokke, and by those whom he represents, do not incline that way. In allusion to the transcendental character of the spirit, he says, "The infinite, the unconditioned is, if I may so say, the mysterious background of its knowing and working, out of which the all-embracing original ideas of the true and the holy proceed, and these, combined with the soul-agreeable in the mind, become the idea of the beautiful. These original ideas are the peculiar impulse of the spirit, the utterances of its being; they are the unsetting suns of its own inner world, whose resplendence overspreads their archetypes or ideals" (*Selbstschau*, part ii., pp. 217, 218). Howbeit the infinite, the unconditioned, the beautiful, and whatever other ideas of a like nature the author may embrace in the term "original ideas," are no more "the peculiar impulse of the spirit, the utterances of its being," than any other of our ideas are. They are indeed peculiarly characteristic of the mind's subjective capacities, which compare and combine the objective impressions of the senses, and produce emotions as peculiar as themselves; but these are certainly not the original ideas of the spirit.

The rhapsodies, in which some indulge, as to the

sublime powers of the soul the above writer transfers
to the spirit, and expresses in terms of personality.
"It is superior to nature; it is the link between her
and a more exalted state of being; its foot dips
into her depths; its head is in the splendour of a
realm of being superior to nature" (part ii., p. 220).
Like many others, and without the claim of poetic
licence, he impersonates the subjective ideas of the
mind; as if such ideas constituted the characteristics
of a being not personally identified with the natural
body. In truth these ideas rather represent than
constitute our own personal capacities, as much so as
they shall in the spiritual body. Such language
makes our objective ideas represent one body, and
our subjective ideas represent another co-existent
personality.

Our subjective ideas, being fundamentally constituted of and resolvable into objective ideas, can
no more be severed from the latter, than the latter
themselves can be separated from the personal senses
of the individual. The dreams and visions recorded
in Scripture, although supernaturally suggested, are
no exception to this theory, but corroborative of it.

Ezekiel's vision of the Cherubim and vitalised
wheels is composed of natural elements, conveying
a symbolic signification. All the symbols of the
Apocalypse are so many verbal hieroglyphs, pregnant with ecclesiastical or historic suggestions under
the impulse of inspiration. They are explicative of
doctrines previously acquired upon the same subjects,
but preternaturally and prophetically developed.

That, which is called knowledge and wisdom, is resolvable into objective ideas; and by the subjective combination or separation of them, the ideal processes are distinguished. All are, therefore, ultimately referable to the objective impressions of the senses. These impressions, however, are only converted into cognitions by the synchronous force of the spiritual agency; wherefore, wisdom and knowledge are characteristically attributed to the spirit. Without this agency, we should be like the idols of the heathen; which have mouths, but they speak not; and which have eyes and ears, yet they neither see nor hear.

Thus, all the sublime and god-like conceptions and characteristics of human intelligence are based upon and constituted of sense ideas, and cannot be divorced from them so as to become identified with any spiritual or other constituent part or essence in the concrete being. When anyone speaks of the thoughts and conditions of his *soul*, they are neither more nor less than the thoughts and conditions of his own concrete *Self*. Likewise the emotions, attendant upon these conceptions and modified cognitions, are identified solely with their originators, the subjective ideas and mental processes; and they probably affect the nervous system and heart more powerfully than the mere objective exercise of the senses is capable of doing.

We have already seen in former chapters, that the same constituents of personality are Biblically ascribed to the brute creation, as well as to man.

If the constituents of the whole man (ὁλόκληρος) be comprised by the apostle in the terms " spirit, soul, and body," yet precisely the same terms are employed throughout the original Scriptures to express the constituents of the brute. For, behold, to it and to man there is said to be one spirit; the corruptible body of both is similarly designated; the brute is termed a living soul. Consequently there is nothing in the mere phraseology to establish a psychological distinction.

But when we read, that the brute is without understanding, and that man on the contrary is endued with it—that man is capable of wisdom and knowledge in the highest sense of those terms— we then perceive that a contrast is presented and a difference recognised between the mental capacities of the two. When we also find moral responsibilities imputed to man and not to the brute, we assent to the distinction. Finally, when we are told of future rewards and punishments, we are solemnly impressed with the responsibilities referred to.

Here, then, is at once the parallel and distinction between man and the beast that perisheth. Close as may be the material and objective correspondence, wide is the disparity of the types.

The subjective capacities of the human race at once dissociate man and brute. The longest life is in no proportion to the capacities of the former for good or for evil. He looks for ever onward; and, his faith harmonises with his longings, after holier and undying conditions.

Moreover, the power of language, or of expressing by definite symbols the various objects of the senses, and of thus retaining or communicating them, further distinguishes the human race from all other creatures, and corresponds with its subjective capacities. Indeed these, without language, would be greatly curtailed in efficiency. The voices of brutes are simply the utterances of their momentary passions.

The symbols of language can be more accurately dealt with than the bare and more evanescent ideas of a person born deaf and dumb; such a man rarely attains any great superiority in mental development, notwithstanding the evidences of naturally superior observation and intelligence, and the aid of mental culture. Certain classes of ideas connected with the defective sense are never fully apprehended, and can only be inadequately communicated by artificial instruction. The processes of arranging and modifying the objective ideas, when thus couched in verbal terms, are indefinitely facilitated.

The spontaneity of brutes seems to be confined to the objects of their senses and instincts as externally presented, or as stimulated by some internal appetency.

The spontaneity of man extends abstractively to the individual sense ideas themselves; and, when those ideas are reduced into definite symbols, they can be spontaneously dealt with. Language enables the ideas, connected with any subject which presents itself to the mind, to be digested, like arith-

metical signs, in relation to cause and effect; by it .
we can in suitable terms express the powers, qualities,
distinctions, or other modifications of anything.
Thus the idea of immortality, apart from tradition,
is arrived at by an unnatural and excessive combination of objective ideas, exaggeratory of the
conditions of mortal existence. The duration of
a man's life is the sum of his years. But we may
add years to years beyond all calculation and
definite expression. If life could be commensurately
extended, it would be what we term immortal.
Immortality is therefore the symbol of a subjective
idea, that cannot be represented by any actual sense
idea. The ideas of Omnipotence and Omnipresence
are the result of analogous combinations.

When we analyse the materials of works of
imagination, we discover nothing beyond the arbitrary modifications of sense ideas. We can no
more imagine than demonstrate anything beyond
the scope of the senses and their reflective results.
The most sublime speculations are but composite
ideas of actual cognition and Revelation. The most
heroic or angelic characters are shaped out of those
human or angelic qualities estimated the highest and
best. Homer's gods are but magnificent men; and
Milton's angels are but embodiments of the highest
known or revealed characteristics of human and Divine
beings. Indeed, as words only express symbolically
objective ideas and their subjective compounds, they
are not capable of expressing anything beyond the

s

· objects of perception in their simple or mixed forms.
We cannot express what we cannot perceive or
conceive, objectively or subjectively. Were a
supernatural object presented to us, our language
would fail to express it; much less can we conceive
or express what eye hath not seen nor ear heard,
nor hath entered into the heart of man to conceive.
When we wish to express a transcendental idea,
we can only say that it is something which eye hath
not seen nor ear heard. We may shift the scene
from earth to some far distant sphere; but we can
only then express ourselves in the same indefinite
manner, or picture to ourselves scenes modified out
of what we actually know.

As Longinus says, " Nature has implanted in our
souls an unconquerable desire ($ἄμαχον$ $ἔρωτα$) for
all that is great and most divine. Wherefore, the
entire world does not satisfy the observation and
contemplation of the human mind, but its thoughts
oftentimes transcend the limits of the surrounding
heavens" (sec. 32). We may on paper violate the
laws of optics or harmonics, yet the actual objective
ideas of the senses remain inviolate on the mental
sensorium. We may imagine men, like the Egyptian
hieroglyphics, with birds' or beasts' heads, expressive
of their qualities; or we may imagine trees yielding
golden apples, or any other combination of objective
cognitions, or the parts of them; nevertheless our
objective ideas remain unaltered, and those subjective
compounds never exceed our objective knowledge,

however grotesque or absurd may be the mutations. Hence those works, which adhere the closest to objective nature, actual life, the universal sympathies of mankind, and to the truths of Revelation, retain the most permanent continuance.

In corroboration of the conclusion, that all acquired knowledge and subjective ideas are the result of sense ideas and experience (see Locke, vol. i., page 303), we may adduce the following passage from the learned Max Muller's Lectures on the Science of Language—"The fact, that all words expressive of immaterial conceptions are derived by metaphor from words expressive of sensible ideas, was for the first time clearly and definitely put forward by Locke, and is now fully confirmed by the researches of comparative philologists. All roots, that is, all the material elements of language are expressive of sensuous impressions and of sensuous impressions only; and, as all words, even the most abstract and sublime, are derived from roots, comparative philology fully endorses the conclusions arrived at by Locke."

In fact the ideal itself is but the multiform reflex of the real.

Whilst the mind realises the finite in number, time, space, or personal attributes, because the idea is based upon what is actually known; yet, to say that the idea of the infinite is dependent upon some other faculty than either that of the senses or some subjective process, which we commonly designate

reason or reflection, appears to be as gratuitous as
to say that our ideas of the divine and the heavenly
are innate, or the subjects of some special faculty.
They are not innate, because we know that there
are people who have never attained them. We
cannot realise them as we can the finite; but, by the
aid of reflection on what is known by evidence or
revelation, we form the indefinite idea of something
unknown, infinite, and Divine.

We cannot, therefore, separate the ideas from the
senses, nor the senses from their organs, and at the
same time retain an experimental personality. The
Divine *afflatus*, or causative inspiration, is not represented as imparting a soul, but a living breath. The
body of personal identity, thereupon, became a living
soul and not a spiritual abstraction.

The organic structure of the eye does not of itself
see, but conveys the external impression by means
of the optic nerve to the cerebral sensorium. If
that nerve be severed, no impression is conveyed.
But the sensorium is itself material, and the impression which it receives is a material impression. At
this point alone the ideal functions of the spiritual
co-efficient are developed by a synchronous consciousness of the impressions received; and it has
been already noticed that the ideas stored up in the
memory appear to be permanent physical impressions of some kind, and as liable to be physically
affected as the immediate sense impressions themselves.

If the material and spiritual characteristics and functions be so distinct and diverse, it would seem that to separate them would involve the cessation of all individual identity.

Self-consciousness involves the abstract consciousness of all the senses, capacities, and properties of the whole man in the aggregate as a living soul; and we cannot otherwise realise the idea of self. By dispensing with all these we impute the same attributes to an impersonality, and substitute the ideal hope of the heathen for the sure and certain hope of the gospel.

There must hereafter be more than an impersonal incorporeal or disembodied spirit to realise individual personal identity, to enable him to see the Divine archetype of angels and men face to face, to hear and unite in the songs of the redeemed, and to assume those personally distinctive attributes which are symbolised by the white robe and the golden crown. The Biblical doctrines and Revelations not only respond to each other, but to the psychology of our nature.

Chapter III

PERSONAL PERPETUITY.

"Except a corn of wheat fall into the ground and die, it abideth alone : but if it die, it bringeth forth much fruit" (John xii., 24). So it has remained unchanged, if the accounts be correct, for probably three thousand years in the mummy pits of Egypt, sealed up in its horny case, and excluded from the influences of the external agencies. Although in the region of death, the agencies of death have not affected it; the entire seed remains dormant, like the sleeping beauty of an enchanted cave, to wake up not at the sound of the hunter's horn, but under the quickening influences of the dews and sunshine of another generation. The same result is exemplified in the seed of every harvest; its normal character remains unchanged, until the chemical affinities, by the action of moisture, warmth, and light, act atomically upon it; at the same time the organic functions of the young plant are developed. Incipient disintegration is met by organic growth and replacement, until the entire seed disappears; and, finally, the full ear of the waving corn scatters the seed of another harvest of much fruit.

The whole of life is a career of organic death.

The bodily tissues are constantly being disintegrated and new ones eliminated. Life in a new aspect succeeds the death of the original seed. Life leads to death, and death precedes new life not in the same but in another. The individual dies, the species is perpetuated. *Lex est, non poena perire.* There is not, however, any natural analogy between the development of the plant from the seed and the resurrection body. The analogy intended by the apostle Paul is a phenomenal analogy. " Thou sowest not that body that shall be, but bare grain" (1 Cor. xv., 37). The analogy is in the apparent phenomena ; those of the one being as unlike and unlikely as those of the other.

In the human system, every pulse and every thought produces its wear and tear. The fabric is made up of cells, and every one of them is instinct with life. But the wear and tear of life acts upon the integrity of the being; thus some portions become dislocated, and others consolidated, until by accident, disease, or the exhaustion of nature, some of the organs cease to perform their functions. Then are the normal conditions of the organism destroyed ; breath and life depart; the vital spark has fled ; the agencies of death, no longer resisted, proceed in their work of decomposition, until the original fabric is reduced to the condition of the dust of the earth.

The blood is by a metonymy sometimes denominated the life, in the Greek and Latin classics as well as in the Hebrew writings; but the blood is itself dependent upon respiration for its vitality, and is the medium of its distribution throughout the system. When its circulation languishes, or is impeded, the extremities become cold and lifeless, and ultimately mortify.

By the nervous and muscular powers, the functions of organic life are preserved; but the brain itself is the principal centre and source of those powers in the higher orders of animals.

In some of the lower species of reptiles and insects, the cerebral matter appears to be more distributed throughout the body. We consequently find in them a much greater tenacity of life and of local consciousness and spontaneity, when the head is severed from the body, than in the higher orders of animals, whose nerves concentre more in the brain. All the ganglia are centres of local nervous sensibility. In like manner air is admitted to the systems of the former by air tubes dispersed over their bodies and not by the localised apparatus of lungs.

In warm-blooded animals, when the head is severed from the body, the blood is rapidly effused, and death presently succeeds. In cold-blooded creatures, such as insects, reptiles, frogs, tritons, and the like, no such effusion follows, and the severed limbs retain their vitality much longer; and, so long as vitality remains, these prolong their special functions and obey any special stimulus, but are of course no longer influenced by the stimulus of any separated senses. Yet this continues only so long as the mutilated organism is in a condition to retain or appropriate the elements upon which vitality depends; their tissues are no longer replenished by their wonted aliment, and consequently soon lose their normal condition.

Upon the same principle vitality, under certain conditions, appears to linger for awhile in some organ or portion of the frame of the higher orders of animals, after the decease of the fabric as a whole. The hair and nails sometimes continue to grow under suitable circumstances like parasites upon a tree; and, some organic function may continue for a time to proceed, by the retention of local vitality.

Could such local vitality, under any circumstances, be retained by the brain, then, perhaps, the phenomena of a dream might be continued in the very sleep of apparent death itself; but, as the vitality of the brain and other vital organs is not parasitic like that of the hair, we cannot suppose that vitality in such organs can continue many minutes after its cessation in the heart and lungs. Zschokke and others infer, from this continuation of parasitic life, a distinction between the agency of life and that of intelligence; but, from the fact that such continuance of life in any organ or part of the body only developes the functions of the portion so vitalised, no such inference can be legitimately supported.

T

Local death may take place before the death of the animal or plant itself, as when a limb mortifies or a branch decays; one lung may become morbid and abnormal, but not literally dead, whilst the other continues its functions. By disease or accident some organ ceases to perform its functions; the blood becomes impure or does not efficiently circulate; vitality is interrupted or diminished; the organism is not adequately renewed and invigorated, and its normal conditions are gradually lost; the physical agencies acquire an ascendancy and hasten the dissolution and death of the affected portion, or of the whole of the organic being.

Vitality is only in a secondary sense dependent upon the food we receive; without food, life still continues so long as we can breathe. Animals in a torpid state live through the winter season. A remarkable instance of functional torpor lately occurred in the Zoological Gardens of London, where a python, in a state of incubation, refused all food for upwards of six months. In such instances, the system feeds upon its own fatty deposits when deprived of external aliment.

It is frequently remarked that, in contrast with the declension of the body, the mind becomes in certain diseases more active; but this is not generally the case, and is never the result of general natural decay. Perhaps, the only attestations to this statement are persons sinking under some gradual bodily decline; for this might not immediately debilitate the mental sensorium, whilst some resulting febrile excitement might actually tend to stimulate it, though tending to consume the body. Providentially, the mind in general remains unimpaired by the advance of age or by the ordinary ailments of the body. This is equally the case with regard to both man and brute; were it otherwise, they would become imbecile when they chiefly required ideal support and direction. Generally speaking, they retain their mental faculties until the last. Death is, in most cases, the result of the decay or destruction of other organs than the cerebral or ideal organs. On the other hand, when accident or disease affects the brain we frequently find that the mind partially or even totally succumbs.

So, as long as the vital energy continues, it is difficult to realise the idea of death.

"All men think all men mortal but themselves" (Young).

A very common idea of death is, that to die is to pass away into another state of existence—into a new life of infinite beatitude, exempt from the toils and pains of mortality—to transmigrate from the present sphere to a brighter—to be one moment a wriggling worm, the next a seraphic spirit.

Even Romaine, speaking of the triumphant faith of the patriarchs, says in the language of opinion and not of poetry or of faith, "The moment they expired, they entered the city which God had prepared for them." A similar sentiment appears in the burial and consecration services of our church,

although it is not sanctioned by her articles or creeds;
it is no dogma of the church. The patriarchs themselves expressed no such sentiments; neither did
those who wept and mourned for them.

If the Platonic idea popularly entertained be
really credited, the pathos and force are altogether
lost in such passages (and in many others of a
similar import) as the following:—

Isaiah xxxviii., Hezekiah's prayer, especially verses
18 and 19, "For the grave cannot praise thee,
death can not celebrate thee: they that go down
into the pit cannot hope for thy truth. The living,
the living, he shall praise Thee, as I do this day."

Job xiv., verse 7, "For there is hope of a tree, if
it be cut down, that it will sprout again, and that
the tender branch thereof will not cease." Verse
10, "But man dieth, and wasteth away: yea, man
giveth up the ghost, and where is he?" Verse 12,
"So man lieth down, and riseth not: till the heavens
be no more, they shall not awake, nor be raised out
of their sleep." Verse 14, "If a man die, shall he
live again? all the days of my appointed time will
I wait, till my change come."

Psalm xxxix., 13, "O spare me, that I may re-
cover strength, before I go hence, and be no more."

The heathen, according to their mythology, looked
for a perpetuation of personal identity after decease
in a *manes*, or tenuous corporeity, in a future state.
Those of their philosophers, who did not altogether
reject the doctrine of a future existence, recognised
it in the form of an abstract personality distinct

from the corruptible body, as being the only probable manner in which such a perpetuation of personality could be philosophically supposed, and as being the most agreeable to the aspirations of a rational creature. Where all was uncertain, the poetic faith, whether of Plato or the vulgar, was better than the philosophic doubt; and, even if immortality were doubtful, the eloquent Cicero preferred rather to err with Plato, than to embrace with the Stoics the alternative of individual annihilation, so abhorrent to all our natural instincts and capacities. It was not sufficient that they could not explain the future state of the soul; seeing that there are very many things, even in our present constitution, which we cannot explicate. Notwithstanding the fallacy of the heathen argument about the immortality of man, yet such a hope was at least consolatory and elevating. It, at least, had some support from tradition, and was a substitute for a better faith until life and immortality were demonstratively and surely revealed.

Man feels conscious of his powers, and that the longest life is too short for their full development. From such considerations, or a widely diffused mythological tradition, his aspirations have always been full of immortality. Addison says:—

> "Plato, thou reasonest well!
> Else whence this pleasing Hope, this fond Desire,
> This longing after Immortality!" (Cato's Soliloquy).

Without this hope however shadowy, but more

especially without the revelation of the resurrection state, how wretched would man, with all his subjective capacities of mind, be in comparison with the inferior orders of the animal creation, which are not endued with any such faculties! The brute lives on, enjoying life as it may, without disturbance from the subjective terrors of dissolution. Burns addresses a mouse thus :—

> "Still, thou art blest, compared wi' me!
> The present only toucheth thee:
> But och! I backward cast my e'e,
>   On prospects drear!
> An' forward, tho' I canna see,
>   I guess an' fear!"

Man is the only creature to whom death is awful, or who is even conscious of dying; truly to all others, it seems to be the law of nature.

Animals and plants alike die; life and intelligence in all cease—"The spirit returns to God who gave it." Life in all is equally mysterious; and, death is not less so. Dr. Bennet remarks that, "The vital spark no longer vivifies the human clay, and its complex machinery is hushed for ever. Organic repair has been brought abruptly to a close ; the human fire is quenched ; and, heat no longer being generated, the body rapidly loses its caloric to the surrounding atmosphere; until, after a few hours, the marble cold of death has seized upon the tenement so long the abode of the organic processes" (On Nutrition).

Death (*mōth*) itself implies the withdrawal or

failure of the energy or agency upon which life depends.

From geologic records, death appears to have been the destiny of all before the creation of man; and, if recent geologic discoveries and calculations may be relied on, there were probably races of men who lived and died before the appearance of the Adam of Paradise. The very conformation of the carnivorous tribes implies the work of mutual destruction; in this sense the heathen maxim may be true, "*lex est non pœna perire.*" Of all creatures, man is the only one endued with faculties of universal and eternal applicability, and capable of unlimited progress. Therefore the denunciation of death upon the Adam of Paradise, as the consequence of his disobedience to the Divine command, may not necessarily imply the introduction of a new law of nature, but the deprivation of an intended exemption, in case of obedience, from the natural condition of corporal and personal dissolution.

In the midst of Paradise grew the mysterious Tree of Life; perhaps, this was the traditional hieroglyphic, significant of a state containing within itself the elements of a higher condition of vitality.

> " From these corporal nutriments, perhaps,
>   Your bodies may at last turn all to spirit,
>   Improved by tract of time, and, winged, ascend
>   Ethereal, as we ; or may, at choice,
>   Here, or in heavenly Paradises, dwell" (Paradise Lost, book v.).

So Milton makes the angelic visitant speak.   Purer

and holier, as years rolled on, the gradual metempsychosis of the natural body into the spiritual had
possibly been the peculiar destiny of the human
creation. The translation of Enoch is illustrative of
such a metempsychosis, and was probably intended
to convince and assure succeeding ages of the possibility of its universal application to mankind;
because Enoch's corruptible body could not, according to St. Paul in 1 Cor., xv., inherit incorruption.

Death, or the sepulchral state, is the execution of
a penalty annexed to disobedience, "thou shalt
surely die." It is "the wages of sin." In its natural aspect, how solemn is death! To die, to cease
from conscious existence, to become a negation, to
pass from the embrace of affection, to "sleep in the
dust," to lie down in the grave where "our thoughts
perish," where the voice of praise is silent!

The brute creation also manifests for a season a
discomposure under the severance of its attachments,
whether it be a separation from its own kin or its
human benefactor; but to the brute the separation
is the same, whether the removal be merely local or
by death.

The members of the human family, if only locally
parted, hope to meet again, and still maintain in
most cases that intercourse which unites them at
least in sentiment; but there is no one who does not
recognise the difference between this farewell and
severance by death; there are few who have not
experienced the pangs of parting with some most

dear. How desolate feels the home where the voices of the children are no more heard! How disconsolate the child of whatever age, when the parents, the associates of its existence, are gone; and when, for the first time, it becomes an isolated being! How forlorn the man when he advances towards the bourne of life, when his ancient acquaintances and friends are one by one taken away, until he seems to be the last survivor of his generation; oh! how solitary amidst the crowds of new comers does he often feel. No wonder that the mourners go about the streets; no wonder that our Lord himself wept at the grave of his friend Lazarus. Where is the hope of him whose entire affections are engrossed with such transient things?

It is not unlikely that philosophy, following the tradition of a future state, did something for men like Socrates and Plato; it imparted to them a hope, which, we may again say, was better than none. It led them to look forward to reunion between the great and good of all ages, and with Cicero to say, " *Meipsum consolabar, existimans, non longinquum inter nos digressum et discessum fore*" (De Senec., 23).

The authenticated traditions of the Hebrew Scriptures, not only as to a future state, but also as to a resurrection from the dead, did more than this. Revelation enabled God's people to exclaim with the holy patriarch Job, "I know that my Redeemer liveth, and that he shall stand at the latter day upon the earth : and though after my skin worms destroy this body, yet in my flesh shall I see God: whom I shall see for myself, and mine eyes shall behold, and not another" (Job xix., 25, 26, and 27).

But, "thanks be to God which giveth us the victory through our Lord Jesus Christ" (1 Cor., xv., 57); in His Resurrection and Ascension we see the παλιγγενεσία (being born again) of the mortal type; we see Him, who bore the image of the earthly, assume the image of the heavenly; we long to be "with Him" and to be "at home" with Him. In the meantime "man giveth up the ghost, and where is he?" (Job xiv., 10). The ideal hope of philosophy and the traditionary hope of the patriarchs is converted into the real. The Biblical psychology demonstrates the necessity of the resurrection doctrine; the resurrection of our Lord confirms it. What is all philosophy, what is martyrdom itself, "if the dead rise not?" We may now say with confidence to the dying believer, as well as to his mourner, "sorrow not, even as others which have no hope. For if we believe that Jesus died and arose again, even so them also which sleep in Jesus will God bring with him" (1 Thess. iv., 13, 14)—thy father and mother, thy wife, thy husband, thy brother, thy friend shall rise again.

The question, how the dead shall be "raised up and with what body do they come," is one which has repeatedly been asked since the apostle so concisely put it, and so forcibly replied to it in the sublime eloquence of inspiration. This question has generally originated from those who reasoned upon the physical impossibility of a resurrection of the same atomic body as that which was buried. However, comparing the phraseology adopted by St. Paul upon this subject with the Biblical psychology, a remarkable congruity at once appears, explanatory of the seeming physical impossibility. For, with regard to the body sown or buried, he terms it σῶμα ψυχικὸν, the personal or soul body, intimating very clearly that it is the personal identity which we are to look for in the σῶμα πνευματικὸν, or spiritual body, in which our individuality shall be restored.

Yet how marvellous and well nigh incredible is such a restitution after the disintegration of the body! The restitution of millions in their personal identity is humanly more astounding than the original creation itself. When we consider what personal identity implies, with all its complex idealities, nothing but the Divine assurance and the actual resurrection and ascension of Christ himself is adequate to the establishment of human faith.

The ideal type of the whole creation, including all its modifications and appliances, must necessarily have existed in the Divine mind before its material generation. The Psalmist says, " In Thy book all my members were written, which in continuance were fashioned, when as yet there was none of them." "Thou understandest my thought afar off. Thou compassest my path and my lying down, and art acquainted with all my ways. For there is not a word in my tongue, but, lo, O Lord, Thou knowest it altogether" (Psalm cxxxix.).

Thus, it is quite as much within the grasp of human reason to conceive that the Almighty and Omniscient can re-create, after the pattern of the actual type of the past, as originally to create from the ideal of his own conceptions. The biographer delineates, in some approximate degree, the character of the departed from the records or recollection of his thoughts and actions. The osteologist reconstructs from a simple bone the form and generic character of the extinct fauna of geologic periods. How much rather shall He, who originated all and knows and can do all things, and in whose universal and everlasting mind the individual thoughts and actions of past generations are registered, reproduce everybody in his or her personal identity. Whether such personal identity exist in an individual and independent form, apart from the natural and spiritual body, we may feel assured it exists in the Omniscience of the Searcher of hearts; its life is hid with Christ in God.

As to what constitutes personal identity, there can scarcely be any very important difference of apprehension, if it be admitted that the man of four score is the same person he was at twenty. There may not be one atom of the same matter in his frame; yet he will say he is the same person,

and those who knew him through life will support
his assertion. His lineaments are changed; he may
look like another person; nevertheless there is the
general character, and perhaps the same scar on his
face; he may have lost an arm; yet something of the
former youth remains. He remembers his father's
house and his juvenile pastimes; his parents themselves and his former friends; the thoughts and
events of years gone by; his joys and sorrows; his
hopes and disappointments; and he is conscious
that it is himself who is identified with all the
chequered scenes and mental idealities of his life.
In a few short years, at most, this octogenarian
passes away and becomes mingled with the clods of
the valley, so that not a particle of his former
frame can ultimately be identified. Some of the
elements of that departed form, once the abode of
life and intelligence, and the object of affection and
admiration, may have blended with the common
atmosphere of all; whilst others may have entered
into combination with the structures of other
organisms. The old organism is effectually dispersed,
and can never be reproduced except at the expense
of separate entities; howbeit, should another rise
up with the same, or with some of the same external
characteristics formerly idiosyncratic of the deceased
octogenarian, with all his reminiscences and pecu-
liarities, and, moreover, with the consciousness that
he was the same person as he who had once become
mingled with the clods of the valley, most people

would consider, that here the identification was as
good as that of the man of eighty was previously
so with the youth of twenty. It is also in perfect
accordance with the Biblical doctrine and phraseology concerning individual personality, as expressed
by the *nephesh*, to consider the resurrection of such
an identity as a resurrection of the same person.

Locke's argument concerning personal identity
rests almost entirely upon the proof of self-
consciousness. "The question being, what makes the
same person, and not whether it be the same identical
substance, which always thinks in the same person;
which, in this case, matters not at all. Different
substances, by the same consciousness (where they
do partake in it), being united into one person, as
well as different bodies, by the same life, are united
into one animal, whose identity is preserved in that
change of substances, by the unity of one continued
life. For, it being the same consciousness that
makes a man be himself to himself, *personal identity*
depends on that only, whether it be annexed only
to one individual substance, or can be continued in
a succession of several substances. For, as far as
any intelligent being can repeat the idea of any
past action with the same consciousness it had of it
at first, and with the same consciousness it has of
any present action, so far it is the same personal
self. For, it is by the consciousness it has of its
present thoughts and actions, that it is self to itself
now, and so will be the same self as far as the same

consciousness can extend to actions past or to come; and would be, by distance of time or change of substance, no more two persons than a man be two men, by wearing other clothes to-day than he did yesterday, with a long or short sleep between; the same consciousness uniting those distant actions into the same person, whatever substances contributed to their production" (book ii, cap. 27, sec. 10). As self-consciousness in the morning assures one that he is the same person who fell asleep the night before, so the same self-consciousness, uniting the most distant actions and proofs of identity in the same person, must satisfy him of his soul or self-identity, however long the interval of oblivion, and whatever substances contribute to his reproduction. But this argument loses its force for establishing personal identity by being in general merely applied to a metaphysical incorporeal abstraction.

Can the sole test of self-consciousness for identification apply to persons dying in infancy, before they can be said to possess any ideal consciousness at all? Certainly the personal identity of the octogenarian cannot naturally be established by confining his self-consciousness to the infantile experience of the first year or half-year of his existence. In such a case we are compelled to resort to external rather than internal evidences of identity; to that which appeals to the consciousness of another, instead of to the self-consciousness of the unconscious infant (see Locke, book ii, cap. 27, sec. 20).

In another passage, Locke admits the possibility

of all our ideas being permanent physical impressions. Experience and analogy suggest the same conclusion; and, agreeably thereto, the "personal body" which is sown or buried shall find its counterpart in the resurrection, impressed with all the mental and bodily idiosyncrasy of personal identity; although that counterpart itself shall be identified in a spiritual body.

Yet, an original creation and a future personal restitution are equally inexplicable. The former we personally experience; the latter we are taught to believe by the evidences and doctrine of Revelation, and by its fitness to human psychology.

We are only personally conscious of our personal sensuous impressions and their subjective ideal modifications. I think of what I have personally felt and thought before; therefore I am the same person who have so felt and thought. In the permanence of ideas or impressions upon the mental sensorium, we perceive the continuance of a personal identity, although the sensorium itself be composed of fluctuating material atoms.

Personal identity does not depend upon self-consciousness, but is only evidenced by it to ourselves; that identity may be obvious to other minds, although the individual himself may no longer retain a consciousness of some portion or any of his history. On the other hand, an individual may be conscious of his own identity, yet, after the lapse of years, it may require many infallible proofs to establish it in the mind of others.

Externally, we find the mark of a wound remain for life, identifying the member that received it; and so the prints of the nails and spear identified the resurrection body of Christ, whether regarded as the spiritual body or not, to the hesitating Thomas. These are external tokens, whilst memory is internal and psychological. The perpetuation of the latter in the mind of the risen Christ, manifested in his conversations with his apostles, was equally indicative of His identity, as those outward tokens were. He was recognised by them, "by many infallible proofs, being seen of them forty days, and speaking of the things pertaining to the kingdom of God" (Acts i., 3).

If personal identity continue through life, notwithstanding the perpetual physical changes of the body, it is but a renewal of the same identity in the resurrection body, were it even devoid of every particle of that atomic body from which the spirit parted at the moment of dissolution. There is a physiological, as well as a psychological, personal identity. "Thou sowest not that body which shall be. It is sown a natural body, it is raised a spiritual body."

There is something very striking and sublime in the recognised identity of Christ at his coming, alluded to by St. John in the following passage, "Behold, he cometh with clouds; and every eye shall see him, and they also which pierced him : and all kindreds of the earth shall wail because of him" (Rev. i., 7). The personal identity of the spiritual and glorified body of our Lord Jesus Christ shall be manifest to all, as it was in His natural body.

x

However, the foregoing identity of the resurgent individual does not imply, that the deformities and imperfections, now adherent to many in their present natural and sinful state, shall then constitute a necessary element of identification. For, occasionally in life, we see these more or less removed without interfering with permanent characteristics; there are physical organs and functions, and mental conditions which are not essential to personal identity. Besides, the apostle assures us with respect to the personal body, that "It is sown in corruption; it is raised in incorruption: it is sown in dishonour; it is raised in glory: it is sown in weakness; it is raised in power: it is sown a natural body; it is raised a spiritual body" (1 Cor. xv., 42-44).

One star differeth from another star in glory. Wherefore, we may infer, that individual idiosyncrasy shall equally characterise the spiritual body, as it now does the natural body; because such idiosyncrasy also constitutes a necessary element of personal identity.

Personal identity likewise intimates personal recognition. We shall know even as we are known. Friend shall meet friend, not as a featureless phantom, but in the personal portraiture of identity. It may, indeed, require other evidence, than that of the personal aspect, to establish personal identity in the mind of another; even, at present, this is often needed between friends long parted, or kindred never until now introduced to each other. Elias and Moses are spoken of in terms of personal identity in their glorified bodies upon the Mount of Transfiguration ; and, in like manner, the patriarchs and prophets in the resurrection state (Luke xiii., 28).

There are "also celestial bodies," as well as bodies terrestrial ; and, as the various geologic periods disclose new animal creations or developments adapted to a new cosmogony, so may we well believe that the spiritual body of the resurrection shall be adapted to a celestial or other new and exalted position, in which ". they neither marry nor are given in marriage ; neither can they die any more : for they are equal to the angels ; and are the children of God, being the children of the resurrection" (Luke xx., 35, 36).

The argument of self-consciousness, in support of personal identity, rests entirely upon the phenomena of memory. Supposing there was no recollection of the past (as sometimes happens from disease or other abnormal circumstance), then would our self-consciousness merely testify to a present existence, which might consist equally well with a succession of new creations without reference to personal identity at all. We should, thus, be reduced to mere creatures of the moment, unconscious of our own identity with reference to the past ; but, as the physical influences which affect all the phases of our ideal impressions and operations also affect the memory itself, there seem to be cogent reasons for believing that all our ideal impressions are themselves physical, and identified with our momentary concrete personality. Therefore, our remembrance, of the past in life not only carries our self-conscious personal identity forward throughout this transitory life ; but, by the restitution of personal identity in the spiritual body, memory perpetuates that identity in the spiritual state. Consequently in the Book of Revelations, the resurrection saints are emblematically represented rendering thanksgivings and glory to God for having redeemed them, and brought them out of great tribulation, as well as for his judgments upon His and their enemies— indicating a remembrance of the past, as well as a present consciousness of their triumphant condition.

If throughout life the same substantial personal identity exist in every instant of time, the *Ego* or Self of every moment, although constituted of fluctuating atoms, is complete in its consecutive identity. In fact, the argument of personal identity furnishes a perfect sorites. The atomic corporeity fluctuates, whilst the personal identity (the *nephesh*) remains, until its dissolution in death ; yet, again to be restored in the spiritual body of the eternal state.

We know not, whether the spiritual body shall be constituted of fluctuating parts analogous to the actual body; but, we are taught by the language of inspiration to believe, that in the heavenly state " there shall be no more death ;" and, consequently, that the soul or personal identity is there destined for perpetuation and immortality.

In such a personal perpetuity there is a psychological fitness. The instincts of the inferior orders of the animal creation are perfect in their present state, so that a generic perpetuity answers all the purposes of their being. A greater longevity would not advance their economy. They manifest no subjective capacities, which lengthened experience and exercise improve and exalt, so as by any rational process to comprehend their own position in the scale of nature, or in any way to better it; were they to live for ever, they could never unite in the eternal anthem of the heavenly choir.

The subjective capacities of man, regarded in the abstract, are, on the contrary, never mature, never exhausted, but adapted to a perpetual progressive advancement. His thoughts "wander through eternity." Immortality is alone commensurate with his idiosyncrasy and his hopes. His senses themselves are susceptible of further development, which, we may feel assured, they will receive in the body that is to be raised in power and glory; and, as the senses are the bases of all the subjective capacities and processes of the personal mind, these must participate in the same exaltation. The intelligence and affections of angels will be those of the redeemed in their angelic equality. "Now we see through a glass, darkly; but when that which is perfect is come, then, face to face. Now I know in part, but then shall I know even as also I am known." It is only in such a state, that the rational being can fully and adequately apprehend and adore the glories of Him, by whom and for whom he was created.

CHAPTER IV.

THE REAL AND IDEAL.

In countries where the heathen mythologies have been superseded by Christianity, the philosophic or ideal soul has generally taken the place of the mythologic shade in the popular mind; and, from the ascendancy of the Platonic philosophy in the early ages of Christianity, the philosophic, as well as the popular, idea of the soul has become essentially Platonic.

The intellectual soul or demon of Plato constituted a personality distinct from the body, having a pre-existence of its own, and ultimately also a future existence, yet one scarcely so distinct as that of the mythologic shade. The body is thus popularly treated as the citadel of the soul. The senses are represented as its windows or instruments of external communication. The soul itself is reduced to an abstract idea personified, nevertheless endued with all the functions and characteristics of concrete personality. The body, it is said, may be injured or impaired, but not this immortal demon. Insanity and idiocy are said not to affect the soul. It is further assumed, in recognition of a Platonic pre-existence, that the soul is released by death from all the trammels and sorrows of human nature, to return home to its native skies. So Archbishop Leighton says of the souls who have long dwelt in these earthly tabernacles, "Like exiles, they earnestly wish to regain their native country."

What the patriarchs sought was a fatherland ($\pi\alpha\tau\rho\iota\delta\alpha$, Heb. xi., 14), where, like our common parents at the first, they should hold personal communion with their heavenly Father; and such a restitution was the object of their faith.

An ideal pre-existence is sometimes the subject of generally admired passages in our best poets; thus Wordsworth, in his Intimations of Immortality from Recollections of Early Childhood, says:—

> " Our birth is but a sleep and a forgetting;
> The Soul that rises with us, our life's Star,
> Hath had elsewhere its setting
> And cometh from afar:
> Not in entire forgetfulness,
> And not in utter nakedness,
> But trailing clouds of glory do we come
> From God, who is our home:
> Heaven lies about us in our infancy !"

Yet this is but the doctrine of the pre-existence of the soul idealised. We admire the dawn of intellect in childhood; there is a sublimity in its genuineness, its simplicity, and artlessness, that disappears in the conceits, disingenuousness, and corruption with which the experience of life invests the adult. The innocent and happy child, "fresh

from its Maker's hands," is indeed a fitter representative of the kingdom of Heaven than the man
of sin and sorrow. Notwithstanding, glorious as the
child is, its communications are all of the earth and
not of heaven, or of any former state of existence.
The Immanuel, who spake of the glory which he
had with the Father before the world was, could
alone testify of a glorious pre-existence.

The same Platonic idea is pursued by Young, in
the Complaint, to its fuller development in death :—

> "This is the bud of being, the dim dawn,
> The twilight of our day, the vestibule.
> Life's theatre as yet is shut, and death,
> Strong death, alone can heave the massy bar,
> This gross impediment of clay remove,
> And make us, embryos of existence, free.
> From real life but little more remote
> Is he, not yet a candidate for light,
> The future embryo, slumbering in his sire.
> Embryos we must be till we burst the shell,
> Yon ambient azure shell, and spring to life,
> The life of Gods, O transport! and of man" (Night I., lines 123-134).

It is not quite clear, from the above, what the
poet regarded as the shell, whether the "impediment
of clay" or the "ambient azure." If the former, then
the Platonic demon is the embryo; if the latter,
then it may be the resurrection body; but if so,
then it is not death which makes us free, but the
resurrection.

Many further illustrations might be adduced from
congregational hymns, as well as from *belles-lettres*,
were it requisite.

The Platonic idea is thus perpetuated to its full extent; and, being poetical and pleasing, it is more popularly captivating than the Biblical mysteries of death and a resurrection. However, the Platonic idea is just as much opposed to the Biblical doctrine, as the Stoical is.

The created being, whether angelic or human, cannot be said to have had an individual pre-existence before his individual creation.

Aristotle's psychology approached much nearer to that of the Bible than the Platonic. Aristotle was no materialist, although perhaps a pantheist; he required little more than the knowledge of the resurrection doctrine to elevate his hopes above those doubts which clouded the conclusions of the Grecian philosophy.

Zschokke's views of soul and spirit may be considered to be little more than a verbal modification of the popular ideas upon the same subject; he was a very popular German sentimentalist, and probably developes the common popular idea of the soul more fully than any other writer. Whilst he allows the same soul to man and beast, he arrogates for man alone a spirit, to which is attributed all his rational powers and subjective ideas. "It is superior to nature; it is the link between her and a more exalted state of being; its foot dips into her depths; its head is in the splendour of a realm of being superior to nature" (*Selbstschau*, part ii., p. 220). He thereby imputes our objective ideas to the objective soul, and our subjective ideas to the

Y

spirit. At the same time he treats the soul, as if it were a subtle body of some kind clothed with the substance of the natural body, yet being itself the body of the spirit (*Die Seele, das ihm Nächste im Naturwesen, bildet gleichsam des Geistes Leib.*, part ii., p. 311). By his theory, therefore, the soul of man partakes of immortality by its union with the spirit, although it is at the outset ranked with that of the brute, whilst the latter is altogether denied a spirit. Treating the human soul in this manner, as the vehicle or body of the spirit, he creates an ideal demon as complete, and as independent of a future resurrection, as that of Plato or any other philosopher. But those ideas and powers, which Zschokke ascribes exclusively to the spirit, are really as much identified with the senses as our objective ideas themselves are; the former ideas are the modified resultants of the latter. Not less does the exercise of the senses affect their physical powers, either beneficially or injuriously, than the exercise of reason itself does; the highest intellect is sometimes by undue exertion irretrievably upset. Nor can an idiot experience the subjective emotions, which are the result of a sound organism and cultivated understanding, any more than a blind man can enjoy the pleasures dependent upon perfect vision.

The physical analogies of all our ideas, feelings, and emotions are referable to the bodily senses, and are modified by their idiosyncrasy. They are thus identified with the concrete soul of Scripture.

The attributes of the spirit, on the contrary, are

vitality, spontaneity, and consciousness, which alone
do not possess any material analogy.

The Pythagoreans, among whom was Plato himself, regarded the soul and body as antithetical, and
in the abstract mutually independent; considering
that into whatever body the soul might after death
be obtruded, it still would retain its own personal
identity. But from the distinctive characteristics of
the soul and spirit, it is in truth they which are
antithetical.

A confusion in relation to the ideas concerning
soul and spirit created the real difficulty in the
controversy between Locke and the Bishop of Worcester (Essay, vol. i., p. 162); and it is often painful
to hear from the pulpit a minister's laboured efforts
under the same perplexity. The Bishop, as well
as Locke, conceived that the soul was spirit. But
Locke supposed, that the soul consisted of some
spiritual substance within us, in which the personal
faculties might inhere; for we cannot conceive of
faculties otherwise than being attached to some
substance. The worthy prelate thought, that such
a doctrine savoured of materialism. But the philosopher taught otherwise. He did not say, that the
powers of the mind were properties of matter, but
that soul, although of a spiritual nature, must
be something substantial in which those powers
could inhere. Howbeit, according to the Biblical
psychology, this very substance for which he sought
is no other than the soul, body, or self of the

individual; to the various functions of whose organs, the spiritual agency imparts the faculties of
spontaneity and consciousness.

Zschokke's soul is in some degree analogous to
Locke's spiritual substance, yet only so far as the
sense ideas are concerned. The spirit supplies the
subjective ideas of his theory; and, from the manner
in which he treats of its sublime nature and thoughts,
he seems to regard it in the light of the rational
soul of Plato. But, in order to perpetuate individual
identity, he considers the animal soul as its body,
and so renders them consubstantial.

The object of such theories is, in the first place, to
account for the distinction between man and the
brute ; and, in the next place, to account for personal
immortality. Notwithstanding, the Biblical doctrine
makes no similar distinction; but, on the contrary,
the Holy Scriptures denominate men and brutes
alike living souls, and declare that they have both
one spirit. At the same time, however, the Bible
plainly and repeatedly recognises the great and important difference betwixt the understandings and
destinies of the two.

Locke and subsequent writers have shown, that
all our complex or subjective ideas are exclusively
composed of our simple or objective ideas, and that
the mental distinction between men and brutes is
that the former have the power, which the latter
have not, of combining and modifying their objective
ideas or cognitions; that, in short, brutes have neither

universal nor abstract ideas. The spontaneity of man extends beyond the mere objective application of his senses. It extends to the abstract reproduction of his sense cognitions individually ; so that he may combine and modify them in *rapport* with any given subject. Wherefore, it is superfluous to introduce any other than the spiritual agency, to account for the distinction between man and brute. In addition to these foregoing distinctions, all creatures have their organic specific idiosyncrasies.

The ideal theories, adverted to, have tended to mystify all metaphysical and even theological subjects, so as in a great degree to retard their development, and conduce to render them unpalatable and unpopular. Whereas, the Biblical psychology treats man as we find him, a concrete being, endued by his spiritual consubstantiality with subjective as well as objective spontaneity, enabling him to arrange his ideas or cognitions in relation to the several moral and scientific subjects, which for the time engage his attention. Thus, reason expresses the logical process of ideal arrangement and imagination, an arbitrary process of the same spontaneous character, modified in every individual according to the higher or lower development of some or all of his ideal senses in correspondence with their idiosyncrasy.

If the human spirit can dispense with a body, whether physical or spiritual, in respect of individual personality, there is no apparent reason why the spirits of brutes may not do the same ; since to both are given " one spirit" (Eccl. iii., 19). The objective ideas of the brute are analogous to those of man. But the subjective ideas of man are entirely dependent upon his objective ideas. So that, if the latter are assumed to inhere in a spiritual substance denominated the soul, we are left to infer that the same spirituality attaches to the brute as to man to the extent of their respective objectivity. The heresy of the Essenes consisted essentially in their holding, with the heathen philosophers, that the spirit was better without the body, and survived it in a personal sense, whereby they superseded the doctrine of a corporeal restitution.

Archbishop Leighton, in discoursing of the soul, does but adopt the popular argument, when he says, " Does not that noble neglect of the body and its senses, and that contempt of all the pleasures of the flesh, which these heavenly souls have attained, evidently show that in a short time they will be taken from hence, and that the body and soul are of a very different and almost contrary nature to one another ; that therefore the duration of the one depends not upon the other, but is quite of another kind ; and that the soul set at liberty from the body, is not only exempted from death, but in some sense then begins to live, and then first sees light ?" Here he adopts the term soul precisely in the Platonic sense, and not in the Biblical sense. But, apart from this, the high thoughts and delights, to which he adverts, do not prove the immortality of the soul otherwise, than the arguments of the heathen philosophers would have done. They only indicate that, in the religious mind, spiritual exercises are esteemed more than carnal, and that the subjective capacities of the rational being are superior to the objective. Yet, there is nothing in these subjectivities to show, that we are personally exempt from death, or that they themselves will survive personal dissolution. Nevertheless, from these lofty capacities, we may well infer a superior destiny. Howbeit, the Archbishop cherishes a still further hope for the sake of the body, as if it constituted a personality distinct from the soul, and were susceptible of an individual existence and happiness of its own, as "the faithful attendant and constant companion of the soul through all its toils and labours in this world." Therefore, "as an instance of the superabundance and immensity of the Divine goodness," he now admits the body to a share and participation of the heavenly and eternal felicity of the soul, as a distinct entity, which, so far as the soul was concerned, he had just said, was "capable of enjoying a perfectly happy and eternal life without the body." Yet, the Scriptures do not say, that the body, which accompanies the soul upon earth, shall be raised, but that the soul-body or same personality shall be raised a spiritual body.

The soul, in the popular sense, seems to be understood to represent that part of man, which distinguishes him from the lower animals; that,

which is identified with his rational or spiritual
faculties; that, which occupies itself with things
rational and divine, in contradistinction to the
merely bodily or animal propensities. There are
animal propensities, which are not essential to personal identity. When the spirit is itself withdrawn, we
are not taught that it retains any relative personal
identity, and to imagine any other personality, or a
divided personality, would not supply personal identity. A personal resurrection, therefore, as Biblically
taught, would appear to be a psychological necessity
in the future perpetuation of personal identity,
and furnishes the true solution of the future destiny
of mankind, to which mythology and the arguments of philosophy indistinctly point. It assigns
to life its true value, whilst it establishes the hope
of the Gospel.

The wide-spread tradition of a future state goes
far to favour the truth of an original Divine revelation of such a doctrine; yet it does not necessarily
depend upon a revelation. It might suggest itself
crudely to the human mind, however barbarous, by
the vivid ideal reappearance of departed relatives
or acquaintances in dreams or visions. But, in the
absence of the revelation of a future state, the
popular belief does not establish, nor could the
wisest prove with mathematical precision, the truth
of the proposition. Neither does it present itself as
an intuition, because this revelation is neither universal nor congenital with us.

By many persons, the body is still considered impeditive to all our powers of thought and rational enjoyment; and, yet, they profess, that the resurrection body shall augment the same powers for the purposes of happiness or misery. But, so far as revealed to us, the latter body shall resume all the characteristics of personal identity, leading us to conclude, that either a natural or spiritual body is essential to a personal identity; and, therefore, that a body, as such, is not itself the impediment, but the constituent of personality. The lapsed condition of the natural body must necessarily derogate from its powers, in contrast with the immortal and glorified body, yet not in any other sense.

All perplexities about the physical analogies of the mind apparently arise either from regarding the mind as a property of matter, or from considering the soul to be an inner spiritual personality enshrined in the outer man, endowed with ideal senses and ideal organs—an ideal man within an organic man. In the latter case, the bodily organs are viewed as the media of communication between that inner man and the outer world, and the entire body is treated as an impediment and encumbrance; but, if the body be in itself an encumbrance, we should have been better without it, and the Pagan conclusion, that we were sent into the body as a state of punishment, would seem to find a reasonable solution.

The outer man of Scripture is the man of sense;

Z

the inner man is the man of faith. The one is objective; the other subjective.

We cannot scientifically say, in the language of the Platonic dialogue, the second Alcibiades, that any one of our organs or senses is like a tool in a workman's hands, or that it is not a part of the *Ego*, but a tool employed. The fallacy of such a paradox is in making the *Ego* a mental abstraction. Each several organ and sense in the natural body is essential, not only in a corporeal, but intellectual or spiritual sense, and is a portion of the conscious *Ego*; and the entire personality of the *Ego* is the complement of all its organs. The atomic personality may change; but, if each atom be replaced by another possessing the same ideal impressions and personal attributes as that which it succeeds, the same personal identity, in contradistinction to atomic identity, still remains; and the permanent *Ego* or Self remains in its permanent spiritual consubstantiality.

The old idea of a tool is, however, perpetuated in the terms of Zschokke, " the spirit has received from nature its perishable veil. But this veiling is yet only a tool, through which it effects a union with her, and stands in reciprocal relation to her" (*In Wechselwirkung zu ihr steht, Selbstschau*, part ii., p. 215). Here the spirit constitutes the person, and the body his tool. Yet, according to the author's theory, the spirit is only the rational part of the person, and the animal soul is its complement.

He leaves us as much at a loss as ever to discover in what respect this animal soul, common alike to men and brutes, differs from the animal body. It remains a pure ideal. He further observes that "we know upon earth no diversity of higher and deeper spirits, but only a great diversity of men in their inclinations, works, knowledge, and faculties. But this diversity manifestly proceeds not from a dissimilarity in the spiritual being, but from the dissimilarity of the work-tool imparted by nature" (p. 216). But, if this difference depend upon the diversity of the work-tool or body, we are left after all to the inference, that the dissimilarity of men and brutes depends upon their different concrete idiosyncrasies.

It was well observed by Aristotle, that all the affections of the mind were necessarily identified with the corporeal organs, and that, therefore, the mind, in a spiritual sense, could not be separated from the body, so as to retain the same personal affections and faculties. Φαίνεται δὲ τῶν πλείστων οὐθὲν ἄνευ σώματος πάσχειν οὐδὲ ποιεῖν (De Anima, cap. i., sec. 1., sent. 9, 10).

Animos enim per se ipsos viventes non poterant mente complecti: formam aliquam figuramque quærebant (Cic. Tusc., lib. i., cap. 16., sec. 37).

The heathen philosophers were, no doubt, perplexed by their own arguments concerning a future state. But on the other hand, if we adopt the theory of the Platonic demon, or the poetic *manes*, we bring ourselves into' equal perplexity with regard to the doctrines of our own Hagiographa. In short, man without a body would be nobody. The individual Self, or *nephesh*, would be superseded and lost.

Consciousness and spontaneity are synchronous with our personal impressions and agency; so that whatever consciousness and spontaneity may be characteristic of the spirit as an agency, apart from its physical consubstantiality, the personal individual identity seems to be dependent upon the continuance of the concrete soul, or self, in its present, or some future condition.

The characteristic idiosyncrasy of all the orders of the animal creation seems to consist in their respective peculiar organisms; and the spiritual co-efficient is in each developed accordingly.

Angels, so far as revealed, appear to possess bodies not totally devoid of material properties in some modified form, analogous, perhaps, to those of the resurrection state. They are active, and not merely passive beings, represented as acting upon, and communicating with, material beings. The angelic equality, spoken of in the Gospels, refers not only to a state, but to personal conditions and similitude.

As the circumstances of creation vary, whether in our own or other spheres, so (we may be certain) will the modifications of Divine power and goodness, as partially illustrated in the infinite varieties of organic life with which our lower orb abounds. The millions of species of animalcules present some of such modifications; the vegetable and animal tribes others; and man, himself, is another of such forms. Again, the natural body in its transmutation into the spiritual, or, as it may be termed, into the personal restitution in the spiritual, transfers the human personality into the category of the angelic.

Without these forms with their attendant characteristics, the personality of each would vanish. The vital or spiritual agency would no longer be a personal spontaneity and consciousnes, but a universal spirit, identified in at least a secondary sense with, and merging into, the universal τὸ ἕν of the Stoics, or the Divine spirit of the Buddhists.

A universal agency can only become an individual agency by its being reduced to a corporeal personal agency. We can no more conceive the spiritual agency, divested of the personal organism, to produce personal phenomena, than, by material analogy, the agency of steam, detached from the machinery which it propels and regulates, to perform the functions of that machine. Therefore, as well from Revelation as from experience and analogy, there seems to be sufficient reason to conclude, that a concrete body of one kind or another constitutes each kind of personality, adapted to the conditions under which it exists—the spiritual as well as the natural body.

We only read of two kinds of bodies ascribed to the human personality in Scripture. The one is the natural body, and the other the spiritual body of the resurrection. It is more difficult to realise in the mind the idea of an individual personality without a body, than that of a miraculous personal resurrection. As the archetypal similitude was inherent in the original creation of the natural body, so is it perpetuated in the spiritual body. "As we have borne the image of the earthy, we shall also bear the image of the heavenly."

But the ideal soul possesses no archetypal *rapport.* The substance of the image is lost. An indistinct shadow of we know not what is all that remains. There is not even an analogy either to the earthy or the heavenly. It is neither consistent with nature nor Revelation, but is rather a counterpart of Milton's impersonation of Death : —

> "If shape it might be called, that shape had none
> Distinguishable in member, joint or limb;
> Or substance might be called that shadow seemed,
> For each seemed either."

It is this tendency to confound the ideal with the real, that peoples earth and air with phantoms of affright, and so often leads astray the popular mind in regions of spiritualism more incongruous than the heathen mythology.

It is the privilege of the poet to create new worlds, in which the mind may expatiate, or look through a glass darkly at things which eye hath not seen nor ear heard.

> "Wollt ihr hoch auf ihren Flügeln schweben,
> Werft die Angst des Irdischen von euch;
> Fliehet aus dem engen dumpfen Leben
> In des Ideales Reich!" (Schiller).

Omniscience and Omnipotence, the Eternal and

Supreme, are realised to the mind of the reader by ideal creations. The Soul, divested of its human nature, is poetically invested with more than human attributes. Of such creations, and of such alone, can it be appropriately said, in the pyrrhonic language of Berkeley, that they only exist in idea.

Thus, the ideal supplements the real and the revealed, in the relation of the subjective to the objective. Thus it is in the higher works of imagination; in which a congruity between them is, or ought to be, maintained.

Revelation tells us of mansions not made with hands, eternal in the heavens; of a second advent; of a restitution of all things; of a resurrection and a future destiny.

The intermediate state or condition is the region of death. It is a desert in our individual soul-being, which the poets and philosophers have peopled with the sublime and beautiful creations of their own imaginings, reasonings, and aspirations. What the ideal is in art, faith is in religious dogma and experience. The one is grounded in our nature; the other is founded upon Revelation.

The telescope of faith brings heaven to earth, and realises the substance of things hoped for; the future in the present. Death and the intermediate state are swallowed up and abolished. The mighty dead are yet alive. *Non cum corpore extinguuntur magnæ animæ.* To be absent from the body is to be present with the Lord. We walk by faith, not by sight.

Bunyan's pilgrim sees the Eternal City full in view, and the angels in the foreground waiting to receive him.

> " Sweet fields beyond the swelling flood,
> Stand dressed in living green" (Isaac Watts).

Whilst "*infiniti guai,*" from the *Valle Dolorosa,* assail the mind of the great southern bard in his Inferno.

There are ideas and emotions, which cannot be adequately symbolised by the reality of nature alone. But let us not confound the ideal with the real or revealed.

PART III.

——:o:——

BIBLICAL DEMONOLOGY.

——:o:——

A 2

PART III.

BIBLICAL DEMONOLOGY.

CHAPTER I.

BIBLICAL DEMONOLOGY.

THE Spirit-world is a region in which the poets of all periods have delighted to expatiate. The heathen mythology has peopled earth and air with phantoms of poetic creation. The nymphs, fauns, satyrs, gods and goddesses of classic celebrity are identified with the groves, fountains, rivers, and landscapes of Greece and Italy. In like manner, fairies and supernatural beings of various orders perform no unimportant part in modern literature. Popular superstition has thus, in all ages and countries, attested a sense or tradition of something more than is seen by mortal eye—that there are or have been influences, operating in the midst of us, of more than human or material origin. The demons of the ancient pagans were of this traditionary character; and, being accounted favourable to men, they bore some analogy to the Hebrew angelic ministrations.

It is not probable (as supposed by the atheist) that the supernatural of tradition is entirely the creature of imagination. The creations of imagination are purely plastic modifications of objective ideas. The idea of another world and a higher order of intelligences, as matters of primeval and nearly universal belief, would be unlikely to arise without some analogous experience suggestive of them. The existence of traditions of the supernatural amongst the most barbarous, as well as civilised, peoples points to a realistic origin; but, the phantoms of superstition or imagination being once originated, it no longer follows that they are themselves real.

According to Mede, the philosophers, before the times of the apostles and also contemporaneously with them, regarded the demons as angelic ministers between heaven and earth. The Academics and Stoics seem to have held a similar doctrine. Some of these demons were regarded as the souls of deified men (Newton's Dissertations, fifth edition, vol. ii., page 439, &c.).

Plato, in Sympos., defines a *daimonion* to be a being intermediate between the supreme God and man.

Hesiod, as quoted by Newton, introduces them in this sense as attendants upon mortals.

Plato, in his Timæus, calls the soul of man a demon, in a strictly personal sense (Stall. Pla. 359).

Euripides uses the word δαιμονῶντας for those possessed with demons, in the sense of a divine inspiration or frenzy.

Although, in the times of the ancient Greeks, the *daimonia* were regarded in a favourable aspect, yet, in the gospel period, they seem to have been viewed, by the Jews at least, as the enemies of man. The Pharisees in particular, as manifest in the later Talmuds, had not only embraced much of the Greek philosophy, but had blended with it certain of the magian doctrines of good and evil spirits. They believed in bad as well as in good angels (Josephus Ant. Jud., xiii., 9).

The heathen in different ages and countries have very commonly attributed human ailments to demoniacal agency or possession; and some of them do so at the present day.

It is not necessary for our present argument to traverse, with Howitt, the vast historic domains of the supernatural. The recorded instances may be accepted as evidences of a universal abstract belief in supernatural powers and influences without establishing any particular superstition. It does not follow, because the pagan and popular demonology may be disbelieved in part or in whole, that, therefore, the supernatural is rejected in the abstract, or Biblical spiritualism is discredited.

The American Indians have their medicine man, who is employed in special cases of bodily or mental affliction to exorcise the patient by various grotesque

gestures and mysterious incantations. The Veddahs
of Ceylon when sick "send for devil dancers to drive
away the evil spirit, who is believed to inflict
disease" (Sir J. E. Tennant's Ceylon, vol. ii., page
442). Amongst other receipts of a Tamul doctor,
referred to by Sir James, is one " to possess with a
devil," analogous to the pretended spells of witchcraft. The modern Hindoos similarly personify the
disturbing cause occasioning disease. The frantic
prophetess, described by Virgil (Æneid, lib. vi.),
somewhat resembles these modern exorcists.

In the New Testament, the instances of *daimonia*
adduced are those of unclean or evil spirits. The
phraseology, by which they are termed, no doubt
expresses the character in which they were popularly
regarded. The demoniacs also believed themselves
to be possessed ; and, like the heathen of their own
time and our day, they spoke and acted in that
character. As such they came or were brought
to Jesus, who alone had power by his *fiat* to heal
diseases and cast out demons.

The heathen exorcists, in the time of the apostles
and of Josephus, assumed to deliver the afflicted
from such possessions ; but probably the scene
enacted when the seven sons of Sceva did so, may
furnish an example of their contemptible reputation.

The opinion held by some eminent persons that
these possessions, like those of the present day, were
merely modified forms of insanity or disease, does
not in the opinion of Campbell and others account

for the special phenomena. On the other hand, many excellent persons appear to be shocked at every suggestion, which does not admit, that they were the literal possessions of the bodies of men by personal agencies from the unseen world. Whatever they may have been, they must harmonise in their doctrinal aspect rather with Biblical psychology than with the pagan. If in a physical sense they were diseases, they might in a psychological sense be inspirations, yet, scarcely in the corporeal sense in which the quaint illustrators of not very antique editions of the Scriptures have represented them.

There are many words and phrases in Scripture, which are popularly understood in a different sense from that which the general tenor of Scripture warrants. Our enquiry, therefore, should be directed rather to the apostolic than to the popular sense.

The Bible is totally opposed to the popular opinion concerning demons; and, whilst there was really no other way in which the narrative could be intelligibly recorded than in the vernacular language, it is probable that both Christ and his apostles would thus colloquially make known the doctrines which are ascribed to them. In short, those infirmities, which were popularly ascribed to the pagan demons, are in the Scriptures attributed to none other than to Satan himself. Thence, it is said of Christ, in the Acts of the Apostles, that he "went about doing good and healing all that were oppressed of the devil."

At the same time, we shall see reason to suppose that, in some instances, these possessions were apostolically classed with ordinary maladies; and, in others, that the satanic influence was rather doctrinal than special.

Two possessed with demons came out of the tombs exceeding fierce, like the λυκανθρώποι of the ancient Greeks, who, as Virgil says, *implerunt falsis mugitibus agros.* These demoniacs, as if they had been informed who Jesus was, cried out, saying, " What have we to do with thee, Jesus, thou Son of God?" (Matt. viii., 29.)   It does not appear that they possessed any intuitive or supernatural knowledge.   In Luke, only one demoniac is mentioned; but he calls himself Legion, and thus becomes the mouth-piece of plurality, according to the characteristics developed (Luke viii., 30).   The narrative then proceeds to state that the demons besought our Saviour, if he should cast them out, to suffer them to enter the herd of swine which were feeding at some distance off.   As the Greeks believed that their mythological deities could inspire men and brutes, our Lord practically demonstrated, to the astonishment of those around, that he could also transfer the demoniacal or satanic inspiration from the man to the unclean swine.   In this instance, and in some others, the demons themselves are said to have addressed our Lord, or to have cried out.   But, from the general context it seems, that the possessed himself personified the demon, and acted as his mouth-piece, the latter never appearing in any visible or recognised aspect. Again, in the Gospel of St. Mark, a man with an unclean spirit cried out, "Let us alone; what have we to do with thee, thou Jesus of Nazareth? art thou come to destroy us?" And then concluded in terms appropriate to his own personality, "I know thee who thou art, the Holy One of God" (Mark i., 24).

Again, when demons came out of many, crying out, "Thou art Christ, the Son of God" (Luke iv., 41), the dispossessed were themselves the spokesmen; phraseologically the personified demons are said to speak, because the possessed believed themselves to personify the influences under which they spoke. Thus, in Acts xix., 16, "the evil spirit" and "the man in whom the evil spirit was" is the same person.

Those out of whom the demons came are apparently included amongst those "sick with divers diseases," mentioned in the preceding verse (Luke iv., 40). And, in the Gospel of St. Matthew (viii., 16-17), demoniacal possessions are apparently classed amongst human infirmities and sicknesses; also in Matt. ix., 32-35. Moreover, we read of a deaf, dumb, and blind spirit; the possessed being deaf and dumb, or blind; probably attended with mental imbecility.

In one instance the possessed is said to be a lunatic (Matt. xvii., 15). In a parallel passage he is said to have a dumb spirit (Mark ix., 17). And in another place, the spirit is called unclean, and a *Daimonion* (Luke ix., 42).

When the Jews said of Christ, "he hath a demon and is mad" (δαιμόνιον ἔχει καὶ μαίνεται, John x., 20), they only expressed the common notion that madness indicated a possession, or in other words, that the demon was the occult cause of mania. It would thus appear, that even lunacy and phrenzy were popularly treated as possessions, as they were by the Greeks and others.

If, at one time, we find the lunatic identified with the possessed, and at another time spoken of distinctively, or, if the possession is sometimes treated as an infirmity or disease, and at other times as a demoniacal or satanic influence, we may not unreasonably seek a solution of the difficulty in the different aspects in which they were regarded, whether physically or psychologically, whether merely as diseases, or with reference to their occult causes.

The diseased, the possessed, the lunatic, were brought to our Lord and "He healed (ἐθεράπευσεν) them" (Matt. iv., 24). The daughter of the Canaanitish woman who was "grievously vexed with a demon," was said to be "made whole" ἰάθη (Matt. xv., 28). Thus, the possessed were sometimes said to be healed, and sometimes to be made whole, as if mentally or bodily diseased; and, at other times, the demon is said to be cast out or exorcised. On another occasion, mentioned by St. Luke (iv., 35), our Lord rebuked (ἐπετίμησεν) the demon, and he came out of the possessed; and, in the same chapter, we read that, when Simon's wife's mother was taken with a great fever, he rebuked the fever, and it left her.

By casting out the popular demons, our Lord did not sanction the heathen doctrines concerning them, but vindicated his own power over the bodies and minds of men even upon popular grounds. He probably did not attempt to controvert argumentatively their superstitions; but, by the exercise of Divine attributes, Jesus attempted to establish his own authority, and thereby to vindicate his own and his apostles' teaching. Yet, on some occasions, he expressly attributed to Satan that which was popularly ascribed to the demons. It may, therefore, be conjectured, that Christ and his disciples were not altogether silent concerning the prevailing pagan superstition upon other occasions, although not recorded in the brief narratives. In the minds of the heathen, the demon symbolised psychologically an occult agency. In the minds of Christ and his apostles, as we shall presently see, the same term symbolised the spirit of him "that worketh in the children of disobedience."

It is not the miracle, but the psychology which is in question. It is as great a miracle to restore by a word a lunatic to his right mind, as to cast out a legion of devils. After the ascension of our Lord, the apostles continued to perform similar miracles, expressed in the same phraseology (Acts v., 16).

At different periods during the Christian era,

mental phenomena, not very dissimilar from those
of the Gospel possessions, have been recorded, and,
on that account, have been likewise so denominated.
The Camisards of the Cevennes, in Savoy, in the
16th century, were thus characterised; and, so, also
used to be considered certain cases of witchcraft
or fanaticism in this country. More recently, the
fanatical epidemic of Morzine, in 1857 and several
successive years, presented similar instances of
phrenzy. The persons subjected to the attacks
were chiefly ignorant enthusiasts; they became
violently excited, threw themselves down, blasphemed
their bishop, related visions of the Virgin Mary,
and sometimes fancied themselves to have returned
from hell upon missions of retribution; one or two
young men were said to have run up trees and along
the upmost branches and twigs like squirrels! The
latter statement we may at once set down to be
a physical exaggeration; but the others, like the
revivals that have occurred in various times amongst
Protestants in this country and America, present a
feature common to demoniacs in all ages and
countries. The mental phenomena in all are
identified with the most extravagant form of the
prevailing religion or superstition; all believe themselves to be possessed in some sense. The revivalists
conceive, whether rightly or wrongly, that they are
under the special influence of the Holy Spirit; the
others pretend that evil spirits have entered into
them. The ideas of the one class are essentially

evangelical; those of the other class are essentially pagan, tinged with the prevailing popular superstitions. All are more or less convulsionists, wrought into phrenzy by the force of religious or superstitious ideas; neither their communications nor symptoms are preternatural. Their apparent insensibility to pain is probably to be traced to the common cause of analogous phenomena, namely, the absorption of mental attention in another direction.

If the Biblical phraseology conform itself to the vernacular, it is not for the purpose of imparting the authority of the latter to the verbal hagiographa, but in order to impress more intelligibly the popular mind. Likewise, Christ conformed to a popular superstition, when he anointed the eyes of the blind man with mingled saliva and dust. He could have imparted sight to the blind man by his word; but he preferred fixing the popular attention by a recognised popular superstition. The demoniacs could only be recorded *eo nomine*. Thus, he manifested his attributes without startling the prejudices of the people; only on suitable occasions, he ascribed to Satan what they attributed to the demons.

Upon another occasion, Jesus illustrated his rebuke to the Pharisees, by addressing to them the parable of the rich man and Lazarus, in conformity with their own creed founded upon the pagan doctrine of *Hades*.

In such cases we have sometimes to supply an understood parenthesis, " as the people say" or " as the Pharisees say."

By miracles our Lord, and the Apostles in his name, taught the people that he was Lord of life and of all its agencies, that not only the bodies but the minds of men were under his control, and that not only the minds of men but the popular demons were subject to him.

Upon one occasion, the Jews imputed the fervour of our Lord's rebuke to his having a *daimonion* or demon; and, although he denied it, yet, when he proceeded to say that, if a man kept his sayings, he should never see death, or should not see death for ever, they said more emphatically "now we know that thou hast a demon" (John viii., 52). Such was the popular mode of speaking, as it is amongst some of the heathen of the present day, in order to account for what might appear to them a mystery or preternatural assumption. Deeming what he said to be incredible and irrational, they concluded he was mad or had a demon.

St. John is the only evangelist who does not record a single instance of the popular demoniacal possessions; but it has been suggested, by competent critics, that he omitted them, as well as many other equally important transactions, because they had been previously related by the other evangelists.

It may be observed, that the Hellenists attached Greek and magian ideas to Greek words, and that those who spoke the vernacular Syriac dialect incorporated a term *daivo* into their language corresponding with the Greek *daimonion*, in addition to their own *shido*, whilst a distinct designation

was given in both languages to the Hebraistic Satan
—in Greek, *Diabolos;* and in Syriac, *Ochelkarzo* (the
Accuser). In our translation the same term ' devil'
is indiscriminately applied to all. When used in
its special sense, it is discriminated in each language
by the article, to designate the arch-accuser; without the article, the term is equally applicable in its
general sense to man himself.

The heathen were only acquainted with 'demons;'
these designated or personified occult agencies
diverse from the known and natural agencies, being
the *daimonia* of the Greeks, the *shaidim* of the
Canaanites, or the *shidee* of the Syrians. Hence,
when a person was affected either in mind or body
in an unaccountable manner, these heathen personified in him the unknown agent or demon, to
whom they ascribed such extraordinary influences.

With respect to such of these possessions as were
of a preternatural character, or were only such in a
doctrinal sense, we are more likely to find the
apostolic apprehension of them in the apostolic
teaching, than in the vernacular phraseology of the
narrative. Although "God wrought special miracles
by the hands of Paul : so that from his body were
brought unto the sick handkerchiefs or aprons, and
the diseases departed from them, and the evil spirits
went out of them" (Acts xix., 11, 12) ; yet, St.
Paul does not, in any of his epistles, sanction the
popular doctrines of demonology, but cautions the
churches against their reception. Doctrinally, the

apostle adverts solely to "the prince of the power of the air, the spirit that now worketh in the children of disobedience" (Eph. ii., 2). He also expressly exhorted Timothy to caution the early Christians against the doctrines of demons (1 Tim. iv., 1), popularly current amongst the pagans; he says nothing even about the demons being the agents of Satan, as suggested by some writers upon the subject.

There do not appear to be sufficient Scriptural, nor any psychological grounds for supposing, that the δαιμονια (demons), or the ἀκαθαρτα πνευματα (unclean spirits) were unpurged human spirits, as intimated by some of the patristic writers; such views approximate closely to the philosophical doctrine of a metempsychosis. The phrase "unclean spirit" is a parallelism with δαιμονιον (demon); for the scribes charged our Saviour with casting out unclean spirits by the prince of the demons, and thereby accused him of having "an unclean spirit" (Mark iii., 30).

The application of 'demon' to the human soul or spirit, by Chrysostom and others, is clearly the Platonic doctrine. Likewise, the expressions translated "doctrines of demons" (1 Tim. iv., 1) and "spirits of demons" (Rev. xvi., 14) have reference, as before noticed, to the pagan doctrines concerning demons.

In the New Testament, we not only read of persons being demoniacally possessed, but also of their being so in the sense of a plurality of evil spirits. Out of Mary Magdalene went seven demons. Another demoniac styled himself Legion on the same account.

The popular demon expresses the occult cause of corporeal or mental infirmity, or wickedness. The apostolic doctrine teaches us, that a satanic influence, either special or congenital, is the real originator of all these evils. Hence, when a plurality of evil spirits or demons are spoken of in a personal sense, we may surmise, either that the same person is afflicted in several mysterious ways, or that, by numerical emphasis, some extraordinary degree of phrenzy or wickedness is implied. For example, in the parable of the Unclean Spirit returning to a man with seven other spirits more wicked than himself, our Lord illustrated in a popular manner the sevenfold wickedness of the generation whom he addressed (Matt. xii., 45). The same numerical emphasis of 'seven' is here adopted as in the instance of Mary Magdalene. In an analogous manner, he upbraided the Pharisees with compassing sea and land to make one proselyte, "and when he is made, ye make him twofold more the child of hell than yourselves" (Matt. xxiii., 15).

Yet, seeing that the leading idea of the word 'demon' is implicative of a Genius or knowing and heroic character, and hence of a superior being in a good or evil sense, and seeing that this word was ultimately transferred by the heathen for the purpose of personifying or expressing an occult agency, it might not be inappropriately adopted by our Lord with reference to the spirit of him that "worketh in the children of disobedience." Jesus evidently applied the term 'demon' in this sense, when he answered those who imputed his power over the demons to be by means of the co-operation of the Prince of Demons—"How can Satan cast out Satan?" (Mark iii., 23). There was thus a philological propriety in the adoption of this very word, notwithstanding its perversion by the ignorant. At the same time Christ, by using 'demon' in preference to any periphrasis, did thereby more popularly establish his own authority; whilst he confounded the vain pretensions of the exorcists with the apposite question, "by whom do your sons cast them out?" (Luke xi., 19).

The remarks of the learned Parkhurst and of some of his authorities upon δαιμονιον may be usefully consulted.

Judas Iscariot is denominated a devil (*diabolos*) after the spirit of Satan had entered into him (John vi., 70, and xiii., 27). With special propriety might he be called the accuser or calumniator of his Divine Master. Christ also ascribed to Satan the oppression of the woman bound with infirmity (Luke xiii., 16). Peter, adverting to the cures effected by our Lord, describes him indiscriminately as "healing all that were oppressed of the devil" *diabolos* (Acts x., 38).

A certain damsel is mentioned in the Acts of the Apostles as "possessed with a spirit of divination" πνεῦμα Πύθωνος—a spirit of Python, the traditional Serpent of the heathen (Acts xvi., 16). Perhaps she was an oracular Pythoness, reputed to be inspired with the spirit of the god Apollo, or in other words stated to be "possessed with a spirit of divination." This person was exorcised by St. Paul in the same manner as the demoniacs.

Similar to this soothsayer was the character of those we read of in the Old Testament called *Ovoth*, or those who had familiar spirits. And, classed with these men, there were the *Zidonim*, or wizards—called in the Septuagint ἐγγαστριμυνθοι, ventriloquists —pretending to supernatural knowledge and influences (Lev. xx., 27).

Simon, the sorcerer, is said to have "bewitched the people of Samaria" (Acts viii., 9) ; however, we have no reason to believe, that he was any more than a pretender, who himself wondered beholding the really great miracles which were wrought by the Apostles.

Although we read of diviners, enchanters, wizards, witches, and necromancers in the Scriptures of the Old Testament, they are only mentioned by way of narrative, or for the purpose of condemnation (Deut. xviii., 10-11-12). They did but imitate the miracles wrought by God, of which they had heard or been witnesses. They resorted to what, in the Acts of the Apostles, are termed "curious arts." Contrari-

wise, the People of God were to be perfect before
him, and were not suffered thus to mock him. Nor
is it any denial of Scripture to deny the authenticity
of such vain pretenders to the possession of supernatural gifts, which the Scriptures themselves in
nowise sanction. If they ever possessed supernatural
inspiration, it must, according to the Biblical doctrine, have been through him that "worketh in the
children of disobedience." Yet the miracles ascribed
to Satan are termed "lying wonders." He himself
is termed the father of lies, or a liar (John viii., 44).
And sorcerers are, in the Book of Revelations, comprised in the same category with "whosoever loveth
and maketh a lie" (Rev. xxii., 15).

The very names, by which sorcerers, diviners, and
similar characters are designated, imply nothing
more than the character of their pretensions. The
Mecashaif (sorcerer or wizard) performs his enchantments pharmaceutically; the *Chartûmim* (diviners)
were hierogrammatists, interpreters of hieroglyphics, and astrologers; the *Shoail Ov* (consulter with
familiar spirits) puffed and swelled himself out as if
inflated by some inspiration, like those in the Greek
and Roman classics. Virgil describes the frantic
Sibyl thus:—

> * * * " Subitò non vultus, non color unus,
> Non comptae mansêre comae : sed pectus anhelum,
> Et rabie fera corda tument ; majorque videri,
> Nec mortale sonans : afflata est numine quando
> Jam propiore Dei" (Æneid, lib. vi., v. 47–51).

The *Zidonim* (wizards) or wise men resembled the wise women of a recent period; and the *doraish el hamaithim* (necromancer), like the witch of Endor or some of our modern spirit-rappers, appears to have held only an ideal communion with the dead. The *manes* or shades of the old mythology were the representatives of the latter, and similar are the ghosts or spirits of haunted houses and solitary places. But, if these be visible or otherwise cognizable by the senses, it must be in a body; and, if the ghost or shade be corporeal, it must either be in the natural body or in the spiritual body; however the latter body is that of the resurrection only. Under no other conditions are we led to believe, that the departed can hold any personal intercourse with the living; and, therefore, we cannot look for such communion until the resurrection of the dead. Wherefore, supposing that the prophet Samuel were really raised by the Witch of Endor, it must have been in his natural body; since we nowhere read of his translation into the spiritual state. If he appeared like an old man with his mantle around him, he must have been visible to King Saul equally as well as to the Witch of Endor. Howbeit Saul was made to know *(vayaidha)* Samuel himself, seemingly immediately after the frightened shriek of the *Baalath Ov.* It was the profession of this woman to practise oracular pretensions and ventriloquism; but she appears, from the narrative, to have been allowed no time to counterfeit, after that Saul

"said, Bring me up Samuel. And when the woman
saw Samuel, she cried with a loud voice" (1 Sam.
xxviii., 11, 12). The time was night, when discern-
ment is slow. How humbled was the witch with
her impostures before a real appearance. She could
say and do nothing, but only betray her fear. She
acknowledges her want of penetration by exclaiming,
terrified, " Why hast thou *deceived* me?" She did
not even recognise Samuel, when she saw him. She
performed no part in the drama, other than that of
an inactive, silent spectator. *Samuel himself* was
the spokesman, announcing his final message on
earth directly to King Saul without any person's
intervention. The strange scene may have been
enacted under the starry heavens. *Samuel*, the truly
inspired Prophet of God—and not the false prophetess, the sham Witch of Endor—foretold the
coming events of the morrow, the victory of the
Philistines and the death of the King of Israel with
his sons. The Man of God says, " To-morrow shalt
thou and thy sons be with me" (1 Sam. xxviii., 19);
this strongly corroborates the supposition, that
Samuel did not appear in his spiritual, but in his
natural body; he would have again (like Lazarus
had) to return to the grave. Now mark the great-
ness of Saul's fear; he " fell straightway all along
on the earth and was sore afraid, because of the
words of Samuel" (verse 20)—*not* because of anything uttered by the witch. She appears to have
fled to a little distance, in dread, during the col-

loquy; for the next verse (21) says, "The woman came unto Saul, and saw that he was sore troubled." This very judgment on Saul is attributed in part to his having consulted "one that had a familiar spirit to enquire of it, instead of enquiring of the Lord" (1 Chron. x., 13). The event is, no doubt, historically true and graphically delineated; but any supernatural characteristics, except the temporary resuscitation of Samuel, are self-condemnatory, and repugnant to the Divine counsels and prerogatives.

The modern demonology of spirit-rapping, in which tables and chairs are made the media of intercourse between the visible and invisible, cannot, according to the Biblical doctrine, be a communion between departed and living human intelligences; because the human personality of the former no longer exists, and the period of the spiritual has not yet arrived. It is contrary to the whole tenor of Scripture that angelic beings of any order should pander to human curiosity, or should avail themselves of inorganic matter to make those communications imperfectly which they could effect so much better face to face; or should trouble themselves to tell us things not worth knowing, or which are better known by living men.

No apparition of a fallen angel (except of Satan himself), or of a disembodied spirit is Biblically recorded; nor is any miraculous influence ascribed to any other than to Satan as the instigator of "the Man of Sin," "with all power and signs and lying

wonders." Yet, it is doubtful whether these are
to be regarded as real miracles, rather pretended
miracles and "lying wonders." Paley, Douglas
Bishop of Salisbury, and other eminent writers notice
the same Biblical fact. Except where a special
satanic influence is Biblically recognised, we perhaps
ought not to introduce it; where sin and deception
in their natural sense are sufficient to explain the
phenomena, we need not—nay, peradventure, should
not—suppose supernatural workings. Even the
enchantments of the Egyptian magicians are not
ascribed to any special satanic influence.

The *Chartûmim*, diviners or hierogrammatists,
simulated miracles by their incantation fires *(bela-
hataihem)*; perhaps their incantations and imitations
deceived the people for a time. The magicians
themselves ultimately acknowledged that the finger
of God was in the Mosaic miracles. St. Paul, in
his second Epistle to Timothy, mentions Jannes and
Jambres amongst the number of these magicians, and
compares with them certain heady and godless characters who by a form of godliness led captive silly
women; but, he says, they shall proceed no further,
"for their folly shall be made manifest unto all men,
as theirs (the magicians) also was." Here, the
apostle seemed to consider that the magicians had
succeeded in deceiving the people for a time, until
their folly or deceptive arts became detected and
manifest; their characters were an abomination to
the Almighty; they were the makers of lies and

forgeries and a parody of the Divine prerogatives, "Thou shalt be perfect with the Lord thy God" (Deut. xviii., 13).

The influences of Satan upon mankind are doctrinally described to be the communication of an evil energy. There are only two recorded instances of objective personal communion; the one was with the Adam of Paradise, and the other was with the second Adam, Jesus Christ—in the former Satan triumphed, by the latter he was vanquished. To no other order of evil spirits is there a similar influence with mankind ever ascribed, or a personal intercourse ever represented. On the contrary, the demoniacal influences themselves are in some instances expressly ascribed to Satan, and appear to be all embraced in the category of those who are "oppressed of the devil."

At the same time, we are never informed, that Satan professes the attribute of ubiquity in the same sense as it is applied to the Holy Spirit; yet, wherever the human race extends, the fallen nature as Satan's work is co-extensive; nor is the foregoing inconsistent with the Evil One's exercising special influences in individual cases.

Some writers have considered that the sons of God, mentioned in the sixth chapter of Genesis, were evil angels; but such an opinion is not sanctioned by any parallel passage in Scripture nor by its doctrinal tenor; on the contrary, the nature of angels is represented to be such that they "neither marry nor are given in marriage." Wherefore, the inference is that the intercourse referred to must have been human.

The judgment of fallen angels, recorded by St. Jude, is an illustration of the Divine condemnation of sin, even in angelic natures; he does not confuse the sins of angels with those of the flesh, or the spiritual with the natural body. We do not even read in Scripture of incorporeal or disembodied spirits.

Although it is said by some that the popular belief in demons continued so late as the second century, yet it appears historically, that the popular demon (like the Pagan oracles and augurs) gradually disappeared with the extension of Christianity and popular intelligence; in the same manner, similar superstitions amongst the heathen, in the present day, vanish in the light of evangelical illumination.

Fontenelle combats the once popular idea, that the ancient oracles were delivered by demons. It is but due to the Divine character of our holy religion to endeavour to clear it of those glosses, which are incongruous with its general teaching, and which are calculated to disparage it in an enquiring age. Consequently, we have ventured to combat opinions concerning the demoniacs, which appear to savour rather of a Pagan and mystical character than to harmonise with those doctrines which are more plainly enunciated. The same author concludes his *Histoire des Oracles* with the following causes of their decline, which are in a modified degree equally applicable to the doctrines of demons—*D'abord de grandes sectes de philosophes Grecs qui se sont moqués des Oracles, ensuite les Romains qui n'en faisoient point d'usage, enfin les Chrétiens qui les détestoient, et qui les ont abolis avec le Paganisme.*

Chapter II.

The hidden invisible agencies of the natural world manifest their presence by their phenomena. The raging billows of the ocean proclaim to all a spirit that still sways upon the face of the deep, whilst the thunder and lightning reveal a subtle and sublime agency, ruling in the clouds above and the earth beneath.

These and other physical agencies are developed by their phenomena in the material world; but, although truly surprising in their results, and apparently supernatural in some instances when beyond the grasp of popular apprehension, they are still so invariable in their laws of action as really to identify themselves with the ordinary and universal physical agencies of the visible universe.

The psychological phenomena, as distinguished from the former, are identified with what is termed a spiritual agency. It is that which produces the phenomena of life, spontaneity, and consciousness in organic beings. In its ordinary phenomena, it is as much a natural agency as the former. Yet, according to the Biblical revelation as well as tra-

ditional superstition, there are unseen powers of a
spiritual character, which in some mysterious way are
represented to originate exceptions to the natural
laws of the physical as well as spiritual agencies.
Those which call down fire from heaven, cause
iron to float in water, repel the action of fire, or
heal the sick by contact, are some of the instances
which are physically miraculous.   Those which
communicate prophetic inspiration, which influence
the hearts and minds of men contrary to their
natural dispositions, expel the popular demon or the
satanic influences, and produce the various ideal
phenomena whether of visions of the night or in
the conduct of individuals, are recorded in evidence
of a superintending providence who overrules and
regulates the world of mind as well as that of matter.

However, it is not every act or influence termed
'spiritual' which is miraculous, or that is effected by
means beyond the explication of the ordinary moral
and intellectual laws which govern the human mind
and character.   For the term 'spirit,' although itself
primarily significant of a pneumatic unseen agency,
is also specially and metonymically applied to those
works and doctrines which are characteristic of the
Divine Spirit and his inspired teachings.   They are
thus placed in apposition to the natural inclinations
of the fallen creature.   The former are specially
termed 'the fruit of the Spirit' (Gal. v. 22); the
latter are the 'works of the flesh' or 'of the devil.'

"The works of the flesh"—adultery, murders,

drunkenness and such like—are objectively at
variance with the subjective teaching of the moral
or Divine law. "The fruit of the Spirit"—love,
goodness, temperance and the like—is the reverse.
"And these are contrary the one to the other" (see
Galatians v.). "In this the children of God are
manifest, and the children of the devil" (1 John
iii., 10). Thus, except where special and miraculous
influences are mentioned or implied, the Spirit of God
and the spirit of the devil are respectively symbolised
by doctrine and conduct. In like manner, a man
is popularly said to manifest a good spirit or a bad
spirit. But, in a special as well as primary sense, the
Biblical doctrine and phraseology point to the
direct spiritual agency of the Deity or of his
adversary or calumniator Satan or τοῦ διαβόλου.
Sometimes these agencies are characterised as powers
and energies proceeding from the agent.

If we cannot explain what those agencies or
powers are, it is because their phenomena are alone
matters of experience and demonstration; but these
phenomena, including those of life itself, are as
surely demonstrative of a mysterious cause and
agency, as if the agency itself were manifested. This
inference has been supplemented by the revelation
of the existence of controlling spiritual agencies,
primarily and personally identified with the Deity
himself or his apostate angel. To these the Biblical
language always refers either literally, metaphysically,
personally, or morally and doctrinally.

In the scene of our Lord's Temptation, Satan
appears as a personal agent. He is generally
adverted to as an invisible malign being. "Your
adversary the devil, as a roaring lion, walketh about,
seeking whom he may devour" (1 Peter v., 8). He
is alluded to also as producing an evil influence upon
men. "The prince of the power of the air, the
spirit that now worketh in the children of disobedience" (Eph. ii., 2). The phrase "prince of the
power of the air" has apparently some reference to the
primary signification of the διάβολος or devil, termed
in the Esse language *diabhail* or the god of the air.
A parallelism is recognised by the ancient Greeks, as
well as by the Hebrews, between the expressions
ἀὴρ and πνεῦμα. Aristotle, *De Mundo*, says that
'air' is also called 'spirit;' and, in the passage of the
Epistle just quoted, it is evident that the phrase
"prince of the power of the air" is parallel with the
following word "spirit," expressive of the power
that "worketh in the children of disobedience." So
God is called "the Father of Spirits," or of those
who are under the influence of His Holy Spirit. An
influence experimentally felt by all who have been
"born again."

The evil spiritual power, with which believers
have to contend, is again adverted to under its
different manifestations as "the wiles of the devil"
(τὰς μεθοδείας τοῦ διαβόλου), more specifically
characterised in the following verse: "For we
wrestle not against flesh and blood, but against

principalities, against powers, against the rulers of
the darkness of this world, against spiritual wickedness in heavenly places" τὰ πνευματικὰ τῆς πονηρίας
ἐν τοῖς ἐπουρανίοις (Eph. vi., 12). The precise
meaning of the latter clause as translated is somewhat
obscure ; and, in times of mysticism and superstition,
the language has often received a corresponding
interpretation. The Syriac, not having any word of
similar terminology with πνευματικὰ (spiritual things
or influences), has substituted " evil spirits (*ruchee
bishotho*) which are beneath heaven." The modern
Greek has needlessly followed this. The French
translation is similar; but, if possible, it is still more
in accordance with a very popular notion, " *les esprits
malins dans les airs.*" However, none of these constructions can be said to be either literal or agreeable
to the context. The word ἐπουράνιος is only used
by Homer with reference to the Gods.; and he
employs οὐρανος to signify the vault of heaven,
above which is the seat of the gods. The use of the
same word in the New Testament in the plural
number is probably a Hebraism, and generally
denotes the spiritual kingdom of God. Thus, in
Matt. iv., 17 and elsewhere, the expression ἡ βασιλεία
τῶν οὐρανῶν signifies the spiritual kingdom of God
in this world, probably so called because of its relation
to the heavenly. Hence the passage, in Eph. iii., 10,
seems to refer to the same kingdom, embracing
Gentiles as well as Jews, wherein the apostle by his
preaching was engaged to make known the mystery

of godliness to the Gentiles, "To the intent that now unto the principalities and powers in heavenly places (ἐν τοῖς ἐπουρανίοις) might be made known, by the church, the manifold wisdom of God;" but, instead of "heavenly places," the plain sense of the words seems rather to imply "in heavenly things" or in things relating to the kingdom of God. The whole tenor of the passage seems to have reference to the work of the church in God's kingdom upon earth. In a patristic gloss upon Matt. vi., 33, we find the same expression αἰτεῖτε τα ἐπουρανια (ye ask heavenly things). Wherefore the former passage, "spiritual wickedness in heavenly places" (τὰ πνευματικὰ τῆς πονηρίας ἐν τοῖς ἐπουρανίοις), seems to imply the spiritual influences of evil in heavenly things, or in things relating to the kingdom of God. The "wiles of the devil" may, therefore, be characterised as moral and political influences and agencies against which believers have to contend. The Christian wars a spiritual battle against the rulers in this dark world, against pride, superstition, ignorance, bigotry, and all kinds of wicked influences prevalent in God's moral kingdom upon earth, specially ascribed to the devil as their originator (ὁ τοῦ κόσμου τούτου ἄρχων, John xiv., 30), without any allusion to other apostate spirits; "the armour of God" is specially adapted for the sons of God to wrestle against and withstand such malign agencies.

Thus the demoniacal possessions, which are so frequently mentioned in the gospels, may well refer to the similar subjective working of the same spiritual influence of the devil in the person possessed; the person himself for the time personating the popular *daimonion*, or what the apostle calls the spirit that worketh in the children of disobedience —being the mouthpiece as well as victim of a spiritual influence, whether such influence be supposed to be special or doctrinal.

The opinion of St. Augustin does not assist us in this matter, being founded upon a purely Platonic theory.

The persons, whom Christ was said by Peter to go about healing, were similar to the preceding, having been brought under the power καταδυνασ- τευομένους of the devil (Acts x., 38).

Again, it is said, that the devil "put into the heart" of Judas Iscariot to betray Christ (John xiii., 2); and also that, "Then entered Satan into Judas" (Luke xxii., 3); and again, by a metonymy, he is denominated "a devil" or adversary (John vi., 70). These phrases are evidently parallelisms. Upon one occasion St. Peter himself is rebuked by the name of Satan, with reference to the unsub- missive spirit he had manifested (Matt. xvi., 23). Satan is represented as the agent, and the individual's conduct characterises the agency to which that con- duct is imputed.

In the Iliad, we find Neptune assuming the similitude of Calchas; and, in the Odyssey, Pallas takes the form of Mentor. In other words, the character of the Deity inspires the man.

Sometimes we find other terms used equivalent

to inspiration; for instance, Herod believing Jesus Christ to be John the Baptist risen from the dead, inferred that, therefore, supernatural powers wrought in him—*αἱ δυνάμεις ἐνεργοῦσιν ἐν αὐτῷ* (Matt. xiv., 2).

When Jesus healed the diseased who came out of all Judæa and Jerusalem, and from the sea-coast of Tyre and Sidon, and those who were vexed with unclean spirits, it is said "there went virtue—*δύναμις* —out of Him and healed them all" (Luke vi., 19); and, when the woman with the issue of blood touched the border of Christ's garment, the issue was immediately staunched, and He remarked, "somebody hath touched Me: for I perceive that virtue—*δύναμις*—is gone out of Me" (Luke viii., 46). The word here translated "virtue" is the same one that is applied to the power of healing diseases and casting out demons. This power or virtue is a Divine prerogative, which our Lord exercised with supreme authority; but He imparted it occasionally to His apostles, so that by their hands miracles were wrought—not by any inherent power, but as the vicegerents of Divine authority.

Also, "God wrought special miracles—*δυνάμεις*— by the hands of Paul: so that from his body were brought unto the sick handkerchiefs or aprons, and the diseases departed from them, and the evil spirits went out of them" (Acts xix., 11, 12). Here we have the miracle of the cure of the issue of blood repeated in another form; instead of touching the apostle's clothes, they brought their own hand-

kerchiefs into contact with the body of St. Paul.
Probably it might be said that virtue proceeded
from the apostle; but it is clearly stated that
God wrought the miracles by the hands of St. Paul
as His instrument. We cannot suppose that the
cure of the issue of blood was effected unknown
or against the will of our Lord; because he said,
literally, "knowing in Himself that virtue had gone
out of Him" (Mark v., 30); nor can we conclude
that it was merely a physical agency, for δύναμις
implies ἐξουσία. Consequently, our Saviour's power
was not analogous to the virtue of a healing plant,
or of medicine, or of mesmerism; but it implied the
authority of a Divine *fiat*.

As, in the philosophy of Aristotle, δύναμις and
ἐνέργεια concur in every scientific workmanship to
produce what mere undeveloped potentiality does
not manifest, so the Divine power's development is
enforced by the Divine authority or *fiat*. The
ἐξουσία is the supreme and illimitable Divine puissance (Luke xii., 5, etc.); the δύναμις is the same
supreme puissance manifested by His works (Rom.
i., 20), or by His servants specially inspired or
authorised to perform them. To ascribe such miracles to mesmerism or animal magnetism or to any
analogous physical agency is at least presumptuous;
and none of these agencies has been attested by
the like decisive and effectual phenomena. The
Biblical cures are imputed to the Divine authority
and agency, and are immediately effective. The

Divine power calls forth or supplies and directs the curative virtue. By some miraculous endowment, or by the intervention of Divine power, the prophets seem to have exercised supernatural gifts. The rod of Moses is made the talisman whereby he confounded the Egyptian magicians, divided the waters of the Red Sea, and brought water out of the rock in Horeb. Elijah called down fire from heaven, he divided the waters of Jordan with his mantle, and ascended the heavens in a chariot of fire. Elisha restored to life the Shunamite's child, and made iron to swim. None of these phenomena accord with those of the known physical agencies, any more than with the known psychological ones.

Those prodigies, manifested by the prophets and some of the demoniacs in preternatural mental affections and endowments, are only reconcilable with the interposition of a preternatural mental agent operating dynamically upon the individual, not through the infusion of supernatural experiences, but through the introduction of a controlling energy. Those miracles, which are characterised as physical, cannot be accounted for by any other hypothesis than that of the extraordinary intervention of the Maker and Ruler of the material universe.

The sacred historians trace the finger of God in everything relative to His peculiar people, whether it be for their preservation or rebuke. His Spirit enlightens His prophets; and His permissive providence employs the lying spirits of false prophets to distort the mental vision of His enemies by a judicial blindness, so that "their eyes see not and their ears hear not." No evil spirit in a personal form appears or is requisite, beyond that which is manifested in the persons of the false prophets themselves.

The phrases "good spirit" *(ruachka hatova)*, "evil spirit" *(ruach raah)*, "unclean spirit" *(ruach hattamea)*, "spirit of wisdom" *(ruach chokmu)*, and the like, are all of similar construction. "The Spirit of the Lord" is equivalent to "the spirit of wisdom and understanding, the spirit of counsel and might, the spirit of knowledge, and of the fear of the Lord" (Isaiah xi., 2); because the Holy Spirit is doctrinally the giver of those precious gifts, displayed specially in the inspired writings of the servants of God, and prized by all His people.

The spirit of antichrist is manifested in unbelievers (1 John iv., 3); the unrighteous are the children of the devil (1 John iii., 10).

"The Spirit of the Lord departed from Saul, and an evil spirit—*ruach raah*—from the Lord troubled him" (1 Sam. xvi., 14). We cannot attribute the evil spirit to God as a personal influence. Saul had been an instrument under the Divine agency in the political economy of the Israelites, but was now rejected on account of disobedience. He was surrendered to his own natural spirit or to a satanic influence, like the blasphemers in the apostolic churches, for their own ultimate correction (1 Cor. v., 5, and 1 Tim. i., 20). In the same sense, "God

sent an evil spirit between Abimelech and the
men of Shechem; and the men of Shechem dealt
treacherously with Abimelech" (Judges ix., 23).
Micaiah imputed the perversity of the King of
Israel to the influence of a "lying spirit" in the
mouth of false prophets. His address assumes the
Oriental form of a visionary parable, in which "there
came forth a spirit, and stood before the Lord, and
said, I will persuade him. I will be a lying spirit"—
ruach shaker, or spirit of faslehood—"in the mouth
of all his prophets" (1 Kings xxii., 21, 22). Elymas,
the sorcerer, is denominated in the Acts of the
Apostles "a false prophet," and also "child of the
devil" and "enemy of all righteousness," perverting
"the right ways of the Lord."

In the dramatic Book of Job, Satan, as an accuser
or adversary, is in terms of personality charged with
being the author of that holy man's afflictions—
perhaps in the same sense as the *daimonia* of the
New Testament. The Devil appears also to be
alluded to in Zech. iii., 1. The same designation is
employed metaphorically in several places with
reference to a human adversary. So our Lord
applies the term to Judas Iscariot and to Peter.

Precisely analogous to the foregoing are the
doctrinal manifestations of the spirit, such as the
spirit of wisdom and of knowledge; or, on the
contrary, the spirit of antichrist, the spirit of
divination, the spirit of error, a lying spirit, and
the like. The characteristic spirit is the moral
characteristic.

Thus we find a great variety of spirits mentioned, each of which is characterised and characteristic. With respect to those that are of a dynamical character, St. Paul expressly denominates them diversities of gifts and operations; yet he attributes them—not to different spirits but—to the same spirit of God, whose influences they represent. "There are diversities of operations; but it is the same God which worketh all in all" (1 Cor. xii., 6). So all those operations of an opposite character are imputed to Satan.

It is manifestly a Biblical doctrine that the Deity, through the agency of His Holy Spirit, influences the minds of whom he will—"I will dwell in them" (2 Cor. vi., 16); "It is not ye that speak, but the Spirit of your Father which speaketh in you" (Matt. x., 20). Christ, with reference to his humanity, said, "The word which ye hear is not mine, but the Father's which sent me" (John xiv., 24).

In like manner, Satan works "in the children of disobedience;" the demoniacs were said to be "under the power of the devil;" and it is written, "he that committeth sin is of the devil."

According to the Hebrew psychology, the word "spirit" is always expressive of an agency, in relation to some personality with which it is identified. With respect to the emanation of the "spirit," it is either of God or of Satan; concerning the operations of the "spirit," it influences man.

The fallen angels are never spoken of otherwise, than being "reserved in everlasting chains under darkness, unto the judgment of the great day" (Jude 6 and 2 Peter ii., 4); "chains" apparently imply some state of personal restraint. Satan only is represented to be at large; and, therefore, it is only correspondingly necessary, for the apocalyptic angel to lay "hold on the dragon, that old serpent, which is the devil, and Satan" (Rev. xx., 2). His liberty is, perhaps, allowed by a permissive providence for the probation of the human race. Since Satan is to be "laid hold on," he must previously have been free.

The hypothesis, that the world was originally the abode of Satan and the fallen angels, and ultimately the scene of their rebellion and downfall, is historically inconsistent and improbable.

There is not a single instance throughout Scripture of any personal manifestation of a fallen angel unto men; corroborative herewith, spiritual possessions and evil influences are doctrinally ascribed to Satan, as already demonstrated. Moreover, this is clearly intimated by our Lord, when the seventy disciples "returned again with joy, saying, Lord, even the demons are subject unto us through thy name;" because our Saviour's reply was, "I beheld Satan as lightning fall from heaven. Behold, I give unto you power to tread on serpents and scorpions, and over all the power of the enemy" (Luke x., 17-19)— thereby ascribing in figurative language the popular demoniacal possessions themselves to Satan, including apparently all the forms of moral depravity.

In Christ's next words, verse 20, " Rejoice not, that the spirits (τὰ πνεύματα) are subject unto you," these various forms of evil are expressed by the common term " spirits," used here in its popular sense as parallel with "demons." All the forms of moral depravity are metaphorically characterised under the different appellations of " the demons," " serpents or scorpions," and " all the power of the enemy."

The passage, in Psalm lxxviii., 49, translated "evil angels" *(mishlacheth malachai rayim)* in reference to the Egyptian plagues, is susceptible of another rendering more in accordance with the historic facts and the literal import of the context. After enumerating the various plagues, the Psalmist seems to characterise them as " messengers of evil" *(malachai rayim)*, executing the fierce anger of God. Neither Satan nor his angels are declared, by Moses, to have been instrumental in punishing Pharaoh and his servants ; it is unlikely that the devil would further the cause of God's people, Israel, by troubling Jehovah's enemies.

We must advert to the characteristics of the popular possessions, in order to apprehend their actual nature. The demoniacs were blind or deaf and dumb ; they were lunatic ; they were phrenzied, and sometimes thrown into fire and water; they were agonised in mind or body ; or, like John the Baptist, they might be merely austere, of whom the people said, nevertheless, that he had a demon.

They did not evidence any supernatural powers or revelations. The persons possessed sometimes addressed our Lord in impassioned, yet not preternatural terms. In one instance there was a transference of the demonical influence. When the possessed were healed, the blind and dumb both saw and spake, to the amazement of the people; the lunatic, the phrenzied, and maniacal were brought to their right mind.

Many individuals, like St. John and our Lord, were only popularly said to be possessed. Those persons, treated by our Lord and his apostles as actually possessed, were, in the apostolic language, said to be brought in some sense under the power or influence of the satanic spirit.

When, therefore, the possessed ones personified the popular *daimonia*, the afflicted persons themselves acted and spoke under an evil influence beyond the controul of reason and of ordinary means. When the two men, mentioned in the eighth chapter of St. Matthew, coming out of the tombs exceeding fierce, cried out, "What have we to do with thee, Jesus, thou Son of God? art thou come hither to torment us before the time?" the men gave utterance, under a satanic influence, to their own distracted sentiments. They had evidently learnt whom Jesus was represented to be; they also were apparently acquainted with the doctrines of future rewards and punishments; the Baptist had taught them, that he who should come

after him would "burn up the chaff with unquench-
able fire;" and Christ himself had already said, that
in the day of judgment there were many to whom
he would say, "Depart from me, ye that work
iniquity." They believed, and were tormented with
unsanctified convictions.

The influences, Biblically ascribed to Divine or to
satanic power, are in all respects consistent with the
characteristics of the human mind. Its objectivity
and subjectivity are intensified or restrained, but no
incongruous powers are conferred. The prophets
pretend not to penetrate the secrets of the heart,
or by clairvoyance to see through a stone wall by
perceiving that which is not objectively presented
to the senses; although, to a marvellous and preternatural extent, they forecast the tendencies of both
individual and national character and events.

But, when one of the brute creation is made the
mouth-piece of a higher power, a miracle is involved;
because the powers of speech and sentiment are
incongruous with the inarticulate and purely objective characteristics of the animal employed. If
the "dumb ass" literally addressed Balaam (as
indubitably understood by St. Peter), and not
metaphorically, it was a miracle, manifesting the
extraordinary interposition of the Lord of nature.

The narratives of Scripture are always quoted or
referred to, by our Saviour and his apostles, substantially in the language and forms in which they are
recorded in the Hebrew writing. This was sufficient

for all doctrinal purposes, and most emphatically vouches for the authenticity of such records; whether they were susceptible of any verbal exposition was in this respect unimportant.   It is possible, that some of these narratives may have originally been transferred from hieroglyphic records, like the Sinaitic or other similar inscriptions, in language which rather expressed the apparent than the latent significance of the symbols.   Such suggestions are offered with reverence and reserve, whilst the effective result must be essentially the same.

Without a miracle, the Mosaic serpent could not have literally conducted the colloquy with Eve as recorded.   Yet, we do not find that any real miracle was ever ascribed to satanic influence.   Spiritual influences or energies are attributed to Satan, but such influences manifest themselves in accordance with the idiosyncrasy of the being in whom they work.   In man, they are developed subjectively as well as objectively—for instance, those who were possessed, and the "lying wonders" ascribed to the devil's inworking.   In brutes, being devoid of subjective capacities, they could only, without a miraculous intervention, be developed objectively; as, when the spiritual influence was transferred from the demoniac to the herd of swine.   They did not remonstrate with our Lord, like the demoniac had done, or the "dumb ass" did with Balaam, but were impelled headlong into the lake as by a preternatural stampede.

If the "old serpent" of the apocalypse were the

traditional hieroglyphic of Satan, we may infer that it was the latter himself who suggested, in some way, or addressed the fatal questions which shook the faith of the woman in the Divine command prohibitory of her eating the fruit of the Tree of Knowledge. The selection of the serpent for the type of sin appears suitable, amongst other considerations, from Max Müller's remarks upon the Sanscrit word *anhas* (sin), derived from *ahi* and its root *ah* or *anh* to choke. He says, *ahi* means a serpent, equivalent to the Greek *echis* and to the Latin *anguis* (Lectures on the Science of Language, series i., page 383). Dr. Adam Clarke's conjecture, that the word *nachash*, translated serpent, might according to Arabic analogy be rendered some species of man-like ape, does not remove the subjective difficulty, neither is it consistent with the Levitical classification of animals according to their modes of progression. "Upon thy belly thou shalt go," seems to identify the serpent symbol. Going "upon the belly" is distinctive of one genus, and "upon all four" is characteristic of another. *Holaic al gachon vecol holaic al arbha* (Lev. xi., 42). The Mosaic symbol therefore remains undisturbed, and harmonises with the apocalyptic.

Many of the early traditions of our race were handed down in a hieroglyphical form, as on the pillars of brick alluded to in Kircher's Ædipus Ægyptiacus, and as illustrated in the heathen mythology of various nations; of many of which traditions

the true antitypes are, like Satan and the serpent,
only discoverable in our sacred Scriptures.

If the serpent had been selected as symbolical of
Satan himself on account of its being "more subtle
than any beast of the field," it may consistently
be assumed that the Temptation of Eve was conducted by a personal artifice, such as the assumption of the office and language, if not the aspect, of
an angel of light. Nor can the curse, any more
than the colloquy, have a literal application to the
nature of the serpent. We are not aware, that the
serpent is conscious of any degradation in going
upon its belly, or that it is less felicitous than other
objective creatures. Nor does it literally eat the
dust, but such food as is most suited to its well
being. The whole, therefore, seems rather to be an
expletive description of the serpentine symbol, and
through it, the intimation of a curse upon the being
symbolised, significative of degradation and misery.
The phraseology, like the hieroglyphic, is accordingly
typical; and then, in congruity with this, as "the
second Adam" was tempted by Satan personally, so
was the first Adam. The conclusion in the mind
of the woman seems to have been ultimately rivetted
by an artful appeal to the evidence of her own
senses, leading to the inference that the tempter
himself had in her presence partaken of the fruit :
" And when the woman saw that the tree was good
for food, and that it was pleasant to the eyes, and a
tree to be desired to make one wise, she took of the

fruit thereof" (Gen. iii., 6). In accordance with the character of a seducer, Satan first partakes in her presence and then proffers; and, consistently with the original, the woman rather accepted than took what was so insidiously presented *(tikach mepirio)*; in like manner her husband received of the fruit of the tree from her hands. Indeed, if this fruit were itself a hieroglyphic significant of "evil communications," she would of course receive or accept rather than take them. " Who told thee that thou wast naked? Hast thou eaten of the tree, whereof I commanded thee that thou shouldest not eat?"

The universal depravity of the human race, through the original intervention of Satan, is sufficient to warrant the ascription of all evil to him as demoniacal or satanic, without supposing him by the personal agency of himself or of other fallen angels to operate upon every individual in every instance. "He that committeth sin is of the devil; for the devil sinneth from the beginning" (1 John iii., 8). His characteristics are inherited and developed as diversified in each individual idiosyncrasy.

But, in a specially subjective sense, particular instances of depravity or mania are popularly said to result from demoniacal possessions; and apostolically and doctrinally, from "the power of the devil." The influences, thus dynamically imparted, are not idealistic but energetic; they do not convey ideas, but a disposition and energy; the ideas follow in the practical development of the disposition. In like manner, the thoughts and visions, which occur in dreams, are constituted not of ideas imported, but of certain modifications of sense consciousness; these ideas may naturally arise in an abnormal series from the partial wakefulness of some of the ideal senses, occasioned by the state of the sleeper's bodily system or by disturbing causes *ab extra* (see Copland, *Voce*, Sleep).

The predominant thoughts and habits of the individual may prevail as the result of his personal reflections and experience; or they may assume, under the influences of a special Divine inspiration, the emblematic representations of prophetic language and the foreshadowing of events, explicative of ecclesiastical doctrine and premonitory of the Divine purposes. Such probably were the visions of Jacob and Balaam, and of Joseph the father of Jesus, and of the prophets and apostles and others, Biblically recorded as trances, dreams, and visions. A preternatural energy was imparted to the mental knowledge and convictions of the prophet. Balaam knew the history of the Israelites and of their conquests, as well as the existing revelations concerning a Deliverer who should at a future time appear as the Sceptre of Israel; his mind was Divinely directed in the application of such knowledge. At the same time, the prophets are made to use language, respecting future events, so verbally exact, that it might be thought to have been written after rather than before their accomplishment; nothing short of inspiration can satisfactorily explain it; and, unless we deny God's personal interposition in mundane affairs and especially with reference to the future destiny of His people at all times, there is nothing irrational in the supposition. It is through a special spiritual agency or energy that such influences are psychologically produced; and, if we believe in the inspiration of the individual, we cannot discredit the inspiration of his dreams or visions, any more than any of his other ideal developments professing that character and evidencing a congruity with historical and revealed truth. Joseph's knowledge of the character of Herod and the probable motives of his anxious enquiries concerning the young child Jesus might, perhaps, naturally suggest the prudence of flight from his jurisdiction; yet, the warning character of Joseph's dream is specially ascribed to angelic interposition. The visions of St. Peter and Cornelius are the exact counterparts of each other, inducing the one to seek Peter and the other to receive Cornelius. The latter had evidently been the subject of doctrinal instruction and had probably known Peter by reputation; whilst Peter, doubtlessly, had heard something of Cornelius the devout centurion. Nevertheless, the reciprocity of their thoughts is explicitly ascribed to angelic influences.

Thus it is not the material of the dream or vision,

that is imparted; but it is the ideal form and scope assumed, which are ascribed to a supernatural energy or influence.

That such dreams were not a mere natural coincidence of thought, appears from their preternatural exactitude with reference to the fulfilment of ancient prophecies and the providences of God, in a manner not fully apprehended until subsequent to their accomplishment. There are many natural dreams, exhibiting extraordinary coincidence of circumstance; and, like many of the events of life, they may be regarded specially providential. However, those of the inspired servants of God are so in a higher sense, as partaking of the same inspiration as that which characterises their ordinary prophetical communications.

St. John, in the Island of Patmos, beheld his visions in the spirit or under spiritual raptures; and, consequently, we believe his apocalyptic utterances to be of a preternatural character, to be the revelations of One, of whom it is written, "Thou knowest all things" (John xvi., 30), even of our Lord Jesus Christ, to his Body, the Church.

St. Paul's vision of a third heaven is spoken of by himself as an ecstatic rapture, which he could not adequately communicate in human language nor account for with certainty. Yet, the vision was only mental and the subjects were such as had their origin in his inspired reflections.

Perhaps, there are no adequate grounds for ascribing the dream of Eliphaz the Temanite to Divine inspiration. He was apparently a God fearing man, yet there is nothing in the poetic narrative to lead us to ascribe it to special revelation :—

In thoughts from the visions of the night, when deep sleep falleth on
    men,
Fear came upon me, and trembling, which made all my bones to shake.
Then a spirit passed before my face ; the hair of my flesh stood up :
It stood still, but I could not discern the form thereof :
An image was before mine eyes; and I heard a still voice,
Shall mortal man be more just than God ?
Shall a man be more pure than his Maker ?

This vision disclosed nothing new ; its description is artistically unrivalled, but does not indicate any special inspiration.

Whenever special inspiration is not expressly asserted or necessarily implied, there is no reason why we should look beyond natural psychological causes for natural effects. On the contrary, when special inspiration is so asserted or, from the nature of the phenomena, so implied, it is equally consistent with the Biblical psychology and the interposition of a special dynamical agency.

Throughout Scripture there is no converse with disembodied spirits ; no necromancy.

PART IV.

—:o:—

THE SEPULCHRAL

AND

A FUTURE STATE.

—:o:—

PART IV.

THE SEPULCHRAL

AND

A FUTURE STATE.

CHAPTER I.

HADES (HEBREW, *SHEOL*) AND *GEHENNA*.

THE philosophers of Greece, admitting the omnipotence of Deity, might not deem the doctrine of a resurrection as taught by the Jewish prophets impossible; yet, it appears to have been discredited by them, from the startling appeal of St. Paul to Agrippa, "Why should it be thought a thing incredible with you, that God should raise the dead?" (Acts xxvi., 8).

Lord Brougham, in a note on the resurrection at the end of his edition of Paley's Natural Theology, observes, that "Lactantius cites a passage from Chrysippus, which shows that they (the Stoics) considered it clear that there was nothing impossible in the resurrection of the body—δῆλον ὡς οὐδεν ἀδύνατον ἀπκατανασστησεσθαι;" howbeit, it is not clear, that this passage meant anything more than the resuscitation of a dead body.

The doctrine of a General Resurrection was probably nowhere entertained by the ancient sects. Aristotle treats the idea of the soul quitting the body and again returning as an impossibility (*De Anima*, cap. i., sec. 3, sent. 6). Homer, in like manner, reverts to a resurrection as the climax of an improbability :—

Ἦ μάλα δὴ Τρῶες μεγαλήτορες, οὕς περ ἔπεφνον,
Αὗτις ἀναστήσονται ὑπὸ ζόφου ἠερόεντος (Iliad, xxi., 55, 56).

Hence, in the ancient classics, for instance in Homer and Moschus, we always read of death, with regard at least to the natural body, as a perpetual and unwakening sleep. So Catullus :—

Soles occidere et redire possunt;
Nobis cum semel occidit brevis lux,
Nox est perpetua una dormienda.

The patriarch Job expresses himself to the same effect :—"For their is hope of a tree, if it be cut down, that it will sprout again, and that the tender branch thereof will not cease (cap. xiv., 7). "But man dieth and wasteth away; yea, man giveth up the ghost, and where is he?" (verse 10). Nevertheless, Job had a hope beyond the grave; for, he presently adds, "So man lieth down, and riseth not: till the heavens be no more, they shall not

awake, nor be raised out of their sleep" (verse 12).
Then, in a future chapter, he exclaims in the language
of exalted faith, "For I know that my Redeemer
liveth, and that He shall stand at the latter day
upon the earth : and though after my skin worms
destroy this body, yet in my flesh shall I see God"
(cap. xix., 25, 26). Although the doctrine of a
General Resurrection was deemed incredible by the
heathen, none spake more eloquently than they on
the immortality of the soul.

To the soul (in the sense of spirit) they attributed
a personal identity; shadowy indeed, yet a substantial personality—"*tenues sine corpore vitas.*"

Plato recognises both *Hades* and *Tartarus* as the
destiny of departed souls; at the same time he, in
his Republic, treats the popular mythology rather
as a superstition, politically useful, than as a subject
of private opinion. Cæsar, in one of his epistles,
pronounces the popular notions to be altogether
fabulous. Cicero also treated the same superstitions
with contempt; yet, on the whole, he inclined
towards the adoption of the views of Socrates and
Plato upon the immortality of the soul (Tus. Ques.
i., 16). Plato's most matured opinions were probably those contained in his Timæus; where he
treats the soul as a personal demon possessing, with
reference to the body, both pre-existence and post-
existence.

The popular pagan superstitions modified the
opinions of the Jews themselves; who, we learn

from their own prophets, had extensively imbibed the superstitions of the surrounding nations to the utter neglect of their own Scriptures. Even the early Christians retained some of the pagan notions respecting the future condition of the soul; which led, in certain instances, to their severe rebuke by the patristic writers. Some of these, who denied the resurrection of the dead, and looked for an access to heaven immediately after death, were by Justin Martyr and other fathers of the church not accounted worthy of the name of Christians, and considered altogether heretical.

But, although the fathers of both the Greek and Latin churches agreed in regarding the period of the resurrection to be the time of future reward or punishment, yet many of them, as Tertullian and Austin, held certain indefinite opinions concerning an Intermediate State. Origen's views were purely Platonic, in accordance with his philosophy. St. Augustine, in his Treatise on "The Quantity of the Soul," treats it upon the same Platonic principles; he carries the soul through successive stages of intellectual refinement, finally translating it to its highest state of perfection with God himself. Polycarp, Clemens Romanus, and Ignatius considered that the souls of the departed did not immediately enter the highest heaven and receive the beatific vision. Chrysostom thought that according as good or evil were done in the body, so in the body would persons be rewarded or punished; nevertheless he says, in his fourth Homily on Hebrews, that God "had already crowned the departed."

In fact, the question of an Intermediate State of personal enjoyment or misery was an assumption arising from the prevalence of the Greek philosophy. For, supposing the scriptural soul were similar to the Platonic soul, there must have been a continuous personal existence after decease; the incongruity of this doctrine with that of the resurrection was a source of perplexity to many of the early as well as modern divines, and none of them could satisfactorily reconcile it. An ample view of this subject is contained in Dr. Burnet's work, *De Statu Mortuorum et Resurgentium;* in which, after a careful collation of every scriptural and patristic authority, he concludes that an Intermediate State is not a doctrine of Revelation, and remains in doubt as to the personal condition of the soul.

The early fathers appear very generally to have contracted from the Rabbinical Jews and philosophising Greeks those sentiments respecting *Sheol* and *Hades*, and the nature of the soul, which have attached a meaning to the phraseology of the Bible at variance with its teachings concerning them. Hence, the Greek *Hades* and Platonic soul were the subjects of speculation with some; whilst the resurrection was alone accepted by all to be the undoubted doctrine of the Gospel. Even Dr. Burnet, in his chapter *De Statu Mortuorum Intermedio,* treats the soul as a sort of man within a man, which, upon being unhoused, must be disposed of in some *Hades* other than the tomb; he seeks for the soul a place that the Scriptures nowhere provide, being all the time under the perplexity of concluding, from the testimony of both the Bible and fathers, that the beautitude of the saints is dependent upon the resurrection. All apparently overlook the Biblical distinction between soul and spirit; and all seem to treat *Hades*, like the Greeks themselves did, as the abode of departed spirits!

The views, held by the most scriptural of the patristic writers, cannot perhaps be better expressed than in the language of the following protest of the eminent reformer and martyr, William Tyndale:—

"I protest before God and our Saviour, Jesus Christ, and all that believe in Him, that I hold of the souls of the departed as much as may be proved by manifest and open Scripture, and think the souls departed in the faith of Christ and love of the law of God, to be in no worse case than the soul of Christ was, from the time He delivered His spirit into the hands of His Father until the resurrection of His body in glory and immortality. Nevertheless, I confess openly, that I am not persuaded that they be already in the full glory that Christ is in, or the elect angels of God are in, neither is it any article of my faith; for if it so were, I see not but then the preaching of the resurrection of the flesh were a thing in vain. Notwithstanding, yet I am ready to believe it, if it may be proved with open Scripture."

If then the souls of the departed be not with Christ and the elect angels of God in their kingdom of glory, where are they? The Hebrews would have said they were in *Sheol*, the Hellenists would have said they were in *Hades*.

In reference to the place or state of the departed,

in a general sense, the Hebrews made use of the
term *Sheol*, whilst the Hellenists similarly employed the Greek word *Hades*. According to some
writers, *Sheol* is derived from *shal*, to ask or enquire
for; in a general sense it signifies 'sepulchre,' so
called, Stockius supposes, because it seeks all men.
Parkhurst, quoting Cocceius, concludes that the
term *Sheol* is used on account of its being the place
or state of those *qui in quæstione sunt* in reference to
its radical signification, and is therefore analogous to
the Greek word *Hades*, ὁ ἀΐδης τόπος, the Invisible
Place or State. Gesenius considers that the true
etymology of *Sheol* is a Hebrew word meaning ' a
hollow, subterranean place'—like as the German
Hölle (hell) is originally from *höhle, hohl, hollow*. In
this sense it is synonymous with 'catacomb,' from
κατακύμβος, a 'hollow down below.' This latter
etymology appears to be the most probable one;
because it accords exactly with the character of the
ancient tombs in Egypt and Palestine, as well as in
Italy and other places, and corresponds with the
common employment of the word to designate the
place of the dead generally. The dead were deposited
in what might be named a 'City of the Dead,' in
subterranean vaults, the access to each of which
was protected by a Gate or Door. In Genesis
(xlii., 38) Jacob says, "Then shall ye bring
down my grey hairs with sorrow to the grave"
(Sheola), to the catacomb or place of the dead. "I
will go down into the grave *(Sheola)* to my son

mourning" (Gen. xxxvii., 35). David charged Solo-
mon concerning Shimei, " His hoar head bring thou
down to the grave with blood" (1 Kings ii., 9).
The Psalmist says of man, " Shall he deliver his soul
from the hand of the grave" *miyad Sheol* (Ps.
lxxxix., 48) ? " There is no work, nor device, nor
knowledge, nor wisdom, in the grave" *bisheol*
(Eccl. ix., 10). In all these instances the word
grave *(Sheol)* is used generically. "Her feet go down
to death, her steps take hold on hell" *Sheol* (Prov.
v., 5.) " Thou wilt not leave my soul in hell"
bisheol (Ps. xvi., 10). Our Saxon ancestors used
the word *hele* for the grave, derived from *helan*, to
cover. The same phrase is still vulgarly retained
with reference to the death of a person, although,
according to modern phraseology, liable to be understood in a damnatory sense.

In the above, and innumerable other instances,
Sheol simply expresses the region of the grave in an
Oriental sense. With a figurative application, it is
also used for the catacombs in the following instances :—" Therefore, the catacomb—*Sheol*—hath
enlarged herself" (Isaiah v., 14). " There are three
things that are never satisfied, yea, four things say
not, It is enough. The grave"—*Sheol*, the catacomb
(Prov. xxx., 15, 16). "It is as high as heaven ;
what canst thou do ? deeper than the catacomb
Sheol ; what canst thou know" (Job xi., 8) ? "If
I ascend up into heaven, Thou art there : if I make
my bed in the catacomb *Sheol*, behold, Thou art

there" (Ps. cxxxix., 8).   God is omnipresent; there
is no escaping from His presence, either by going
underground or by ascending the loftiest mountain
top.   The destiny of all the dead is in the Creator's
mind and power.   In like manner, Amos (ix., 2, 3)
the Prophet says, "Though they dig into hell—
Sheol, the catacomb—thence shall mine hand take
them; though they climb up to heaven, thence will
I bring them down: and though they hide themselves in the top of Carmel, I will search and take
them out thence; and though they be hid from my
sight in the bottom of the sea, thence will I command the serpent, and he shall bite them."   Here
the place of the dead, the lofty heavens, Mount
Carmel, and the sea, are equally shown in parallelism
to be impotent to afford an escape from the God of
Justice.   "For a fire is kindled in mine anger, and
shall burn unto the lowest *Sheol*" (Deut. xxxii., 22).
Similar to this the New Testament says, "Thou
Capernaum, which art exalted unto heaven, shalt be
brought down to *Hades*" (Matt. xi., 23)—*Sheol* or
Hades, the grave, being the most abject state, a state
of nonentity or finality of existence.   "*Sheol* from
beneath is moved for thee" (Isaiah xiv., 9).   By a
bold prosopopeia, the dead kings of the nations are
here represented to be stirred from their royal state,
in the catacombs, to welcome their oppressor, the
King of Babylon, now fallen and become in the
grave like unto themselves.   Corruption, of course,
occurs whenever the process of embalming the dead

is not adopted. Hence the reference, in the foregoing chapter of Isaiah, to the worm, "The worm
is spread under thee, and the worms cover thee"
(verse 11), demonstrative of the complete humiliation of the once haughty tyrant. With respect to
this state of weakness and helplessness, so contra-
distinctive to the vigour of life, the word *rephaim*
is applied to the dead. The translation of *rephaim*
by dead is evidently correct from the allusion to
the worms in the context. *Rephaim* is also used
parallel with *maithim* in Isaiah (xxvi., 14), and
Psalm (lxxxviii., 11), and elsewhere. There is no
countenance in the Bible to the Rabbinical, or
rather Pagan, notion of the shades in *Hades*, "For
the living know that they shall die : but the dead
know not anything" (Eccl. ix., 5).

The same generic word, *Sheol*, is used in all these
and similar connexions ; and apparently all with
reference to the insatiable, profound, awe-inspiring,
or levelling character of the sepulchral state. It
is neither the place of joy nor of sorrow, but of
silence, corruption, and oblivion.

When a particular grave is spoken of, as my
grave, his grave, or the sepulchre of an individual,
the word *keber* is employed. *Kivrai David* (Neh.
iii., 16). *Keber Avnair* (2 Sam. iv., 12). *Kivroth
hamelachim* (2 Chr. xxi., 20). Likewise, when referring to an act of burial, as "they buried Abner in
Hebron," *yikberoo eth Avnair bechebron* (2 Sam. iii.,
32). Jehoiakim "shall be buried with the burial of

an ass," *Kevoorah chamor yikkavair* (Jer. xxii., 19).

Thus *keber* is used in a specific sense with regard to a particular burial, whilst *sheol* is employed in a generic as well as figurative sense, expressive of the personal state of the dead when buried or entombed. They are no more seen. They are in *Hades*, as the Greeks would say, in the Invisible Place. The Hebrews say they are in *Sheol*, the sepulchral state, which in the Septuagint and New Testament is always translated by the classical word *Hades*.

The expression, "Gates of the Grave," *Shaarai Sheol* (Is. xxxviii., 10), indicates with historical precision the literal meaning of *Sheol*, alluding to the form of the ancient Jewish sepulchres, which were either hewn in a rock, or formed in subterraneous caverns; the entrance to them was by a narrow door or gate, sometimes locked with a key. " I have the keys of death and of *Hades*" (Rev. i., 18). We find the corresponding expression, πύλαι ᾅδου, in Matt. xvi. 18 ; here Christ, in reference to the ultimate triumph of His church over death at the general resurrection, says, " the gates of *Hades* (the grave or catacomb) shall not prevail against it." The same phrase is met with in Homer, in allusion no doubt to the like Oriental custom.

The expression ἐν φυλακῇ " in prison," applied by the Apostle Peter to *Hades*, is by no means a solecism (1 Peter iii., 19). *Hades* was, in the Grecian mythology, represented as being presided over by

Pluto, who was depicted with a key in his hand. The
embalmed dead were locked up in the gloomy region
of the sepulchre, according to the Oriental custom,
as in a prison. Consonantly with this usage Christ
—being the Resurrection and the Life—is represented emblematically with " the keys of *Hades* and
of Death" (Rev. i., 18). Virgil describes the shades
in *Hades* to be in a dark prison *carcere caeco*
(Æn. vi. 734). Shakspeare, also, makes the ghost
in Hamlet say :—

> " But that I am forbid
> To tell the secrets of my prison-house,
> I could a tale unfold, whose lightest word
> Would harrow up thy soul ; freeze thy young blood."

When, therefore, St. Peter uses φυλακῇ parallel
with *Hades*, there is a classical fitness in the term
" prison" being applied in a Hebrew sense to the
sepulchral state. The "spirits" or (rather, as before
shown in this work, pp. 116 and 117) the " souls,"
symbolically preached to by Noah, were in the grave
or the sepulchral state when the apostle wrote his
epistle ; in plain language, Peter says in the next
chapter that the gospel was preached " to them that
are dead" (1 Peter iv., 6). Cowper brings out this
Scriptural truth in the hymn :—

> " Israel, in ancient days,
> Not only had a view
> Of Sinai in a blaze,
> But learned the Gospel too :
> The types· and figures were a glass,
> In which they saw a Saviour's face."

Likewise, with reference to the Resurrection, St. Paul says, "O grave—*Hades*—where is thy victory?" (1 Cor. xv., 55). The name of him who sat on the pale horse (Rev. vi., 8) was Death; and *Hades* followed with him—in the natural order of sequence. At the General Resurrection, Death and *Hades*, both again used generically, deliver up the dead which are in them; and Death and *Hades* are cast into the Lake of Fire, the Second Death (Rev. xx., 13, 14). By comparing these with other texts we shall find that, in Scripture, *Hades* and *Sheol* are parallel terms; and they both alike refer generically to the state of the dead. A similar parallelism exists between the words *keber* and ταφος or μνημεῖον, being specifically used in relation to any particular sepulchre, as the tomb of Lazarus in John xi., or that of Jesus in Matt. xxvii., 61.

In the books of the Old Testament we nowhere find any reference to a penal hell, in the sense in which the word *Gehenna* is employed in the New Testament writings.

There was a place called Tophet in the Valley of Hinnom, that was wont to be the scene of dreadful human sacrifices to Baal by those who followed the idolatrous practices of the heathen. And, on this account, the Israelites frequently incurred the severe denunciation of their prophets, accompanied with threatenings that the time would come when their descendants should themselves be slaughtered there in Divine retribution. Thus Jeremiah says :—" Behold, the days come, saith the Lord, that it shall no more be called Tophet, nor The valley of the son of Hinnom, but The valley of slaughter; for they shall bury in Tophet till there be no place" (Jer. vii., 32).

We find references to the practices alluded to both in the books of Kings and Chronicles, as well as in Jeremiah.

In some of the Chaldee Targums the word *Gehinnom* is introduced, compounded of the words *Gai Hinnom*, or Valley of Hinnom, and applied by them to the place of the damned, indicating that it was used in this sense in our Saviour's time, as noticed by Parkhurst. By this use of the word, the burning alive of human victims in the Valley of Hinnom was rendered typical of that *Gehenna* where the fire never shall be quenched (Mark ix., 43). Thus we read, " Shall be in danger of hell fire γεενναν του πυρος" (Matt. v., 22). " How can ye escape the damnation of hell της γεεννης" (Matt. xxiii., 33) ? " Fear Him, which after he hath killed hath power to cast into hell εἰς την γεενναν" (Luke xii., 5). In these and similar passages the word *Gehenna* is evidently expressive of a penal state.

In the following, *Tartarus* is applied in a sense synonymous to the sense in which it was also used both by Greeks and Romans :—" If God spared not the angels that sinned, but cast them down to *Tartarus* ταρταρωσας" (2 Peter ii., 4). It is remarkable that *Tartarus* is the place where Hesiod says the rebellious

Titans were confined in chains, as if founded upon
some tradition of the former event.

In the Epistle of St. James, *Gehenna* is alluded to
as the source of evil influences, the tongue "setteth
on fire the course of nature; and it is set on fire
of hell ὑπο της γεεννης" (St. James iii., 6). And,
addressing the Pharisees, Christ says, in the like
sense, that after making one proselyte, "ye make
him twofold more the child of hell υιον γεεννης
than yourselves" (Matt. xxiii., 15). Thus, we
observe, the same uniform consistency in the use
of terms pervades the New as well as the Old
Testament; the word *Hades* invariably having
reference to the grave, in the generic sense of the
region of the dead, or the sepulchral state; and the
word *Gehenna* equally precisely referring to a state
of evil or of punishment.

Dr. Campbell, in his Preliminary Dissertation to
the Four Gospels, observes truly that, in the Old
Testament, the word *Sheol* signifies the state of the
dead in general without regard to their particular
character or condition. Yet, whilst some critics,
such as Dr. John Taylor, consider that the word *Sheol*
means no more than *keber*, Campbell not only admits
the generic character of the former word, but conceives that it has a meaning analogous to the Greek
Hades. In short he refers, like most others, to the
Pagan-Greek construction of the word, in order to
define the sense and even situation of the Hebrew
Sheol; whereas the real question is, not as to the

Pagan, but as to the Hebrew meaning; by this latter meaning the Hebrew word *Sheol*, as well as the Greek word *Hades* adopted by the Septuagint and New Testament writers, should be construed. He remarks that, both by Jews and Pagans, *Hades* is placed in the lowest parts of the earth, and that its inhabitants are synonymous with the καταχθονίων of the Epistle to the Philipians (ii., 10); and, as a proof of the coincidence of the Hebrew and Pagan notions concerning the nature of the place, he cites Virgil's description of it from the eighth book of the Æneid. In fact, throughout Campbell's Dissertation, the mind of the writer is evidently impressed with the Pagan sense of *Hades*, and only in this sense perceives a distinction between the words *Hades* and *taphos* or *Sheol* and *keber*.

By reversing the process of construction, and first of all enquiring as to the distinctive import of the Hebrew words, a much more consistent and probable distinction between *Hades* and *taphos* or between *Sheol* and *keber* becomes obvious.

Thus *Sheol* and *Hades* are never used in the plural, because they refer to a generic condition of the departed, as in an Oriental sepulchre or catacomb, extended metonymically to all the dead, whilst the words *keber* and *taphos* are adopted specially with reference to a particular grave. *Gehenna*, on the other hand, refers to a place or state of torment known only under the Christian Revelation.

Thus viewed, all difficulties of construction vanish.

The passage in Acts ii., 27, is expounded by a personal resurrection, by which the departed soul or person (*nephesh*) is no longer left in the sepulchral state (*Sheol* or *Hades*), whilst the perishable body (*nevailah*) passes to corruption in the grave (*keber* or *taphos*) where it was interred. The Rabbinical and Heathen *Hades* is in no danger of being confounded with the Biblical *Gehenna*; and the Gates of *Hades* shall present no barrier to the Christian faith in a glorious Resurrection. Nor are the Gates of *Hades* confused with the Gates of Death (*vide* Job xxxviii., 17); whereby a believer in the promises made to the seed of Abraham contemplates the abstract mysteries of Death. The Scriptural metaphors and impersonations of *Sheol* and *Hades* receive an intelligible and consistent solution. The καταχθονίοι (those under the earth, Philip. ii., 10) are identified with the sepulchral tenants of *Hades*, in apposition to those in life upon earth or in heaven.

When we refer to Jewish history at the time the Gospels were written, and even before, we find that the mass of the people were little, if any, better than the Pagans intermingled among them. Their Rabbis had substituted their Targums for the Bible, and had actually adopted modified Greek notions concerning the destiny of the departed. As the Greeks translated *Sheol* by *Hades*, so the Rabbis returned the compliment by attaching to their own elder phrase a Greek meaning totally opposed to the context and doctrines of all their Holy Books. A fate precisely analogous to the preceding attended

our Saxon word *hele*, which translators have frequently substituted in the Old and New Testaments
for *Sheol* and *Hades*, whenever, according to the
misconceptions of a superstitious and dark age, they
fancied something more than the grave was meant.
The sect of the Pharisees believed in a resurrection, yet not the resurrection taught in the Bible.
They confined their resurrection to the good, whilst
the wicked would be left in the lower region of their
Rabbinical *Sheol*, to which they attached the idea
of the Greek *Orcus* (the lower region of *Hades*), the
upper region being assigned to the good until their
resurrection.   It is this *Hades* referred to in the
Rabbinical illustration of the rich man and Lazarus,
Jesus having adopted it for the purpose of rebuking
the covetous Pharisees.   The Essenes denied the
resurrection doctrine, considering that the soul
would live after death; they, like the former sect,
did thus appropriate Greek and Pagan ideas.
The Sadducees repudiated all these opinions, and
held death to be an eternal sleep.   (See Josephus
and Jennings' Jewish Antiquities.)

Hence, these Hebrew phrases lost their original
significance; and henceforth, although our Saviour
and his Apostles employed them in their original
Hebraic sense, we are to be prepared to find them
interpreted, by Jewish as well as Gentile proselytes,
in a Pagan rather than a scriptural sense.   St. Paul
prepares us throughout his Epistles to guard against
the prevalence of this Greek philosophy : "Beware,
lest any man spoil you through philosophy and vain

deceit, after the tradition of men, after the rudiments of the world, and not after Christ" (Col. ii., 8). "Not giving heed to Jewish fables and commandments of men, that turn from the truth" (Titus i., 14). "Who concerning the truth have erred, saying, that the resurrection is past already" (2 Tim. ii., 18) was Paul's warning to Timothy.

Again, when we turn to the pages of Heathen mythology, a similar phraseology is met with. Tooke quotes an unnamed author, who gives the following definition of Elysium:—"'Απο της λυσεως, *a solutione; quod animae piorum corporeis solutae vinculis, loca illa petant postquam purgatae sunt a levioribus noxis quas contraxerant.*" The sentiments of Philoponus, concerning the purification of the soul, are not dissimilar.

Virgil gives an elaborate account of the infernal regions visited by Æneas:—

"Quisque suos patimur manes; exinde per amplum
Mittimur Elysium, et pauci laeta arva tenemus" (Bk. vi., 743, 744).

Hades is, by the ancient poets, converted into a place in the infernal regions, and as such is referred to in the *Iliad*. In fact, these views of the soul and of Hades pervade so many of the ancient classics, and are so familiar to every scholar, that it is needless here to do more than advert to them.

"Omnes eodem cogimur: omnium
Versatur urna, serius, ocius
Sors exitura, et nos in aeternum
Exilium impositura cymbae" (Hor. lib. ii., ode 3).

Pythagoreans, Platonists, and Epicureans alike

attributed a living personality to the soul after death, as well as a locality to *Hades*, in quite a different sense from that discoverable in either the Old or New Testament writings.

The poets of different countries make frequent allusion to some place, where the souls of the departed are received into a state of immortal happiness. Thus, the spirits of the Egyptians were supposed to be consigned to some region beyond the Nile; where they would be arraigned before the Divine tribunal, and disposed of according to their merits, in some manner, until they should at length be allowed to repossess the bodies so carefully embalmed. The ancient Greeks and Romans had their *Fortunata Insola*, their hence and Elysium. The Hindoos have their heaven of Indra; the Persians their Peristan or fairyland, "with its city of diamonds and its country of Shadiam, so named from love and pleasure." The Mahommedans look, in the hour of death, to being received into a voluptuous heaven. The Indians of the prairies anticipate their celestial hunting grounds. And the Esquimaux believe in a sunny region beneath the ocean, where there shall be no more hunger or thirst.

But the very fact, that all these and other aspects of the Pagan *Hades* are depicted in the language of human experience, demonstrates their human origin and invention. Because, where Revelation is silent, no man could describe anything not ever perceived by mortal eye or heard by mortal ear.

Howbeit such traditions are quite consistent with, and even corroborative of the primordial disclosure of a Future State; and they are in perfect harmony with those aspirations of our nature which arise in reflective minds. We will not call them 'Intuitions;' since, if they were so, all should possess them.

The popular belief in the Platonic soul—even if the doctrine of a Resurrection be held—necessitates a recurrence to the Pagan *Hades*, or the substitution of an undefined and undefinable Intermediate State.

The authors of the Books of the New Testament, under Divine guidance, accommodated Grecian phraseology to Hebraistic ideas; but the Jewish Rabbis, ignorant of their Scriptures (as charged by our Saviour), imported the mystical doctrines of Oriental philosophy into their teaching. It may be said, they reverenced the Talmud more than the inspired volume in their modern theology.

Whilst, in Apostolic times, the Jewish converts attached Hebrew ideas to Greek phraseology, the later Christians (with whom the Greek language was vernacular) adopted the Grecian ideas and philosophy. Consequently, we find these speak of the soul and of *Hades* in the same way that the Pagan Greeks themselves would have done, except in the application of their dogmas to Christian instead of to Pagan theology. This is evident from the mode in which they treat the soul as a spiritual personality distinct from the body, and *Hades* as the place of the soul's separate existence after death.

It is not uncommon to hear it stated that the soul of Christ, after his crucifixion, descended into *Hades*, the separate place of departed spirits, and there comforted them by his manifested presence. Yet we do not find anything of this kind in Scripture. Christ's humanity died. He resigned his spirit into his Father's hands. But the spirit of Jesus, being the fulness of God, and one with the Holy Spirit himself, continued his deity intact; and Christ, on the third day emerging from the Sepulchral State, resumed, in his risen body, the life which He had laid down of himself.

The Grecian ideas, imbibed by succeeding generations from European devotion to Greek and Roman literature, and especially the attractions and popular style of the Platonic writings have so imbued the minds of Christians in general, that the minds of all have become prepossessed in favour of that way of thinking and speaking. Our lexicons, commentaries, and metaphysics are all consequently accommodated to the same phraseology and views. So much is this the case, that many consider the questioning of their propriety to be heterodoxy. Dante's *Inferno* is based upon an ideality similar to that of the descent of Æneas to the infernal regions. Indeed, he takes Virgil for his cicerone. Sentiments, derived from similar classical sources, pervade a large portion of the most popular European poetry.

In like manner, at one period, it was generally

believed by Christians, that the ancient oracles were
actually delivered by demons, as professed by Pagan
writers. Thus, Fontenelle observes, in his *Histoire
des Oracles*, "*On a cru, dans les premiers siecles du
Christianisme, que les Oracles étoient rendus par des
Démons; il ne nous en faut pas davantage pour le
croire augourd'hui. Tout ce qu' ont dit les anciens,
soit bon, soit mauvais, est sujet à être bien répété, et ce
qu'ils n'ont pu euxmêmes prouver par des raisons
suffisantes, se prouve à présent par leur autorité
seule.*"

It has thus become habitual to construe the scriptural phraseology as to ψυχη and ἀδης by Pagan
analogies, instead of by the Biblical doctrine and
contexts. Thus, the passage already quoted from
Matt. xi., 23:—"Thou, Capernaum, which art exalted
unto heaven, shalt be brought down to hell." The
words ἑως ᾁδου (unto the grave) are translated by
Beza, "*ad inferos*," but, in the Syriac version, "*edamo
lashiul;*" the Lutheran translation is like our own—
" to hell."

The quotation from the 16th Psalm, in Acts ii.,
27, "thou wilt not leave my soul in hell," (εἰς ᾁδου),
is in the Latin rendered *apud Inferos*, but in the
Syriac *bashiul*.

The same Greek word "*Hades*," in 1 Cor., xv., 55,
"O grave, where is thy victory?" is, on this occasion,
rendered by Beza, *O Sepulchrum;* and the order of
the sentence is reversed. In the Syriac we find,
zochuthech shiyul. In this place the Latin gives the

true meaning of *Hades;* whilst *Inferos* is at least liable to misconstruction.

In Rev. xx., 13, 14, the Latin version gives a third rendering of the same word "*Hades.*" For, where the original has "Death and *Hades*" gave up their dead and "Death and *Hades*" are cast into the lake of fire, the Latin supplies *mors quoque et Infernus.* The Syriac gives *mawtho vashyul.*

The English, German, and other modern translations are equally equivocal with the Latin. The various editions of the Vulgate have similar and other discrepancies; some of them, perhaps, with a design. The preceding furnish an example of the different senses which may be thus conveyed. The words of the Latin version clearly detect the Greek idea. But the same Grecising tendency is discernible in most of the theological and metaphysical literature of all Christendom.

It is somewhat surprising that the Syriac version has not been more consulted than it seems to have been in translating from the Greek; because it generally gives better than any other version the Hebraistic vernacular sense of the Greek words. Even in the Hebrew version of the New Testament the Syriac appears to have been disregarded.

The consequences of this misconstruction of Scriptural phraseology are, that some of the most characteristic doctrines of the entire Hagiographa are misapprehended and weakened. A sort of moral vacuum is created in the Greek *Hades*, which

must be supplied. Hence the errors of the Pharisees and Essenes. Hence also the absurd Popish
doctrine of purgatory; and the equally unscriptural
Protestant doctrine of an Intermediate State of
personal happiness or misery. Hence, moreover,
the difficulty which many Christians express in
receiving the clear Biblical doctrine of the Second
Coming of Christ, to be glorified by his saints in
their resurrection state, when taught to believe that
God's children are already glorified with Him in
heaven. Whereas, upon the scriptural hypothesis,
the former is the comforting hope of all the evangelists. Death is abolished; and faith substitutes
the "substance of (or subsisting on) things hoped
for." All look and point solely and exclusively to
the day of the Coming of Jesus, and not to any
indefinite previous state. The Bible teaches the
Resurrection to be a condition precedent to the
personal beatitude of the sons of God, and as their
only hope of immortality. Whilst, in a metaphysical aspect, the misconstructions referred to are
not less obvious and important.

In a poetical sense, it is very pleasing to contemplate the gate of the sepulchre as the gate of heaven;
since it is so to the believer, although not by an
immediate transition.

It is also, in the same sense, very pleasing for
man's flesh to regard the death of an infant as the
transplanting of a flower from earth to Paradise.
It is also pleasing to picture the departed spirit of

a parent as still hovering around the family circle. And, no doubt, it would be a relief to all to be assured that death was an immediate transition or translation to heaven. But, when these sentiments are understood literally, and become articles of faith, they supersede the truth or detract from its importance, which, properly understood, is the most comforting of all, because it carries with it the conviction of reality. And, when philosophy itself adopts Pagan theories and poetic phraseology as expressive of philosophic and religious axioms and dogmas, it is equally perplexing to philosophy and religion.

Never is the language of poetry so impressive as when it is in conformity with truth and nature. Consistently with truth and Scripture, we may dwell with the deepest pathos upon the solemnities of death and the sepulchre; and, equally consistently, we may triumph with the apostles in the hope set before us in the Gospel, and enlarge in the language of faith upon the realities of the resurrection and heavenly state. We may reduce our future hopes to a present assurance, and see things which are not as though they were, yet all in perfect harmony with the important and peculiar doctrines of our religion and the principles of a philosophy in accordance therewith, justifying the ways of God to man.

When we consider that there is neither in nature nor revelation any foundation for the abstract or

Platonic idea of the immediate translation, as it were, of the individual to a higher state of personal enjoyment directly upon the decease of the body, we are led to attach a greater importance to life itself. It is natural to cling to life, as a drowning man clings to a straw. But the tenor of Biblical doctrine, as well as its psychology, also favours this natural instinct. Instead, therefore, of treating life with indifference, we are induced to denounce, as the greatest of follies and wickedness, all those courses which shorten existence and are productive of bloodshed, diseases, and cruelty, militating against God's laws of creation. Nevertheless, under the assurance of a better state, of a heavenly Fatherland, the believer is ever prepared to risk even life itself in the path of obedience.

CHAPTER II

THE HOPE OF ISRAEL.

UNDER the Old, as well as under the New Dispensation, the believer had a Hope beyond the grave; but it was less clearly announced, and, consequently, less apprehended, under the former than under the latter Dispensation. Moreover, this Hope did not constitute any distinct doctrine under the Mosaic Law.

It is certainly surprising that the patriarchs, who were the channel of the Divine Revelations, should have transmitted comparatively so little information concerning a Future State; whilst the heathen nations should have nearly all possessed so many traditions concerning it. Yet, perhaps, the patriarchs' belief in the Apocalyptic character of the tradition, and, therefore, their reverence for it as such, was what restrained them and the prophets from exercising the same poetic license that originated, in the Heathen Mythology, such wild expansions of a like tradition. The simplicity of the Jewish tradition may thus be considered evidence of its genuineness. Wherefore, whilst the Revelation of a Future State is sufficiently obvious in the

Jewish writings, it is of a very different nature from the speculative character of what the Heathen imagined. All the Pagan Paradises are purely imaginative; each nation, according to the habits or genius of its people, assimilates the Elysium or Future State to their ideas of supreme earthly felicity.

The actual nature of the Future State it would probably be impossible to convey in the language of mortals. It is something that eye hath not seen, nor ear heard, nor hath it entered into the heart of man to conceive. The absence, therefore, of any details is rather confirmative than otherwise of the genuineness and truth of the sacred records; these confine themselves solely to what can be said, namely, the promise of a Deliverer for man from the abnormal condition of the grave and of his personal Resurrection from the Dead.

The translation of Enoch and Elijah afforded an assurance of another sphere of existence. Our Lord himself adverted to the God of Abraham, Isaac, and Jacob, who were then dead, as an argument for demonstrating to the Sadducees the promise of a resurrection. Jehovah could not be the God of the dead without the certainty of a Resurrection. The patriarchs themselves sought, by faith, "a better country, that is, an heavenly" (Heb. xi., 16). David, Job, and the Prophets all concur in the Hope of a Resurrection from the dead; nevertheless, they proceed no further. It was through the Gospel alone that life and immortality were explicitly brought to light; there we find nothing voluptuous or carnal, but something symbolic and spiritual, and consistent and analogous with what we might conceive of the Resurrection state. Instead of a Peristan and City of Diamonds, we have the City whose Gates are pearls; instead of a leisurely Elysium of sunny banks and human gratifications, we have a pure River of Water of Life, clear as crystal, proceeding out of the throne of God, and on either side of it the mystic Tree of Life; instead of the light of the sun, God himself is that city's glorious light; in it there is no more curse, and the holy ones shall reign for ever. The whole of this is emblematic—a sublime vision, symbolical and not descriptive of a higher and resurrection state.

The patriarchs are said to have "given up the ghost" (Gen. xxv., 8; xxxv., 29; xlix., 33); Jacob "was gathered unto his people" (Gen. xlix., 33); and "David slept with his fathers" (1 Kings ii., 10). The phrases "thou shalt go to thy fathers" (Gen. xv., 15), and "was gathered to his people" (Gen. xxv., 8), arose from the Eastern custom of burying families for successive generations in the same sepulchre or locality. The phrases were synonymous, and thus became in time significant of burial generally; they were applied, even when an individual was not interred in the same sepulchre with his fathers, as occurred unto Abraham himself. The expression 'sleep,' being at this early period applied to the state of death, is a strong intimation that it was then not regarded as a state of extinction, but of temporary dissolution or repose.

The Psalmist says of man, "His breath goeth forth, he returneth to his earth; in that very day his thoughts perish" (Ps. cxlvi., 4); and again, " The dead praise not the Lord" (Ps. cxv., 17); "Like sheep they are laid in the grave," *Sheol* (Ps. xlix., 14); "In death there is no remembrance of thee: in the grave who shall give thee thanks" (Ps. vi., 5). Had David believed in an immediate transition to a place of felicity after death, he could not have thus expressed himself with any degree of propriety. Yet that he believed in a future resurrection is apparent from such passages as the following:—" My flesh also shall rest in hope. For Thou wilt not leave my soul, *naphshi*, in hell," *Sheol* (Ps. xvi., 9, 10). This passage is, in the Acts of the Apostles, expressly applied in proof of the doctrine of a Resurrection (Acts ii., 26, 27). It is there referred to the Resurrection of Christ, and spoken of as being fulfilled in that event; " for David is not ascended into the heavens" (Acts ii., 34). The Resurrection of Christ is also intimated in the twofold character in which the Messiah is spoken of in the prophets, as the suffering Messiah in the days of His humiliation (Isaiah liii.), and as the triumphant Messiah on His Second Coming (Isaiah xi.), the latter being the resurrection character of the former. Again, the Psalmist says, "I shall be satisfied, when I awake, with Thy likeness" (Psalm xvii., 15); "God will redeem my soul from the power of the grave," *Sheol* (Psalm xlix., 15); "Thou shalt guide me with Thy counsel, and afterward receive me to glory" (Psalm lxxiii., 24). Hosea says, "I will ransom them from the power of the grave, *Sheol;* I will redeem them from death" (Hosea xiii., 14). In this last verse the expressions 'grave' and 'death' complete an emphatic parallelism; and, whether the terms themselves are to be regarded as doctrinal metaphors or not, their force depends upon the traditional Resurrection. And Isaiah, in prophetic rapture writes, " When the Lord of Hosts (personified in Christ) shall reign in Mount Zion, and in Jerusalem, and before His ancients, gloriously" (Isaiah xxiv., 23). " He will destroy in this mountain the veil spread over all nations. He will swallow up death in victory; and the Lord will wipe away tears from all faces" (Isaiah xxv., 7, 8). Apparently the preceding are the same period and events symbolised, by a prosopopeia, in the twenty-first chapter of the Apocalypse.

But, whilst the inspired Preacher in the Book of Ecclesiastes, is impressed with the solemn certainty of that night which comes upon all, " when no man can work" (John ix., 4), it is quite consistent to suppose that he held the common faith of his father on the future destiny of his race. Therefore, he says, " Whatsoever thy hand findeth to do, do it with thy might; for there is no work, nor device, nor know-

ledge, nor wisdom in the grave, *Sheol,* whither thou
goest (Eccl. ix., 10). "Then shall the dust return
to the earth as it was; and the spirit *ruach* shall
return unto God who gave it" (Eccl. xii., 7).

All the promises announced by the prophets have
reference to a triumphant Messiah, when the Seed of
the woman shall bruise the Serpent's head, and, as
in the Books of Isaiah and Daniel, when "Thy dead
men shall live" (Isaiah xxvi., 19); and, when "Many
of them that sleep in the dust of the earth shall
awake, some to everlasting life, and some to shame
and everlasting contempt" (Dan. xii., 2). The
vision of dry bones in Ezekiel (c. xxxvii), however
allegorical, conveys a sublime intimation of the idea
of a Resurrection. Although these and similar
passages primarily convey a moral meaning, nevertheless that meaning is illustrated by the evident
recognition of the Resurrection doctrine. And Job
with singular distinctness exclaims, "Though, after
my skin, worms destroy this body, yet in my flesh
shall I see God : whom I shall see for myself, and
mine eyes shall behold, and not another; though my
reins be consumed within me" (Job xix., 26, 27).
Equally explicitly the heavenly voice in Daniel's
vision, addressing him, says, "Go thou thy way till
the end be, for thou shalt rest, and stand in thy lot
at the end of the days" (Dan. xii., 13); nothing is
here intimated respecting any Intermediate State,
but that he should rest till the end. And Job,
adverting to death, says, "So man lieth down, and

riseth not : till the heavens be no more, they shall
not awake, nor be raised out of their sleep (xiv., 12).
The learned author of the Divine Legation has
certainly shown that some of the passages here cited
from the Psalms and from the Books of Job and
the Prophets are capable of a construction with
reference to temporal deliverances only.   The whole
tenor of his argument tends to demonstrate that the
Jewish religion and people were without the sanction
of the doctrine of a future state of rewards and
punishments.   Yet the translation of Enoch and
Elijah must have at least pointed the hopes of the
faithful beyond the present.   Moreover, we find that
the faith of Abraham and the Patriarchs is in the
Epistle to the Hebrews expressly attributed to their
looking forward to a better, that is a heavenly
country; and, we find certain passages in the Psalms
expressly quoted in the Acts of the Apostles as
having reference to the doctrine of a Resurrection ;
also other passages from the Old Testament history
and the Prophecies are cited in the Gospels and
Epistles, as having direct allusion to the Messiah,
" Of whom Moses in the law, and the Prophets, did
write" (John i., 45), and as having reference to
Christ's future kingdom.   Consequently, we cannot
otherwise conclude than that, throughout the prior
dispensation, the doctrine of a Resurrection State
was a subject of faith with at least the most eminent
of God's people ; however dimly it might be entertained by Israel at large.   St. Paul, in his oration

before Felix, enunciating his Hope in the Resurrection of the dead, expressly asserts the belief of the Pharisees of that period in the same doctrine, "That there shall be a resurrection of the dead, both of the just and unjust" (Acts xxiv., 15). Indeed, Dr. Warburton's argument purports chiefly to show that the doctrine was not popularly apprehended during the earlier Mosaic legislation, and that there were good reasons why this should be the case under the extraordinary dispensation of a Theocracy. And further, that, although the ceremonial rites of the Mosaic Law were typical of the offices of Christ and the relationships of his people, yet they do not appear to have been popularly understood then in that light. The later sect of the Sadducees repudiated as well the doctrine of a Resurrection as of the existence of spirits. Thus, Dr. Warburton says, in book vi., s. 5, "Though it appears that a future state of rewards and punishments made no part of the Mosaic dispensation, yet the law had certainly a spiritual meaning, to be understood when the fulness of time should come : and hence it received the nature, and afforded the efficacy, of prophecy. In the interim, the mystery of the Gospel was occasionally revealed by God to his chosen servants, the fathers and leaders of the Jewish nation ; and the dawning of it was gradually opened, by the prophets to the people."

It may be said that the doctrine of a Resurrection to a Future State was latent in the Old Testament Scriptures, but was brought to light by the New.

Under the Old Dispensation, there existed no proof to which to appeal if the doctrine had been distinctly announced; and, therefore, in the then heathenish state of the Jewish mind, the mere promulgation of such a doctrine might have prejudiced the people against the teaching in general of their own priests and prophets. It was, therefore, reserved until the fulness of time, when Christ himself should put it to the proof by His own personal sacrifice and resurrection. To this proof He himself, and more especially His apostles, afterwards constantly appealed.

Under the Old Dispensation, therefore, the people were addressed by types, such as the building of the ark, the command to Abraham to offer up his only son, the pilgrimage to the promised land, the sacrificial rites of the law, and similar foreshadowings of promises calculated to generate faith in the promises of God, but of which the antitypes were then not generally perceived. Thus, we seldom find the doctrine of a Future State distinctly stated, and that only by the most eminent and later prophets.

Perhaps some may consider that Dr. Warburton pushes his argument further than necessary, when he infers, from the silence of Job's comforters as to his Hope of redress in a Future State, that they merely had a future temporal hope. Their silence might proceed from their want of a suitable reply, not being men of like faith with Job. The fitness of the sentiment itself consists in its being the

sublime climax of the failure of all temporal consolation. The argument of his friends was that
the wicked receive their punishment in this life;
Job's on the contrary was, that so far from this
being the case, "One dieth in his full strength,
being wholly at ease and quiet; and another dieth
in the bitterness of his soul." Therefore, he placed
his Hope beyond the grave; "For I know that my
Redeemer liveth, whom I shall see for myself."
And, perhaps, the Doctor may be thought as going
out of his way, to impute to the author of the Book
of Ecclesiastes the sentiments of the Grecising Jews,
merely because of an apparent analogy between the
Spirit's return to God and the philosophic doctrine
of the refusion of the soul into the universal spirit.
The analogy may exist; and yet, unless we impugn
the inspired character of the Book, we must take
it as a scriptural text parallel to other texts in the
New Testament, in which Christ and believers com-
mend their departing spirits to God; although the
author of that Book might not himself have embraced the resurrection doctrine.

The scriptural distinction between soul and spirit
is not generally preserved by Dr. Warburton. In
book vi. of the Divine Legation, he finds it necessary for his argument to advert to the true meaning
of living soul in the original, as implying merely
the living animal, and, therefore, not conveying the
idea of immortality; here he confesses the soul's
distinctive character, whilst in general he employs

the term soul, in its popular sense, as equivalent to spirit.

In like manner, in book v., he says that *Hades* in the Old Testament signifies the receptacle of dead bodies; in the New, the receptacle of living souls. But this it has been shown is merely the popular distinction, arising from the prevalence of the Greek philosophy, which attributed a Greek meaning to a Greek word adopted as an equivalent to the Hebrew word *Sheol*. The sense of the term *Sheol* was, by the context, evidently intended to be transferred to the word *Hades;* this will become still more apparent, when we inspect the detailed doctrines of the New Testament.

As we approach the era of the latter dispensation, we find the doctrine of the Resurrection still more popularly entertained than in the Books of the Old Testament. We have seen that by the more eminent of the patriarchs and prophets the doctrine was clearly recognised ; but in the time of the Maccabees it was a popular belief. Thus the mother and her seven sons, so cruelly put to an excruciating death by Antiochus for refusing to forsake the law of Moses, encouraged each other under their agonies by the Hope of a Resurrection. One of them said to the king, " It is good, being put to death by men, to look for Hope from God to be raised up again by Him. As for thee, thou shalt have no Resurrection to Life." So the mother said to her sons, " Doubtless the Creator of the

world, who formed the generation of man, and found
out the beginning of all things, will also of His
own mercy give you breath and life again" (2 Mac.
vii., 14, 23).

Chapter III.

LIFE AND IMMORTALITY.

IN passing from the Old to the New Dispensation we at once enter upon a further development of the hopes of the departed. Life and immortality are fully "brought to light." Our Saviour says, in the Parable of the Tares, that at the end of the world whilst His angels shall cast them which do iniquity "into a furnace of fire," the righteous shall "shine forth as the sun in the kingdom of their Father" (Matt. xiii., 42, 43); and again, concerning the same period, He says, "When the Son of Man shall come in His glory, and all the holy angels with Him, then shall He sit upon the throne of His glory" (Matt. xxv., 31); and, after depicting the separation of the sheep from the goats, Jesus adds, " These shall go away into everlasting punishment: but the righteous into life eternal." Upon another occasion, speaking of the Resurrection of the dead to the Sadducees who said there was no Resurrection, Christ says, " In the Resurrection they neither marry, nor are given in marriage, but are as the angels of God in heaven;" and then, in illustration of that doctrine, reminding the Sadducees how God spake

to Moses in the bush, Jesus asks whether they had
not read of God saying, "I am the God of Abraham,
and the God of Isaac, and the God of Jacob? God
is not the God of the dead, but of the living" (Matt.
xxii., 32); thus giving the Sadducees to understand that the Resurrection of the dead was so sure
an event, that God actually spake to Moses of dead
Abraham and Isaac and Jacob as if their resurrection had already taken place. If the verse, lastly
quoted, implied the continued personal existence of
the Patriarchs independently of a Resurrection, it
would have confirmed instead of confuted the
Sadducees' prejudices. See further hereon before,
pages 117, 118. In like manner, St. Peter, alluding
to the language of the Psalmist, "My flesh shall
rest in hope; because thou wilt not leave my soul
in *Hades*," demonstrates that the Resurrection of
Christ and not of David was here referred to; St.
Peter states, David "is both dead and buried" and
"is not ascended into the heavens" (Acts ii., 29, 34).

To his disciples, Jesus says, "Ye which have
followed me, in the regeneration, when the Son of
man shall sit in the throne of His glory, ye also
shall sit upon twelve thrones, judging the twelve
tribes of Israel" (Matt. xix., 28). "For the Son of
Man shall come in the glory of His Father, with
His angels, and then he shall reward every man
according to his works" (Matt. xvi., 27); this latter
declaration was made in answer to the question,
"What shall a man give in exchange for his soul?"

(Matt. xvi., 26). Nor did the Messiah teach his disciples to pray for an immediate reward, but "Thy kingdom come" (Luke xi., 2). And, after mentioning certain signs indicative of the approach of His Second Coming, he says, "They shall see the Son of Man coming in the clouds of heaven, with power and great glory. And he shall send His angels with a great sound of a trumpet; and they shall gather together His elect from the four winds, from one end of heaven to the other" (Matt. xxiv., 30, 31) —a phrase synonymous with a gathering from all nations, as is evident from the same expression being applied in the promise contained in Deut. xxx., 4, concerning the future gathering of the Israelites from all the nations whither they may be scattered.

By the Parable of the Talents, we are further taught, that Christ's return to receive His kingdom will be the time for rewarding His faithful servants, and punishing the negligent (Matt. xxv., 14-30). And, in another discourse with His disciples, He exhorts them to watch for the signs of the coming day, and to "pray always, that ye may be accounted worthy to escape all these things that shall come to pass, and to stand before the Son of Man" (Luke xxi., 36).

At another time, asserting His power before the Jews, He says, "Marvel not at this: for the hour is coming, in the which all that are in the graves shall hear His voice, and shall come forth, they that have

done good, unto the Resurrection of life; and they
that have done evil, unto the Resurrection of damnation" (John v., 28, 29). And, on a future occasion,
addressing the people, He declared that it was His
Father's will, "That of all which He hath given
me I should lose nothing, but should raise it up
again at the last day. And this is the will of Him
that sent me, that every one which seeth the Son
and believeth on Him, may have everlasting life:
and I will raise him up at the last day" (John vi.,
39, 40). Again, "No man can come to Me, except
the Father which hath sent Me draw him: and
I will raise him up at the last day" (John vi., 44).
And again, "Whoso eateth my flesh, and drinketh
my blood, hath eternal life; and I will raise him
up at the last day" (John vi., 54): and afterwards He demonstrated His power, by calling
Lazarus from the tomb; the dead natural body
was restored to life (John xi.). This was not
the Resurrection to eternal life, of which Christ
himself became the first fruits; nevertheless, the
restoration of Lazarus, who had been dead for four
days in a warm climate, manifested the right of Jesus
to the title of the Resurrection and the Life: what
Jesus could do then, He would be able to do at the
last day. The characteristic of the General Resurrection will be, that the natural body shall be raised
a spiritual body. It shall be a victory over death
and the grave, which Christ's miracles of revival
were not, inasmuch as mere resuscitation afforded
a double conquest for death and the grave.

Our Lord surprised His disciples by speaking of death as of a sleep—"Our friend Lazarus sleepeth." He then explains himself by saying plainly, "Lazarus is dead." Of Christ himself it is said, by St. Paul, that He is "become the first fruits of them that slept" (1 Cor. xv., 20). And again, "Them also which sleep in Jesus will God bring with Him" (1 Thess. iv., 14). Of the dying Stephen it is said, "he fell asleep" (Acts vii., 60). During sleep there is no personal consciousness. Therefore, if death be like unto sleep, the dead can have no consciousness; otherwise death is not like sleep. Again, the two resemble each other, by our being able to be restored from each to a state of personal consciousness. The doctrine of the Resurrection fulfils this condition more literally than any other interpretation ever propounded. And the use of the term "sleep" in reference to death, is a strong corroboration of the doctrine itself. Chrysostom says, in reference to the burial places of the early Christians, that "on this account this place is denominated κοιμητήριον (a dormitory or sleeping place); in order to teach that those who have departed, and are laid there, are not dead, but sleeping and taking rest." But death is called "sleep" in the Old as well as in the New Testament; in the former, David, Jeroboam, and others are said to have "slept with their fathers," indicating a peculiar harmony of doctrine and expression.

Whether the application of the expressions "unwaking sleep" and "endless sleep" to death by

the ancient heathen were partly borrowed from
tradition or adopted from the resemblance of death
to falling asleep, yet in no sense was it so appropriately applied to death by the disbelievers in a
Resurrection as by the believers in the traditional
faith.

The early Christian doctrine of the sleep of the
soul, in the sense of the Platonic demon, was inconsistent with its supposed psychological character;
in the Biblical sense alone is the term intelligible
and relevant. The spirit, as the immortal agency
of life and intelligence, cannot be said to sleep.
To the 'soul,' as expressive of personal identity, is
the figure of 'sleep' only appropriate, in connection
with the certainty of the believer's future Resurrection
to a glorious and everlasting life.

Neither Lazarus, nor the damsel (Mark v.), nor
the widow's son (Luke vii.), who were resusci-
tated by Christ, nor has any other person restored
to life ever made any recorded disclosures concerning
the sepulchral state; no one has even pretended
that they had anything to narrate. Moreover, the
conduct and conversations of Christ himself, both
before and after His Resurrection, entirely negative
any supposition to the contrary. Jesus himself
controverts the construction of the thief being
promised to be in Paradise on the day of his death;
since, in the conversation of Mary Magdalene with
her risen Lord, "Jesus saith unto her, Touch me not;
for I am not yet ascended to my Father" (John xx.,
17).

Before actually raising Lazarus from the dead,
Jesus did not attempt to console the sorrowing
Martha, by assuring her that her brother was then
in a better place or otherwise in a state of greater
felicity than he would have been in life, but that
"thy brother shall rise again;" and further that He,
who addressed her, was himself "the Resurrection
and the Life." "He that believeth in Me, though he
should die, yet shall he live" (κᾶν ἀποθάνῃ ζήσεται);
and whosoever liveth and believeth in Me shall not
die for ever" (οὐ μὴ ἀποθάνῃ εἰς τὸν αἰῶνα), John xi.,
25, 26.

After Christ's Resurrection, "Many bodies of the
saints which slept arose, and came out of the graves"
(Matt. xxvii., 52, 53). This is also confirmatory of
the Biblical doctrines of death being a sleep, the
grave being the only Intermediate State, and of the
possibility and truth of a Resurrection. There is no
intimation of the ascension of these revivified saints
into heaven; they may have died again like Lazarus;
at any rate, their Resurrection from death unto life
was one more testimony to the Lord of Life.

Of the rejecter and unbelieving he saith, "The
word that I have spoken, the same shall judge him
in the last day" (John xii., 48).

After signifying to his apostles, at the Last Supper,
that God was about to glorify him, he added, "Little
children, yet a little while I am with you. Ye shall
seek me: and as I said unto the Jews, Whither I go,
ye cannot come; so now I say to you" (John xiii.,
33). Then, replying to Peter's enquiry, he says,

"Whither I go, thou canst not follow me now; but thou shalt follow me afterwards" (v. 36). Afterwards, he explicitly declares to them that "I will come again and receive you unto myself; that where I am, there ye may be also" (John xiv., 3). Jesus gently upbraids his "little children" for their want of curiosity and searching about his departure, "I go my way to Him that sent me; and none of you asketh me, whither goest thou?" They sorrowed, when they should have enquired of the Lord.

What greater comfort could he administer to his servants under affliction, or in the hour of death, than when he thus addressed them? "Let not your heart be troubled: ye believe in God, believe also in me. In my Father's house are many mansions; if it were not so, I would have told you. I go to prepare a place for you. And if I go and prepare a place for you, I will come again, and receive you unto myself; that where I am, there ye may be also" (John xiv., 1-3). Again, in the same chapter, "Let not your heart be troubled, neither let it be afraid. Ye have heard how I said unto you, I go away and come again unto you" (v. 27, 28). He does not say that they shall upon their decease go to Him, but that he will come again and receive them. And, in his intercessory prayer, he adds, "Father, I will that they also, whom thou hast given me, be with me where I am; that they may behold my glory, which thou hast given me" (John xvii., 24). He had already told his disciples that He would come

again, and receive them unto himself, that where
He was, there they might be also ; and that in the
regeneration, when He should sit in the throne of His
glory, they also should sit upon twelve thrones, or,
as the Apostle Paul expresses himself in his Epistle
to the Colossians, "When Christ, who is our Life,
shall appear, then shall ye also appear with him in
glory" (Col. iii., 4).

That this was the comforting faith of the apostles
clearly appears from their repeated exhortations to
those whom they addressed, to look forward to "that
day," even " the coming of the Lord." So strong
was their faith that they identified themselves with
Christ as if they had actually died and risen with
Him :—"If ye then be risen with Christ, seek those
things which are above, where Christ sitteth on the
right hand of God. For ye are dead, and your life
is hid with Christ in God. When Christ, who is our
life, shall appear, then shall ye also appear with Him
in glory" (Col. iii., 1, 3, 4). Christ being "the
Resurrection and the Life" of believers, they commit,
when dying, their departing spirits to God or Christ;
thus, St. Paul, alluding to the sting of death and
the victory of the grave, exclaims, "Thanks be to
God who giveth us the victory through our Lord
Jesus Christ" (1 Cor. xv., 57) ; and St. James,
encouraging the early Christians under the persecutions to which they were exposed, says, "Be patient,
therefore, brethren, unto the coming of the Lord"
(James v., 7). St. John exhorted the Christians to

abide in Christ, "That, when He shall appear, we may have confidence, and not be ashamed before Him at His coming" (1 John ii., 28). St. Peter blesses God for having "Begotten us again unto a lively hope by the Resurrection of Jesus Christ from the dead" (1 Peter i., 3); the same Apostle encouraged the elders of the church to the performance of their duties, not for the sake of "filthy lucre," or by the promise of an immediate reward, but that "when the Chief Shepherd shall appear, ye shall receive a crown of glory that fadeth not away" (1 Peter v., 4). St. Jude concludes his short Epistle by commending the converts "unto Him that is able to keep you from falling, and to present you faultless before the presence of His glory with exceeding joy." So St. Peter writes, "Let them that suffer according to the will of God, commit the keeping of their souls (themselves) to Him in well doing, as unto a faithful Creator" (1 Peter iv., 19); he also adverts to the salvation of their souls (not spirits) "at the Revelation of Jesus Christ" (1 Peter i., 9, 13). It is always a personal salvation that the apostles refer to.

With reference to the future state, St. John says, "It doth not yet appear what we shall be: but we know that, when He shall appear, we shall be like Him; for we shall see Him as He is" (1 John, iii., 2). "It is sown a natural body; it is raised a spiritual body. There is a natural body, and there is a spiritual body" (1 Cor., xv., 44). And after showing that, when "this mortal shall have put on immortality, death is swallowed up in victory," St. Paul exclaims, "O death, where is thy sting? O grave, where is thy victory?" And he not only says, "If Christ be not raised, your faith is vain" (v. 17); but (v. 29) he adds, "What shall they do which are baptized for the dead, if the dead rise not at all? Why are they then baptized for the dead?" As Doddridge says, "Why do new converts press forward and offer themselves for baptism in the very face of persecution and death, like soldiers stepping into the ranks of the fallen, if they did not believe in the glorious doctrine of a Resurrection?" And again, "If after the manner of men I have fought with beasts at Ephesus, what advantageth it me, if the dead rise not?" (v. 32). He expresses no satisfaction in the heathen or philosophic notion that an abstract personification, whether called Shade, Soul, or Spirit, mounts up from the possibly mangled or tortured body, but St. Paul places all his reliance upon the hope of immortality through the Resurrection from the dead. "We ourselves groan within ourselves, waiting for the adoption, to wit, the redemption of our body" (Rom. viii., 23). "It is sown a natural body; it is raised a spiritual body." And when the same apostle comforts the Thessalonian converts concerning their departed friends, he does not say that their souls are happy in heaven, or speak of any unscriptural *Hades:* he says, "I would not have you to be ignorant, brethren, concerning them which are asleep, that ye sorrow not, even as others which have no Hope. For if we believe that Jesus died and rose again, even so them also which sleep in Jesus will God bring with him. For this we say unto you by the word of the Lord, that we which are alive, and remain unto the coming of the Lord, shall not prevent them which are asleep. For the Lord himself shall descend from heaven with a shout, with the voice of the archangel, and with the trump of God: and the dead in Christ shall rise first" (1 Thess. iv., 13-16). Also, "For God hath not appointed us to wrath, but to obtain salvation by our Lord Jesus Christ, who died for us, that, whether we wake or sleep, we should live together with him" (1 Thess. v., 9, 10). Because "Your life is hid with Christ in God" (Col. iii., 3). And to the Hebrews he writes, after enumerating several of the Patriarchs, Prophets, and eminent Believers, who had died in the faith, "These all, having obtained a good report through faith, received not the promise: God having provided some better thing for us, that they without us should not be made perfect" (Heb. xi., 39, 40). For, as they of old had not then entered into that rest which God had promised to his people, he concluded that, "There remaineth therefore a rest to the people of God" (Heb. iv., 9). Addressing the Thessalonians, he thanks God who had delivered them from their idols to serve Him, "And to wait for His Son from heaven" (1 Thess. i., 10). "For what is our hope, or joy, or crown of

rejoicing? Are not even ye in the presence of our
Lord Jesus Christ at his coming?" (1 Thess. ii., 19).
And, encouraging them under their trials, Paul adds,
that God would "Recompense tribulation to them
that trouble you; and to you who are troubled, rest
with us; when the Lord Jesus shall be revealed from
heaven with his mighty angels, in flaming fire taking
vengeance on them that know not God, and that obey
not the gospel of our Lord Jesus Christ: who shall
be punished with everlasting destruction from the
presence of the Lord, and from the glory of his
power; when he shall come to be glorified in his
saints, and to be admired in all them that believe
in that day" (2 Thess. i., 6-10) —even *in that day*,
when the redeemed in their angelic equality shall
realize the Apocalyptic prosopopœia and unite with
the angels themselves in the chorus of heavenly
anthems to the glory of the Great God, for whom
all things are and were created.

Not only was the traditional Hope of Immortality
ratified by the doctrines of our Lord and of the
authors of the Gospels and Epistles, but it was still
further confirmed and illustrated by the actual
Resurrection and Ascension of the Crucified One
himself.

The Parable or Fable of Dives and Lazarus, in
Luke xvi., is often understood to be illustrative of
the destinies of the departed: whilst, in reality, it
has no apparent bearing upon the doctrine of the
Future State taught in every other place by Christ.

It rather seems to be an argument or illustration *sui generis* to meet the case of the proud and self-sufficient Pharisees, whom he was admonishing because of their covetousness. Some of the early fathers conceived this parable might have reference to the future relative positions of the Jew and Gentile in relation to the church; but, confining our observations to the subject in hand, we have rather to direct attention towards the popular notion of the Fable referring to the Intermediate State of the dead. It may be supposed that Jesus, in addressing the Pharisees, would desire to place any particular point before them in their own way, according to their received dogmas, in order that he might at once illustrate his own argument, and carry conviction to their understandings; since, if an hypothesis were disbelieved, the argument based upon it would not be considered good. Therefore, as they believed in the existence of a personality after death, independently of the Resurrection of the body, he here represents Abraham as the pater-familias of their heaven or Paradise, where he receives the poor man Lazarus into his bosom, whilst Dives or the rich Pharisee is found to be in a place of torment, from which he has a view of the former. "It came to pass, that the beggar died, and was carried by the angels into Abraham's bosom : the rich man also died, and was buried ; and in *Hades* he lifted up his eyes, being in torments, and seeth Abraham afar off, and Lazarus in his bosom." In

the Bible *Hades* is never, except here, represented
to be a place of torment; *Gehenna* is the final
receptacle of the wicked in the New Testament,
typified by the Valley of Hinnom in the Old Testament. The Jewish Rabbis were deeply tainted with
the superstitions of the surrounding heathen; and
both Pharisees and Sadducees were notoriously
ignorant of their own Sacred Writings.   Christ
attributed the denial of a Resurrection by the Sadducees to their own ignorance of the Scriptures.
The Pharisees' idea of a place of reward or punishment, directly after decease, arose from their assign-
ing to *Sheol* the meaning of the Pagan *Hades*,
instead of their giving to the Greek *Hades* the signification of the Hebrew *Sheol*, and was probably
but the appropriation of the heathen doctrine modified to suit their sophisticated predilections. It is
not the Biblical *Sheol* or *Gehenna* which is described
above, any more than it is the Biblical heaven.   It
is, in fact, the Rabbinical *Sheol*, the counterpart of
the Greek *Hades* or *Orcus*—an imaginary abode,
the upper part of which was allotted to the good,
and the lower part to the wicked.   Hence the conversation introduced between Abraham and Dives.
It is only a Rabbinical allegory adopted by our
Lord.   The rich man and Lazarus are represented
in an embodied state capable of recognition and of
interlocution.   But, seeing that the Bible nowhere
intimates such to be the circumstances of the
departed Spirit (*ruach*) or the deceased Soul

(nephesh), the whole parable is doubtlessly hypo-
thetical in accordance with pharisaical notions,
with which it precisely corresponds. The Pharisees
plumed themselves upon being the children of
Abraham, as sufficient to justify them in their pride
and covetousness. Howbeit, in this fable, Christ
taught them that, however they might deify Abraham, who according to their Grecising ideas would
occupy a prominent place in the upper region of
this Greek *Orcus*, and even could they address
themselves to him under such circumstances as the
fable hypothetically assumes, Abraham himself
would still refer them to Moses and the prophets;
if these servants of God were not obeyed, a Resurrection, like that of Samuel and Lazarus of Bethany,
would avail nothing, would not change disobedient
into obedient children. But the despised, obedient
beggar, whether a believing Jew or Gentile, would
be welcome to the bosom of the Father of the
Faithful, being the offspring of a similar faith. So
Jesus elsewhere says, "Had ye believed Moses, ye
would have believed me: for he wrote of me. But
if ye believe not his writings, how shall ye believe
my words?" (John v., 46, 47).

The allegorical character of this parable is, moreover, manifested from the rich man being represented
to be dead and buried, and yet to be lifting up his
eyes in torments, and from this dead man requesting
the Resurrection of Lazarus as understood by Abraham in Luke xvi., 31; if Lazarus were in Abraham's

bosom, the Father would only require to send his
Son to the earth again. Wherefore, taking the in-
cidents of this parable to be significatory of separate
doctrines, then absurdities oppose us; taking the
parable to be a parable or fable, and the truth
depicted shines into our understandings.

The promise of Christ to the penitent thief upon
the cross (Luke xxiii., 43) is another passage, which
has received a construction at variance with the
otherwise uniform doctrine of the Saviour respecting
His kingdom. The verse reads, in the original,
thus :—'Ἀμὴν λέγω σοι, σήμερον μετ' ἐμοῦ ἔστῃ ἐν τῷ
παραδείσω. The structure is somewhat analogous
in the following sentence :—'Ἀμὴν λέγω σοι, ὅτι σὺ
σήμερον ἐν τῇ νυκτὶ ταύτῃ, πρὶν ἢ δὶς ἀλέκτορα
φωνῆσαι, τρὶς ἀπαρνήσῃ με (Mark xiv., 30)—here,
to make it plain that the denial of Christ by Peter
should happen on that very night, the words are
adjusted in the passage in an unmistakeable manner,
"That this day, even in this night." Had ὅτι σὺ
(that thou) been omitted, the structure of the
sentence would have been similar to that of the
text in question; it would then have read, "I say to
thee to day, in this night, before the cock crow twice,
thou shalt deny me thrice." Thus the time, when
the denial should occur, would have been indefinite.
For the purpose of disconnecting σήμερον from 'Ἀμὴν
λέγω σοι, a structure would then have been adopted
similar to Λέγω σοι, Πέτρε, οὐ μὴ φωνήσει σήμερον
ἀλέκτωρ in Luke xxii., 34. Whence, had it been

intended to separate σήμερον from the introductory
clause in Luke xxiii., 43, either the particle ὅτι
would have been prefixed to the dependent clause,
or the sentence would have been differently constructed. Again, in Luke iv., 21, the Greek has
Ἤρξατο δὲ λέγειν πρὸς αὐτούς, Ὅτι σήμερον "He
began to say unto them, that this day." And
again, in Luke xix., 9, "Jesus said unto him,
That this day is salvation"—ὅτι σήμερον σωτηρία.
Wherefore σήμερον, "to-day," should be read in
construction with the first clause of the sentence
under examination; the punctuation should be thus,
"Verily I say unto thee to-day, thou shalt be with
me in Paradise." Likewise in Matt. xxi., 28, the
invitation is "to-day;" but the son did not go until
afterwards; the verse should be read, "Son, go to-
day, work in my vineyard." The adverb σήμερον is
placed in a similar position in Acts xxii., 3, "As ye
all are this day" καθὼς πάντες ὑμεῖς ἐστε σήμερον.
The word "to-day" is used emphatically and in
reference to the dying thief's faith; he believed Jesus
in the hour of his deep humiliation and seemingly
utter helplessness, and by faith then entered the
Paradise of God—faith being the substance of things
hoped for, the evidence of things not seen. Likewise the believer enters heaven through faith, and
is on the day of his conversion seated with Christ
in the heavenlies. We can scarcely conceive that
Christ would intend to imply a more immediate
prospect of happiness to the dying criminal than

he had on every other occasion held forth to his own apostles.

It is evident that the thief was not only penitent, but that he believed in the future kingdom of the Messiah. He, therefore, prayed, "Lord, remember me when thou comest into thy kingdom;" to this petition the suffering Messiah at once lent a gracious ear, and in his own agony comforted another by the words, "Verily, I say unto thee to-day, thou shalt be with me in Paradise." The expression Paradise is only used by our Lord on this occasion, and is beautifully suggestive. In Eden Paradise was situated, wherein dwelt the first Adam; the second Adam came to restore the ruin made by the loss of Paradise through sin. A flaming sword kept out the first Adam, dwelling after his disgrace in Eden before Paradise. Christ enters through the veil and receives the flaming sword in death, and opens a road to Paradise by the believer's acceptance of the accepted sacrifice. Paradise is restored, but not yet actually a possession; the believer has Paradise now by faith in Jesus. Faith is not bound by time or space. "To him that overcometh will I give to eat of the tree of life, which is in the midst of the Paradise of God" (Rev. ii., 7); similarly, "He that believeth in me hath everlasting life," the Tree of Life in the Paradise of God. It is, "When the Son of man shall come in His glory," that His people shall "Inherit the kingdom" (Matt. xxv., 31, 34)— "When he shall come to be glorified in His saints"

(2 Thess. i., 10). The quotation from Revelation being the only verse in the New Testament where the word "Paradise" receives a definite application, has there reference to the kingdom of the Messiah described in Revelation xxii.

The word "Paradise" is of Hebrew origin *(Pardes)*; it is only used three or four times in the Old Testament, with reference either to "a garden eastward in Eden," or to gardens and pleasure grounds; and, in the latter sense, it was adopted by the Persians and Greeks (see Calmet). But, the Apostle John having pointedly and definitely applied the term to the future kingdom of the Messiah, "The time of the restitution of all things," or the Paradise restored, it was more probably in this sense than in any other adopted by our Lord in responsive parallelism to the prayer of the penitent malefactor. St. Paul employs the term Paradise metaphorically, as parallel to the phrase "third heaven," in his vision of supreme angelic felicity.

Thus the word Paradise, being used parallel with the future kingdom of Christ referred to in the petition of the dying malefactor, necessarily requires and confirms the punctuation of the passage as before suggested. Many of the most ancient copies of the Greek text, as Blackwall remarks, have no accents; and, it may be added, they have no punctuation except at the close of a sentence. Wherefore, the modern punctuation is no portion of the text.

Lastly, we would point those, who believe in the Platonic soul or demon, to the following texts

relating to Christ's soul (or Self):—"Thou shalt make
His soul (Himself) an offering for sin ;" "He hath
poured out His soul (Himself) unto death" (Isaiah
liii., 10, 12); Psalm xvi., 10, "Thou wilt not leave
my soul (Myself) in the grave" (*Sheol*, translated by
Hades in Acts ii., 27). Consequently, the Messiah
himself was not in Paradise on the day of His death,
but made an offering for sin ; His spirit went to God
himself; His soul or Self, having been poured out
sacrificially unto death, was laid in the grave and
saw no corruption. Furthermore, even after His
Resurrection, Christ said to Mary, "I am not yet
ascended to my Father" (John xx., 17).

The body and spirit combined make the *living*
soul, or conscious individual. Adam became a *living*
soul, upon the spirit being breathed into the organic
body ; he was a man before life was given him.
"Glorify God in your body, and in your spirit, which
are God's" (1 Cor. vi., 20) ; Paul is here speaking
to the saints individually, and likewise in the passage, "Be holy both in body and in spirit" (1 Cor.
vii., 34).

The sense of this 43rd verse, in Luke xxiii., is
sufficiently conspicuous by its own context; the
promise of Jesus is a fitting response parallel to
the petition made, as well as in harmony with the
general tenor of our Lord's and the Apostles'
teaching. The parallelism is more demonstrative
than the mere verbal interpretation of either ancient
or modern translators ; the ordinary construction is
repugnant to all.

CHAPTER IV

DEATH ABOLISHED.

IT is a bold figure of speech to say that death is abolished (2 Tim. i., 10), when we daily witness the havock made by it amongst the living. Nevertheless, in a doctrinal sense, Christ is termed the Resurrection and the Life; and those, who believe in Him, are said to have put on Christ. Moreover, Jesus "hath brought life and immortality to light through the Gospel" (2 Tim. i., 10); and faith is designated "the substance of things hoped for, the evidence of things not seen" (Heb. xi., 1). Hence he, who believes in Christ and the Resurrection, appropriates his Resurrection by faith at the very hour of death. Thus death is abolished or neutralized—καταργήσαντος μὲν τὸν θάνατον (2 Tim. i., 10). Through our Saviour's atonement, resurrection, and ascension, he has overcome death in its cause and worst consequences, and has thereby established the believer's faith upon an evident and practical foundation.

All must submit to the act of transition, of dying, of putting off the mortal coil. But θάνατος, death, is not the act of dying; it is the end of dying, the state of death. It is only this, that is capable of

becoming the subject of faith.   In the Apocalypse
of St. John (v., 13), the creature under the earth
ὑποκάτω τῆς γῆς is, upon this bold negation of death,
portrayed with the many angels, the four living
creatures, and the four and twenty elders worshipping
Jesus who liveth for ever and ever.

If we meet with passages difficult to reconcile
with other ones more explicitly revealing what
Divine goodness hath thought right to make
known, we seem to have no alternative, according
to the rules of just criticism, except the interpretation of the more obscure by the more demonstrative doctrine, and of particular passages by their
relative contexts.   St. Peter, when writing to the
church concerning Christ's Second Coming and the
New Heavens and the New Earth, adverted to the
Epistles of St. Paul speaking of these things, and
added "In which are some things hard to be understood, which they that are unlearned and unstable
wrest, as they do also the other Scriptures, unto
their own destruction" (2 Peter iii., 16).   Although
the Apostle here probably alludes more particularly
to those doctrines of salvation, which persons
unenlightened in the general tenor of the Holy
Scriptures are liable to misinterpret; yet in like
manner passages exist, which, from the peculiarity
of their phraseology alone, have perplexed many
good and eminent men.   The rule of criticism
already proposed is the only legitimate one, perhaps,
in the absence of an authentic interpretation.

We may safely assume, that whatever the Apostles wrote with reference to a Future State would, if properly understood, harmonize throughout.

It was the Apostle Paul, who defined faith to be "the substance of things hoped for, the evidence of things not seen" (Heb. xi., 1). Throughout his Epistles, he evinces his faith in the doctrine of the Resurrection and the Second Advent of Christ; to these two things, he constantly directs the hope of all believers. But, it is only in a few passages, where he chiefly realises his definition of faith, by speaking of the Resurrection and of the kingdom of Christ as of events contemporaneous with death itself, as if the latter event, in fact, were merged in the reality of the former.

Paul, after adverting to his own and Timothy's ministerial troubles, perplexities, and persecutions, says, that they are not distressed, or in despair, or forsaken, or destroyed, "Knowing that he which raised up the Lord Jesus, shall raise up us also by Jesus, and shall present us *with you*" (2 Cor. iv, 14). "For we know, that if our earthly house of this tabernacle were dissolved, we have a Building of God, an house not made with hands, eternal in the heavens. For in this we groan, earnestly desiring to be clothed upon with our house which is from heaven" (2 Cor. v., 1, 2). "For we that are in this tabernacle do groan, being burdened: not for that we would be unclothed"—any more than the philosophising Rabbis, who expected that their spirits

would be clothed with another body immediately
after death, desired to die—"but clothed upon, that
mortality might be swallowed up of life" (2 Cor. v.,
4).   This was capable of immediate accomplishment either by a sudden change and bodily translation, like Enoch and Elijah, or by the sudden and
speedy Coming again of Jesus Christ; for this
mortal must put on immortality.   "Therefore we
are always confident, knowing that, whilst we are
at home in the body, we are absent from the Lord:
for we walk by faith"—whilst here in the mortal
body—"not by sight," as we will do, when the Lord
shall appear: "we are confident, I say, and willing
rather to be absent from the body, and to be present
with the Lord" (2 Cor. v., 6-8), as we shall be when
clothed upon, and mortality shall be "swallowed up
of life," and "this mortal shall have put on immortality," and when God, who "Raised up the Lord Jesus,
shall raise up us also by Jesus, and shall present us
with you" (2 Cor. iv., 14).   To the believer, death
is abolished, he having paid the wages of sin through
accepting death in Jesus; and the language of faith
realises, by an immediate transition, that which is
hoped for.

According to the Platonic doctrine, heaven is
the native place of the soul.   According to the
Christian doctrine, that which is born of the flesh
is flesh; therefore "Ye must be born again," born
of the Spirit, to become children of God, and thus
part of the household of the Father of Spirits.

The sons of God have, of necessity, to patiently walk by faith, and "seek a fatherland" πατρίδα ἐπιζητοῦσι (Heb. xi., 14). Heaven is the home of the believer; because it is the home of his heavenly Father. "Ye are of God, little children" (1 John iv., 4). Thus a child, born abroad, when bound for the country of his parents, is seeking his fatherland—the father may never have left his native place. Being "present with the Lord" implies a personal actual presence; this is never promised until the coming of Christ, when the dead and living saints each receive a spiritual and ever-living body—the undying personal identity of the Resurrection State. The creature's personality, as before demonstrated, exists by the union of the spirit with a body. It is often erroneously supposed, that the words "absent from the body" are parallel with the words "present with the Lord;" but the former phrase refers to our fleshly tabernacle in this world, and the latter to a future period of dwelling with the Lord in the new tabernacle or body at His appearing.

The Greek phraseology, in which the preceding passages are couched, is figurative; but they are perfectly expressive of the sense here ascribed to them. The term σκῆνος ("tabernacle" 2 Cor. v., 1), a tent, is applied to the body by Hippocrates and other classical authorities, as well as by the Apostle Paul. The word ἐκδημέω ("absent" 2 Cor. v., 6) is used by the ancient Greeks to signify to be away from one's own people; and, consequently, the passage in this verse, connected with the preceding and subsequent parts of St. Paul's letter, impresses the believer with the importance of him, a Citizen of Heaven, not walking after the flesh, but after the Spirit. Death is not the subject of allusion at all in these verses; for St. Paul has just said, in the preceding fourth verse, "Not for that we would be unclothed, but clothed upon." Of all God's promises, the Saints have now given to them "The earnest of the Spirit" (verse 5). Now St. Paul, pursuing the Greek idea of being away from home ἐκδημέω, uses, in apposition thereto, ἐνδημέω to imply the end of his journey and his arrival at his better home; where he would be "present (or at home) with the Lord."

According to the apostolic doctrine, the Believer is one with Christ, and is by faith risen with Jesus and seated in the heavenlies. Therefore, St. Paul greatly desired the reality of those things hoped for; he yearned for his perishable natural body to be exchanged for an immortal spiritual body. This spiritual body Paul would receive in the place of his natural body, when Jesus should come again as the Resurrection and the Life to receive the faithful; so that, as Christ said, "Where I am, there ye may be also" (John xiv., 3).

The Syriac translation of 2 Cor. v., 9, is, "We desire, that, whether abroad *onudai* or at home *omurai*, we may be acceptable to him." The

Believer is now abroad, wishing for the coming of his Lord and King to take him home to the father-land. "Henceforth know we no man after the flesh" is declared in the following 16th verse. "If any man love the world, the love of the Father is not in him" (1 John ii., 15).

Paul is so bold in his love for Jesus, that the immediate appearance of the Saviour would gratify and not terrify the Apostle. "Wherefore we labour, that, whether present or absent, we may be accepted of Him; for we must all appear before the judgment seat of Christ." The Apostle cannot consistently be supposed to desire for himself any other or more immediate union with Christ, than he everywhere intimates to other believers. Besides, to understand the expression, "Absent from the body and to be present with the Lord," literally and immediately, would prove too much, as Christ is said to be now "seated at the right hand of God;" and, therefore, to be personally present with Jesus in a literal and immediate sense, would involve a present participa-tion in the glorious presence of the godhead. But, in the very context already quoted, Paul avowed his belief "that he which raised up the Lord Jesus, shall raise up us also by Jesus, and present us with you," "At the coming of our Lord Jesus Christ with all His saints" (1 Thess. iii., 13). So Christ himself had previously declared, "I will come again, and receive you unto myself; that where I am, there ye may be also" (John xiv., 3). Indeed this seems to be the plain context of the passage in question, and most in harmony with the entire Scriptures. The difficulty in the reading arises from the elliptical and metaphorical style of the writer.

Another passage, in the first chapter of St. Paul's Epistle to the Philippians, occasions much difficulty to commentators; this letter was written from Rome, when he was suffering and in bonds for his Master's cause—even expecting death.

In verse 7, St. Paul alludes to these "bonds." In verses 12 and 13, he speaks of "the things which happened unto me," and says "my bonds in Christ are manifest in all the palace, and in all other places;" and in verse 20, the apostle talks of "whether it be by life or by death." Evidently Paul is at this time in much affliction and hazard of his life. Now follow the verses, which will have to be particularly considered here. "For to me to live is Christ, and to die is gain. But if I live in the flesh, this is the fruit of my labour: yet what I shall choose I wot not. For I am in a strait betwixt two, having a desire to depart, and to be with Christ; which is far better" (Phil. i., 21-23). Death to Paul would indeed have been a gain, as sleep is to the overworked slave, or even to any tired man. We are reminded here of St. Paul's words to the Corinthians about his troubles :—"In labours more abundant, in stripes above measure, in prisons more frequent, in deaths oft. Of the Jews five times received I forty stripes save one. Thrice was I beaten with rods, once was I stoned, thrice I suffered shipwreck, a night and a day I have been in the deep; in journeyings often, in perils of waters, in perils of robbers, in perils by mine own countrymen, in perils by the heathen, in perils in the city, in perils in the wilderness, in perils in the sea, in perils among false brethren; in weariness and painfulness, in watchings often, in hunger and thirst, in fastings often, in cold and nakedness. Beside those things that are without, that which cometh upon me daily, the care of all the churches" (2 Cor. xi., 23-28). Job, in the midst of his short trial, wished for death—"There the wicked cease from troubling; and there the weary be at rest" (Job iii., 17); much more might St. Paul desire to fall asleep in Jesus. The apostle had fought a good fight; therefore to him, a soldier of Christ, fighting in a foreign land, "To live is Christ, and to die is gain."

Furthermore, a confirmation of the assertion, that for the faithful Christian "to die is gain," appears in Revelation xiv., 13 :—"Blessed are the dead which die in the Lord from henceforth: Yea, saith the Spirit, that they may rest from their labours; and their works do follow them."

Paul's life was useful to Jesus, seeing that he fought Christ's cause so energetically and heroically; whence, "For me to live is Christ." The noble apostle of the Gentiles hesitates between these two, life and death; for the sake of Jesus, he would live : for his own sake, he would prefer death. How many people of the world get sick of life; how much more should this apostle, then, a man not of this world, be weary of it ! If Christians of the present century

laboured for Christ as thoroughly as Paul, they would
not be so astonished at him saying "to die is gain"—
rest is pleasant to the weary hard-working man. The
unselfishness of Paul gleams out through his not
wotting what to choose, whether life or death. He is
in a strait betwixt the two. However, he decides for
life; because, "To abide in the flesh is more needful
for you." What a beautiful spirit is here manifested!

The 23rd verse of this same first chapter of St.
Paul's Epistle to the Philippians depends, for its
explanation, upon whether the Greek words εἰς τό
ἀναλῦσαι should be translated with reference to the
apostle returning to the dust or to the returning
of Christ. At any rate, the present translation
"to depart" is not accurate; because the word
ἀναλῦσαι means "to loose back again," that is, to
return, either the returning of a ship to port, or of
a traveller to his own country, or of a visitor from
supper to his own house. Jesus likens His present
abode in heaven to a man travelling into a far
country, who will return (Matt. xxv., 14). This word
ἀναλῦσαι occurs in 2 Mac. xii., 7, in Luke xii., 36,
and 2 Tim. iv., 6; in these three places the words
can only signify 'return.' In Luke xii., 36, the
authorized version of the Bible has "will return;"
in Tim. iv., 6 it has "departure." But the Greek
meaning in this latter passage is not brought out
by the English word 'departure;' St. Paul is speaking of his death and means "my dissolution (or
returning to the dust) is at hand;" "For dust thou
art, and unto dust shalt thou return" (Gen. iii., 19).

Whence the word ἀναλῦσαι should have its proper English signification affixed in Philippians by the word "returning." But what "returning?" Does St. Paul here allude to his dissolution as in Timothy? Surely not; else he would not have written τὸ ἀναλῦσαι "The Returning." He also affixes, to "The Returning," the result, viz., "And to be with Christ;" this dissipates any doubt. Hence Paul, hesitating betwixt those two things, life and death, writes in verses 23, 24, thus:—"For I am in a strait betwixt those two things (having a desire for The Returning and to be with Christ, which would be far better than either); nevertheless to abide in the flesh is more needful for you." He concludes by confessing it is better for them that he should live; and, therefore, of these two things, life or death, the former must continue. Howbeit, parenthetically he exclaims—"Having a desire for The Returning (of the Bridegroom) and to be with Christ." "For I reckon that the sufferings of this present time are not worthy to be compared with the glory which shall be revealed in us. For the earnest expectation of the creature waiteth for the manifestation of the sons of God"—"If so be that we suffer with Him, that we may also be glorified together" (Rom. viii., 18, 19, 17). "That I may know Him, and the power of His Resurrection, and the fellowship of His sufferings, being made conformable unto His death; if by any means I might attain unto the Resurrection of the dead" (Phil. iii., 10, 11).

The Bible never promises a Resurrection of the fleshly body of the believer; the believer himself, in his or her identity, shall arise with a glorified and spiritual body; St. Paul, not St. Paul's fleshly body, shall rise again. The miraculous resuscitation of the fleshly body, in certain instances, is typical of the future Resurrection of all believers in their several individualities.

The death of the believer is absorbed in the Resurrection Life of Christ. To the Christian, death is no more death; to him, in the language of faith, "Sudden death is sudden glory." Death, as a final and hopeless condition, is abolished. St. Paul would have preferred to be clothed upon rather than to have died; he, however, looked forward with an unfailing hope to the day of the Coming of his Lord, when "this mortal shall put on immortality," and death shall be "swallowed up in victory," the believer then dwelling in the Fatherland at home with Christ. Throughout the Book of Revelation, it is, by the application of this very doctrine of faith in things unseen, that the apostle John is enabled to realise, as he does, the transactions of the risen saints.

By an act of faith, St. Paul passes *per saltum* to the reality of the promises; but he longed with a burning desire for the substitution of sight in the place of faith—for a real, face-to-face look at his Master, Jesus. The apostle's confidence was such, that he was willing to exchange at any moment the corruptible for the spiritual body, and to be present or at home with Christ—not in the Platonic sense of returning to his native heavens or star, but to "be at home" with Christ, when He "who is our life shall appear." By faith, the day of death and the day of Christ's Returning become united. This is the key to St. Paul's subsisting on things hoped for; whilst the Hope, to which he pointed the church, was the advent of Christ as the climax of their faith.

Well might he exclaim, amid his deadly strife and ceaseless warfare, "What advantageth it me, if the dead rise not?" (1 Cor. xv., 32).

We cannot separate the objective and subjective personality, inasmuch as all our objective perceptions and reminiscences are fundamental to the subjective. To disjoin them would be to create an ideal monstrosity, incongruous with personal identity. The assumption, that the spirit unclothed and bodiless retains all the perceptive and other capacities of the individual, is the dispensing with a body altogether, and to supersede the very doctrine of a Resurrection; for the establishment of this, Christ died and rose again.

Confronted with death, personal immortality could never have been established by reason. Plato's assumption regarded a Being of his own imagination. All the ancient philosophers were doubters or disbelievers in a future existence. Their popular superstitions more unequivocally perpetuated a doctrine, that was probably a distorted tradition. The Jewish and apostolic writings alone unfold the true state of the question; and, by their doctrine and evidences of

a personal Resurrection, they establish our Hope of
Immortality, which otherwise had been rather "promised than proved" as remarked by Seneca.

The Scriptural doctrines and psychology harmonise with and establish each other; and the
doctrine of a personal Resurrection or Restitution
is their necessary corollary. But, by faith, which is
"the substance of things hoped for," the promise is
even now realised to the believer. The act of dying
is a matter of experience, and not of faith; the
promises beyond death are alone the subjects of
faith. These do not depend upon experience or
the deductions of philosophy, but upon Revelation.
The intermediate state or condition of death,
θανατος, is ignored and abolished. Where time
ends eternity begins.

In Bunyan's allegory, death is a river through
which all must pass. The act of dying, and not
death, is here allegorised. By faith, the heavenly
Canaan is an actual possession, and celestial revelations burst upon the believer's view. The state
of death is rather a dark region beyond the river;
here the Pagan philosopher was bewildered, and
the infidel is "in endless mazes lost." To the
believer, it is abolished. He is dead and risen with
Christ, and lives for evermore. "O death, where is
thy sting? O grave, where is thy victory?"

> "For ever with the Lord!"
> Amen, so let it be;
> Life from the dead is in that word;
> 'Tis immortality.

CONCLUSION.

From the whole of the preceding considerations, the following are a few of the inferences deducible; some of these are fully discussed in another manuscript:—

1.—Living Man is an independent personality, constituted of body and spirit; and each individual has a distinctive Self.

2.—The body and spirit possess separate functions, and are consubstantial during life, but separable at decease.

3.—The body consists of a physical organism, adapted to personal action; which may be divided into intellectual and mechanical action.

4.—The intellectual organism receives its ideas through the several senses; these ideas are active and permanent physical impressions.

5.—The *nephesh* (soul or self) is the organic personality of man and the individuals of the entire animal creation.

6.—The *ruach* is the spirit of life imparted to each creature, both man and brute, by the divine *afflatus*.

7.—The individual organism of any creature constitutes its idiosyncrasy.

8.—The spirit of life imparts vitality, volition, and consciousness.

9.—The spirit is the co-efficient of the body in the living creature.

10.—The mental characteristics of the spirit are volition and consciousness.

11.—Volition is the active agency of the spirit, being the motive agency of thought and action.

12.—Consciousness is the passive agency of the spirit, receiving and appropriating the ideas impressed on the mental sensorium.

13.—The various processes of the combination and separation of ideas, directed by the active agency of the spirit, are what is commonly called the faculties of the mind.

14.—Personal identity is solely maintained by the union of the spirit with a body, such body being impressed with all the ideal and individual characteristics of personality.

15.—Personal identity is lost, on the separation of body and spirit, by the corruption of the body through the absence of the spirit of life.

16.—The doctrine of a Resurrection implies a restoration of all that constitutes conscious personal identity.

17.—An Intermediate State is not sanctioned by the Bible, and originated from a Platonic interpretation of the Hebraistic phraseology.

18.—Death is a penal state, being the wages of sin; and thereby is intensified the sacredness of life, as well as the horror and criminality of all that abuses or curtails it.

19.—The doctrine of a Resurrection is an assurance of the restoration of personal identity, and is in accordance with the inferences of philosophy as to the adaptation of man to immortality.

20.—The opinion concerning the immortality of the soul is repugnant both to the original language and the doctrines of Scripture.

21.—The previous deductions reconcile revelation with philosophy in accordance with mental phenomena.

22.—The sole dependence of human immortality upon a Resurrection concentrates all the hopes of the faithful in the Redeemer as " the Resurrection and the Life."

INDEX.

Newcastle-upon-Tyne: A. Reid, Printing Court Buildings, Akenside Hill.

www.ingramcontent.com/pod-product-compliance
Lightning Source LLC
Chambersburg PA
CBHW031340070726
47496CB00017B/1343